THE CLASSICS OF WESTERN SPIRITUALITY
A Library of the Great Spiritual Masters

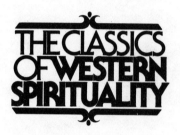
THE CLASSICS
OF WESTERN
SPIRITUALITY

Johann Arndt

TRUE CHRISTIANITY

TRANSLATION AND INTRODUCTION
BY
PETER ERB

PREFACE
BY
HEIKO A. OBERMAN

PAULIST PRESS
NEW YORK • RAMSEY • TORONTO

Cover Art
The artist BETSY ROOSEN SHEPPARD graduated with a Fine Arts degree from
Moore College in Philadelphia. A fellowship winner she went on for further studies in
Europe, at the Arts Students League and The School of Visual Arts in New York. She
lives with her husband and their two children in Newton, New Jersey. Of her cover
painting she says, "I saw Arndt as a warm, balanced person with his feet on the ground
(thus the earth colors) and his head in some heavenly clouds (thus the cosmic stars and
blue tones of mystery)."

Design: Barbini Pesce & Noble, Inc.

Copyright © 1979 by The Missionary Society
of St. Paul the Apostle
in the State of New York

Library of Congress
Catalog Card Number: 78-72046

ISBN: 0-8091-0281-1 (cloth)
ISBN: 0-8091-2192-1 (paper)

Published by Paulist Press
Editorial Office: 1865 Broadway, New York, N.Y. 10023
Business Office: 545 Island Road, Ramsey, N.J. 97446

Printed and bound in the
United States of America

CONTENTS

Acknowledgements

For their help in the processing of the final text, I am indebted to Ann Hovey for her help with typing a rough draft, to Frieda Lepp, my research assistant, and particularly to Nancy Stade, without whose gracious and accurate assistance neither this edition nor the Boehme translation could have been completed with as little difficulty.

Editor of this Volume

PETER ERB was born in 1943 in Tavistock, Ontario, Canada. He is presently Assistant Professor of English and Religion and Culture at Wilfrid Laurier University, Waterloo, Ontario, Canada. Dr. Erb's specialization is in late medieval spirituality. After serving as pastor of the Amish Mennonite Church in Tavistock, he re-entered the academic world, completing his M.S.L. at the Pontifical Institute of Medieval Studies, and his Ph.D. at the University of Toronto. He has published numerous articles, reviews and papers on Protestant spirituality. His books include *Schwenkfeld in His Reformation Setting* and *The Spiritual Diary of Christopher Wiegner*, and he is now working on a book entitled *Toward a Definition of the Contemplative Life*. He is the recent recipient of a Canada Council Grant to complete a book on Gotfried Arnold. Professor Erb has combined teaching and writing with an active career in research on Protestant monastic communities in North America, and Patristic scholarship among the Radical Reformers. Dr. Erb is Director of Library and Archives at Conrad Grebel College, University of Waterloo, Ontario, and Associate Director of the Schwenkfeld Library, Pennsburg, Pennsylvania. He has supervised doctoral and master's students at various universities in Canada and the United States. He resides in Waterloo, Ontario with his wife, Betty, and their two children, Catherine and Suzanne. Dr. Erb is a member of the Ostdeutscher Kulturrat, Kulterwerk Schlesiens, American Society of Reformation Research, American Society of Church History and the American Theological Library Association. He also translated the Jacob Boehme volume in this series.

Author of the Preface

HEIKO OBERMAN, the eminent Church historian, is Director, Institute fuer Spaetmittelalter und Reformation, at Tuebingen University in West Germany. He is one of the major authorities in the world on the Protestant Spirituality of the post-Reformation period. His studies on "Nationalism" have received international acclaim. His works include *The Harvest of Medieval Theology* (1963), *Forerunners of the Reformation: The Shape of Late Medieval Thought* (1966) and *Simul Gemitus et Raptus: Luther und die Mystik*. In Kirche, Mystik, Heiligung und das Natuerliche bei Luther: Vortraege des III. Internationalen Kongresses fuer Lutherforschung. Goettingen (1968)

Preface

I

The fascination with Johann Arndt and with his major writing, *True Christianity* ("Vier Bücher vom wahren Christentum," Spring 1606), is due to the fact that this work is at once protest and program. His protest places Arndt in the unenviable position of waging a war on two fronts: on one front, against the noticeable decay of a self-conscious Christian society held in suspense—and imbalance—long before the military disruptions caused by the Thirty Years War and long outlasting the concluding Peace of Westphalia (1648); and on the other front, against the disputations of an orthodoxy[1] so concerned to protect its purity that the experience of faith and the living signs of the imitation of Christ (*imitatio Christi*) had become at least suspect and at most relegated to a place of secondary importance. Hence, Arndt attacks a double and a doubly dangerous divorce: one between faith and life, another between scholarly knowledge and practical wisdom, a wisdom which was for Arndt the decisively Christian know-how.

It was Arndt's program that saved his protest and saved it from being dubbed the work of a "Puritan"—with all the pejorative connotations of that word in the English-speaking world—or the work of a "Schwärmer"—with all the pejorative connotations of that word in the German-speaking world. Through his program Arndt became "the Father of German Pietism," marking the path from faith and conversion toward rebirth and sanctification. The elements of moralism and obscurantism remained a latent threat,

---

1. Arndt's critique is directed against an arid speculative orthodoxy, not against Lutheran orthodoxy as such which proves to be much more alert to affective theology than the usual designation tends to suggest.

but they materialized only in those fringe pietist groups that first severed, and then excised, social ethical concerns from its roots in the life of the Spirit.

II

The impact of Albrecht Ritschl's impressive three-volume *History of Pietism*[2] has been so overpowering and far-reaching that today, outside the small circle of specialists, pietism is still generally associated with anti-intellectualism, hyper-individualism, and holy-group separatism; untouched by the Reformation, it lived off the "eroticism of medieval mysticism" and the "Pharisaic irresponsibility" of medieval monasticism. From the number of "isms" in this general summary, it is clear that modern research could easily correct Ritschl on many scores.[3] The contemporary assessment of pietism, however, remains stubbornly resistant to the academic *aggiornamento;* thus, "pietism" continues to have an unwholesome reputation on both sides of the Atlantic Ocean.

Admittedly, this judgment is not groundless with respect to those trends in pietism which, since the beginning of the nineteenth century and in bewildered reaction to the Enlightenment, allied themselves with a frightened and fossilized orthodoxy, giving way to that kind of individualistic withdrawal and conventicle separatism that Ritschl regarded as characteristic of pietism as such. But the compelling vision of the first three generations of pietist leaders from Spener (†1705) to Francke (†1727) and Zinzendorf (†1760) retained Arndt's program, developed it, and directed it toward social renewal, cutting through the dead weight of traditional Christianity that had burdened the creative imagination of "faith active in love" (Gal. 5:6).

This new translation of Arndt is published at the very juncture in time when these two kinds of pietism are wrestling with each other and with the spirit of the times. At stake in this struggle

---

2. Bonn, 1880-1886; reprint Berlin, 1966.

3. Manfred Waldemar Kohl, *Studies in Pietism. A Bibliographical Survey of Research since 1958/59*, unpublished Diss., Harvard, 1969; Martin Greschat, "Zur neueren Pietismusforschung. Ein Literaturbericht," in: *Jahrbuck des Vereins für Westfälische Kirchengeschichte* 65 (1972), pp. 220-268; Johannes Wallmann, "Reformation, Orthodoxie, Pietismus," in: *Jahrbuch der Gesellschaft für niedersächsische Kirchengeschichte* 70 (1972), pp. 179-200; see also the collection of articles on German pietism: *Zur neueren Pietismusforschung*, ed. Martin Greschat, Wege der Forschung vol. 440, Darmstadt, 1977.

between "true" and "false" pietism—here so evaluated in view of its historical origins and intentions—is the crucial question: Will the vitality of Arndt's protest and the viability of his program belie and falsify the Ritschlian view and overcome its current cultural and intellectual stigma?

III

In German scholarship the beginnings of the Pietist Movement are usually identified with the publication of Philip Jakob Spener's *Pia Desideria* (1675); but it should be remembered that these proposals for the reform of life (*reformatio vitae*), intended to follow up and to complete Luther's reform of doctrine (*reformatio doctrinae*), were first published as a "Preface" to a work of Arndt. As Spener sees it, Arndt stands in the immediate proximity of Luther, and both men travel the same spiritual path shown by Johannes Tauler (†1361). Through Martin Luther (†1546) the great wheels of the Reformation were set in motion, and while Luther rightly deserves first place, "it is by no means clear as yet through whose books God will be more effective."[4] Spener merely authorized and popularized the earlier designation of Arndt as a second Luther and a third Elias: "At the time of Hus, in the year 1415, the tree of life took root; at the time of Luther, in the year 1517, this tree started to flower; in the year 1618 the harvesters went out to gather in its fruits."[5]

There can be no doubt that Arndt is the hidden and powerful source of a tradition that moved for some time in subterranean channels, surfacing toward the later part of the seventeenth century as German pietism. Yet it should be clearly seen that German pietism is but part of a much larger European phenomenon: Jansenism, precisionism, puritanism, and a widespread chiliastic spiri-

---

4. *Theologische Bedenken*, Halle, 1700, III. 714. The German original version of this free translation is most accessible with Johannes Wallmann, *Philipp Jakob Spener und die Anfänge des Pietismus*, Tübingen, 1970, p. 110, n. 105. In this excellent Spener study Arndt is properly assigned priority vis-à-vis Spener as "Begründer" of pietism. *Ibid.*, p. 14; cf. p. 239.

5. Quoted by Hans-Joachim Schwager, *Johann Arndts Bemühen um die rechte Gestaltung des Neuen Lebens der Gläubigen*, Münster i. W., 1961, p. 95.

6. In the larger European perspective William Perkins (†1602 in Cambridge, England) may well hold the best claim to the title "Father of Pietism." Cf. the basic work of August Lang, *Puritanismus und Pietismus. Studien zu ihrer Entwicklung von M. Butzer bis zum Methodismus*, Neukirchen, 1941, reprint Darmstadt, 1972, pp. 101-131. Lang thus confirmed the earlier thesis of Heinrich Heppe, *Geschichte des Pietismus und der Mystik in der reformierten Kirche*, Leiden, 1979, p. 140. For Dutch pietism in the seventeenth century see Wilhelm

tualism. In England, The Netherlands, Germany, France, Switzerland, and Scandanavia—and, as far as I can see, in this geographical order—these new movements attest to the resilience of European Christianity at the end of the Reformation era, a time when discouragement and new hope mysteriously intertwine, eliciting impressive forms of individual piety and communal revival.[6]

Until this point, the formidable scholarly energy focused on establishing religious pedigrees and on organizing the mass of pamphlets and authors in terms of priority and influence has neglected the crucial connection between the history of religious thought and that kind of social history which can best be described as the analysis of the *Zeitgeist,* the mood of the times. Thus, later historians have refused to see that the political and confessional conformity demanded by all three major European denominations forced a band of kindred spirits to seek shelter with one another. Readings from sources that were often anonymous united people of very different stripe. On either side of the Channel and on both sides of the Rhine, hungry eyes devoured the same passages of Scripture—and came to similar conclusions. The differences between these variants of pietism are intriguing, but they should not lead us to overlook the beginnings of the first phase of a trans-confessional ecumenical movement that would spawn missionary work inside and far beyond the borders of Europe and that would initiate care for the socially underprivileged—long before the malaise of the social structures themselves was uncovered.

IV

Admid this surprisingly cohesive European movement, Johann Arndt assumes a place all his own, performing a double service. The first aspect of Arndt's double service lies in the fact that his *True Christianity* could not have been written and would not have been able to survive the challenges of Lutheran orthodoxy if he had

---

Goeters, *Die Vorbereitung des Pietismus in der reformierten Kirche der Niederlande bis zur labadistischen Krisis 1670,* Leipzig, 1911. The advantage of F. Ernest Stoeffler over against these more detailed and conceptually refined basic studies is his pan-European perspective: *The Rise of Evangelical Pietism,* Leiden, 1971² (1965); *German Pietism during the Eighteenth Century,* Leiden, 1973. The transition to the new world is sketched with a fine pen—and on a much broader canvas than the title suggests—by James R. Tanis, *Dutch Calvinistic Pietism in the Middle Colonies. A Study in the Life and Theology of Theodorus Jacobus Frelinghuysen*'s-Gravenhage, 1967, with extensive sources and secondary literature.

not been such an observant reader and perceptive student of Martin Luther's works. Precisely at a time when Lutherans were understandably intent on defending the heritage of the Reformation by insisting on the *Augsburg Confession* (1530) and the *Formula of Concord* (1577), Arndt discerned behind the theological conclusions of Luther the function of true doctrine as the perimeter around the experience of penance and salvation; in short, he brought to light again the spontaneity of Christian service as the true fruit of a living faith. Arndt is entitled to the honor of being the first "Luther scholar" to see, underscore, and apply Luther's vision that justification by faith alone does not preclude but, to the contrary, unleashes good works in terms of the whole Christian, his action in the Church and in the world.

Long before scholars decreed the mutual exclusion between "Reformation" and "mysticism," Luther himself had ingested and incorporated into his own thinking the sermons of Bernard of Clairvaux (†1153), the biblical piety of his spiritual director Johannes Staupitz (†1525), and the meditations of Johannes Tauler (†1361). The inner suspense and the dynamic contrast between the pains of desolation and the excesses of joy in the experience of untrammeled faith characterize his spirituality, just as the famous formula "righteous and sinner at once" (*simul iustus et peccator*) catches the exact paradox of his doctrine of justification.[7] In this respect Arndt is a second Luther, a *Lutherus redivivus*.

Symbolically Arndt was decisively helped by a 1520 reprint of the 1518 first complete edition of the "German Theology" (the so-called *Theologia Deutsch*) which, with the express permission of Staupitz,[8] had been edited by Luther for the Augustinian press at the Wittenberg monastery. In 1597 Arndt found this precious volume somewhere all dusted over just as Luther had found it some eighty years before. Arndt's writing career and the direction of his thought take a new turn with his re-edition of the "German Theol-

---

7. See Heiko A. Oberman, "Simul gemitus et raptus: Luther und die Mystik," in: *Kirche, Mystik, Heiligung und das Natürliche bei Luther*, Vorträge des Dritten Internationalen Kongresses für Lutherforschung, ed. Ivar Asheim, Göttingen, 1967, pp. 20-59. For the original English version of this article see *The Reformation in Medieval Perspective*, ed. Steven E. Ozment, Chicago, 1971, pp. 219-251.

8. *D. Martin Luthers Werke*. Briefwechsel, vol. 1, Weimar, 1930, p. 160, line 8-10, no. 66.

ogy" in Halberstadt 1597[9] which Arndt is inclined to ascribe—
again, as Luther before him[10]—to Tauler. In using Angela di
Foligno (†1309) and, without knowing it, Valentin Weigel
(†1568),[11] in quoting Raymund of Sabunde (†1436), and in learning
from Johann Staupitz,[12] Arndt harvested "mystical sources" for his
True Christianity. In doing so he did not deviate from Luther but
rather gave access to a more authentic Luther, always grateful for
finding earlier spiritual resources that the later confessional stance
would rule out of court as irreconcilable with the credo of the
Reformation.

V

The second aspect of Arndt's double service is directly related
to this challenging claim of Luther's heritage. Albrecht Ritschl was
not completely wrong in tracing Arndt's lineage back to medieval
monastic and mystical traditions; it is the value judgment that went
with Ritschl's work that deserves reconsideration.

Arndt is not only a faithful student of Reformation theology;
he also proves to be a true disciple of Luther in his awareness that
the medieval Church has achieved much more than "the growth of
papalism" and "the commercialization of penance." The treasures
of piety discovered by Arndt in the mystical sources and in the
monastic experience were not merely to be acknowledged and re-
spected but deserved to be carried into the Reformation era, where
the monastic vows were again shouldered by all Christian men and
where the learned theology of the schools was complemented by an
affective theology accessible as well to the simple and the unlet-
tered.

---

9. Wilhelm Koepp regards this as the "Wendepunkt" in Arndt's life: *Johann Arndt. Eine
Untersuchung über die Mystik im Luthertum,* Berlin, 1912, p. 24.

10. Luther first published an incomplete edition in 1516 (nineteen chapters) and followed up with a complete edition in 1518. Against earlier allegations Luther provides here a
faithful and unchanged version of the best manuscript known. See Steven E. Ozment,
Mysticism and Dissent. Religious Ideology and Social Protest in the Sixteenth Century, New Haven,
1973, pp. 17-60; 18, n. 10.

11. Weigel chose as subtitle for his crucial self-defense "A Treatise on True Saving
Faith . . ." (1572) that of the *German Theology.* Ozment, *Mysticism and Dissent,* p. 204.

12. Staupitz continues to be a highly esteemed author in the Pietist tradition. See *Johann
von Staupitz. Sämtliche Schriften,* vol. 2: *Lateinische Schriften* II, eds. Lothar Graf zu Dohna,
Richard Wetzel, Spätmittelalter und Reformation. Texte und Untersuchungen 14, Berlin,
1979, pp. 10f.

PREFACE

The deep chasm between a medieval mysticism intent to mobilize all human resources for the ascent to God and Luther's discovery of the priority of the descent of God, overcoming man's highest aspirations and received in faith, is not to be denied. But the fascination with Johann Arndt and the lasting significance of his *True Christianity* are due to his harvest of medieval spirituality so staunchly harnessed by the basic insights of the Reformation that he will continue to find a wide and grateful readership across the divisions of language, culture, and confessions.

Tübingen, 1. Advent 1978   Heiko A. Oberman

Introduction

"In my youth," wrote Albert Schweitzer on the four hundredth anniversary of Johann Arndt's birth in 1955, "I gained from my mother a love for Arndt; he was a prophet of interior Protestantism."[1] Schweitzer was eighty-three years of age when he wrote these words, and his comments reflect clearly the extent of Arndt's popularity and influence within the spirituality of German Protestantism. Nevertheless, the 20th century has not been as closely attracted to Arndt's writings as have earlier centuries. At the same time as Schweitzer was listening to Arndt at his mother's side, the modern Protestant antagonism to mystical writing was being established by authors such as Albrecht Ritschl;[2] the antagonism was continued by the Protestant dialectical theologians of this century, chief among whom was Karl Barth.[3]

The antagonism of such modern authors to the word "mysticism" is not recent, however; it can justifiably be traced back to the

---

1. Wilhelm Koepp, *Johann Arndt und sein "Wahres Christentum"* (Berlin, 1959), p. 16.

2. See in particular Albrecht Ritschl, *Geschichte des Pietismus* (3 Bde.; Bonn, 1880–1886). For a translation to his prolegomena see his *Three Essays*, trans. Philip Hefner (Philadelphia, 1972).

3. See Bengt Hägglund, *The Background of Luther's Doctrine of Justification in Late Medieval Theology* (Philadelphia, Pa., 1971), pp. 2–3. Among those who share this distaste are Gustav Aulen, *The Faith of the Church*, trans. Eric H. Wahlstrom and G. Everett Arden (Philadelphia, Pa., 1948), pp. 50–53; Karl Barth, *Church Dogmatics*, trans. G.W. Bromiley (Edinburgh, 1962), IV/3/2, pp. 539–540; Adolph Harnack, *History of Dogma*, trans. Neil Buchanan (London, 1900), VI, pp. 97–108; Adolf Köberle, *The Quest for Holiness*, trans. John C. Mattes (Minneapolis, Minn., 1938), pp. 7–14; Anders Nygren, *Agape and Eros*, trans. Philip S. Watson (London, 1953), pp. 228–29, 700–709, and Albert Ritschl, *The Christian Doctrine of Justification and Reconciliation*, trans. H.R. Mackintosh et al. (3rd ed., n. pl., 1888), pp. 112–114, etc., and cf. Friedrich Kalb, *Theology of Worship in 17th-Century Lutheranism*, trans. Henry P.A. Hamann (St. Louis, Mo., 1965), pp. 178–179. Note, however, the positive stance taken in this regard by Paul Tillich, *Systematic Theology* (Chicago, Ill., 1963), III, pp. 241–243.

1

INTRODUCTION

age of Johann Arndt himself. Arndt was born on December 17, 1555, possibly in Edderitz bei Köthen, and spent his youth, the son of a village pastor, in Ballenstedt in Anhalt-Bernburg.[4] In the year of his birth, the Peace of Augsburg was signed and Lutheranism was thereby given legal status within the Holy Roman Empire, and assured of relative security for the next fifty years. At the same time as it gained such political and territorial security, however, it was experiencing internal theological struggles that would continue in some form throughout the coming centuries.

Prior to Luther's death in 1546, Lutheran doctrine was codified in three major documents: *The Augsburg Confession* in 1530, *The Apology for the Augsburg Confession* in the same year, and *The Smalcald Articles* published in 1538.[5] All three were a center of controversy. No sooner had *The Augsburg Confession* been accepted by the Protestant princes than Philip Melancthon (1497–1560) began to revise the text so as to allow for various interpretations. Melancthon's irenic concerns were directed in the same way to the *Apology*, and allowed only his qualified endorsement of *The Smalcald Articles*. His humanism and ecumenical orientation dictated his position following the Protestant military defeat in 1547.

Following the defeat, Melancthon developed a doctrine that Lutherans might accept the imposition of certain Catholic practices as *adiaphora*, that is, matters not central to faith. In this he was opposed by Matthias Flacius Illyricus (1520–1575) who insisted that there were no *adiaphora* with respect to faith. In 1561 a second controversy—to last for some ten years—was precipitated by George Major (1502–1574), who taught that good works were necessary for salvation. A few years later the Synergistic Controversy arose in which Melancthonians supported a defense of the doctrine that man as man cooperates in his conversion. Flacius Illyricus and

---

4. The fullest study of Arndt's life and thought, its background and influence, is Wilhelm Koepp, *Johann Arndt: Eine Untersuchung über die Mystik im Luthertum* (Berlin, 1912) (hereafter cited as Koepp, *Arndt*). The medieval sources that influenced his work are extensively discussed in Edmund Weber, *Johann Arndt's Vier Bücher vom Wahren Christentum, als Beitrag zur protestantischen Irenik des 17. Jahrhunderts: Eine quellenkritische Untersuchung* (Marburg/Lahn, 1969). See also John O. Evjen, "John Arndt," *The Lutheran Quarterly* 35 (1905): 540–555, and F.J. Winter, "Johann Arndt der Verfasser des *Wahres Christentums*" in *Schriften des Vereins für Reformationsgeschichte* 28 (1910): 30ff.

5. For an outline of these controversies, see F. Bente, *Historical Introduction to the Book of Concord*, in *Concordia Triglotta* (St. Louis, Mo., 1921) and *Die Bekenntnisschriften der evangelisch-lutherischen Kirche* (Berlin, 1930), I, pp. xi–xliv.

the Gnesio-Lutherans opposed Melancthon in both Majorist and Synergistic Controversies, but by 1560 Flacius's pure Lutheranism was leading him into a heresy of his own, in which he insisted against his opponents that the very substance of fallen man was sinful. Although Flacius's opinion was a minority one, discussion on the issue continued to 1575. In 1549 Andreas Osiander (1498–1552) initiated a struggle that was to last into the late 1560s. Upholding a doctrine of infused righteousness through Christ's divine nature, he severely limited Luther's doctrine of forensic justification, and was opposed by nearly all Lutherans at the time. Two other controversies must be noted. The first involved Johann Agricola's (1492–1566) antinomian insistence on the role of Gospel as opposed to Law. The second had more far-reaching results, and was carried on during the 1560s and 1570s over the attempt of the Melancthonians to effect an agreement between Lutherans and Calvinists on the doctrine of Christ's nature and, as a result, on the practice of the Lord's Supper. Through the mediation of two Lutheran theologians, Jacob Andreae (1528–1590) and Martin Chemnitz (1522–1586), the questions raised by these controversies were eventually resolved in the *Formula of Concord* (1580).

In their attempts to support their various positions and in the polemical intra- and interdenominational literature that grew up during the theological controversies, the debating theologians developed a precise theological methodology and vocabulary known as Protestant Orthodoxy or Scholasticism.[6] Its method was rooted in that of Melancthon's *Loci Communes*,[7] and was particularly influenced by the Spanish-Jesuit scholastics of the 16th century.[8] Aside from its methodology and its legalistic insistence on the acceptance of closely worded doctrinal statements of faith, Orthodoxy is difficult to define. To its enemies, such as Arndt, it was seen as a dry,

---

6. On the history of scholastic orthodoxy within Protestantism, see Isaac A. Dorner, *History of Protestant Theology*, trans. George Robson and Sophia Taylor, 2 vols. (Edinburgh, 1871), and Robert P. Scharlemann, *Thomas Aquinas and John Gerhard* (New Haven, 1964), pp. 13–43. A more recent work is that of Robert D. Preuss, *The Theology of Post-Reformation Lutheranism, A Study of Theological Prolegomena*, 2 vols. (St. Louis, Mo., 1970).

Excellent compendiums of scholastic doctrine are available. See Heinrich Heppe, *Reformed Dogmatics*, trans. G.T. Thomsen (London, 1950); Heinrich Schmid, *The Doctrinal Theology of the Evangelical Lutheran Church*, trans. Charles A. Hay and Henry E. Jacobs (Philadelphia, Pa., 1876). See also Winfried Zeller, hrsg., *Der Protestantismus des 17. Jahrhunderts* (Bremen, 1962).

7. See Scharlemann, *Thomas Aquinas*, ch. 5, pp. 22–28.

8. Ibid., pp. 13–22.

polemical, intolerant defense of a single denomination's position, lacking any concern with issues relevant to religious life or the practice of Christian virtue and devotion. Yet, Orthodoxy's opponents often owed much to its form and matter. Interest in personal piety was not neglected by the greater orthodox theologians.[9]

Orthodoxy is commonly categorized according to three historical periods.[10] The first, a Golden Age, extended from Chemnitz to 1618; the second, High Orthodoxy, covered the period of The Thirty Years' War; a third, the Silver Age, lasted to the early 18th century. The major figure in the second was Johann Gerhard (1582–1637). In the third, Johann Andreas Quenstedt (1617–1688), David Hollatz (1648–1713), and the irenic George Calixtus (1586–1656) were the most significant authors.

From its beginnings Lutheran Orthodoxy was opposed by men who were primarily interested in the practice of piety: personal renewal, individual growth in holiness, and religious experience.[11] This practically oriented opposition found a spokesman in Arndt, who was fiercely denounced for heresy by contemporary theologians; although defended by many, including Johann Gerhard, he did leave himself open to charges of unorthodoxy.[12]

Arndt's early education had taken place in Aschersleben, Halberstadt, and Magdeburg, and at twenty-two he went to the university at Helmstedt to study medicine. He took ill, gave up his plans for a medical career, and began to read theology and mystical authors. His studies took him to Wittenberg, Strassburg, and Basel and in 1583 he was serving in the diaconate in Ballenstedt. In the same year he married Anna Wagner. The marriage was happy but the couple remained childless throughout their thirty-eight years together.

---

9. On Orthodoxy's interest in personal piety, see Hermann A. Preuss and Edmund Smits, eds., *The Doctrine of Man in Classical Lutheran Theology* (Minneapolis, Minn., 1962), pp. xix–xxii, but cf. Henrich Schmid, *Die Geschichte des Pietismus* (Berlin, 1863), p. 1, and Martin Schmidt, *Wiedergeburt und Neuer Mensch* (Witten, 1969), pp. 5–6. Above all see Hans Leube, *Die Reformbestrebungen der deutschen lutherischen Kirche im Zeitalter der Orthodoxie* (Leipzig, 1924), and Heinrich Bornkamm, *Mystik, Spiritualismus und die Anfange des Pietismus im Luthertum* (Giessen, 1926).

10. See R. Preuss, *Post-Reformation Lutheranism*, I, pp. 44–47.

11. See Max Goebel, *Geschichte des Christlichen Lebens* (3 Bde., Coblenz, 1852–1860), and F. Ernst Stoeffler, *The Rise of Evangelical Pietism* (Leiden, 1965).

12. See Koepp, *Arndt*, pp. 67–143, for details on the controversy. The scope and duration of the controversy is evidenced by a recently discovered manuscript by a mid-17th century Silesian, which charts the various treatises written for and against Arndt. (See MS Schwenkfelder Library, Pennsburg, Pa., SB33.)

INTRODUCTION

The year following, in 1584, Arndt was pastor in Badeborn, a small village near the larger town Quedlinburg, where he served in the St. Nicholas church shortly after. From the very beginning of his career he was involved in controversy. Firmly Lutheran, he refused to abandon the rite of exorcism before baptism, despite the order of his Calvinistically inclined Duke. Increasing difficulties necessitated his move in 1599 to Baunschweig, where he immediately became enmeshed in the power politics of the city against the Duke. In 1609 he was at Eisleben, and after a short but pleasant pastorate there he was appointed General Superintendent of Celle in 1611. He died in 1621.

In his numerous writings, Arndt's overwhelming interest was with the practice of the Christian life. It was always his concern to describe clearly the virtuous activities to which a Christian in his love for neighbor is obligated, and the meditation, reflection, and prayer to which, in his love for God, a Christian is called. The majority of Arndt's writings are, as a result, works of spirituality and not dogmatic treatises.[13] In 1597 he edited the 1518 Luther printing of the *Theologia deutsch* with a lengthy introduction opposing the polemical publications of the time. The work was reprinted with the *Imitatio Christi* and a shortened introduction in 1605, 1617, and 1621. In 1605 as well he edited Johann Staupitz's *De amore dei* in a German version and the same year saw the publication of the first book of his famous *True Christianity (Wahres Christenthum)*. The work was reprinted in a corrected version in 1606, which with three additional books printed by 1610 comprises the *Four Books on True Christianity*. The work was immediately popular. It went through some 20 editions prior to Arndt's death and over 125 printings before the close of the 18th century. A full listing of 19th-century and American printings remains to be done.[14] In the posthumous printings of *True Christianity*, two books were added, a fifth including Arndt's 1620 tracts *On True Faith and a Holy Life*, *On the Union of the Faithful with Jesus Christ, Our Head*, and *On the Holy Trinity*, and a sixth, comprising his answers to critics, some of his letters, and the two prefaces to the *Theologia deutsch*. Most later printings also included his posthumous *Informatorium biblicum* (1623)—on approaching the Bible—and his two testaments. Next in popularity to his *True Christianity* was his prayer book, *A Paradise Garden Full of*

---

13. For a list of his works, see Koepp, *Arndt*, pp. 297ff.
14. Ibid., pp. 302–306.

INTRODUCTION

Christian Virtues, of 1612. The *Paradise Garden* included material reworked from earlier sources both Catholic (medieval and Jesuit) and Protestant, and from the Scriptures. The prayers in the volume are gathered under five main headings: on the virtues and the Ten Commandments, on the three chief articles of Christianity, prayers of consolation, prayers in time of need, and prayers of praise.[15] His Postills on the Gospels (1615/1616) and his Catechetical sermons (1616) were also influential in later centuries although their popularity was dependent on that of the *True Christianity* and the *Paradise Garden*.

*   *   *   *   *

What has attracted the attention of many readers of *True Christianity* is its extensive use of medieval and other mystical sources. One must take care, however, to define the word "mysticism" properly when applying it to Arndt. "Spirituality" has been described as concentrating "above all on prayer and on everything connected with prayer in the ascetical and mystical life—in other words, on religious exercises as well as religious experience."[16] For Arndt and his contemporaries, "mystical theology" was understood within the context of spirituality as defined above, and embraced both ascetic theology and the theology of mystical union.[17] Within Arndt's circle it was equated with practical theology in opposition to the theological speculation of Orthodox circles. Thus, for him it tended to be equated, although not exclusively, with ascetic theology,

> treating of the exercises required of aspirants to perfection. Ordinarily the soul rises to perfection by passing through three stages. First of all, it gets free from sin by penance and mortification; then it forms inner virtues by prayer and imitation of Christ; and lastly, it advances in the love of God until it reaches habitual union with him. It is for us to enter the path of perfection and to traverse its stages more or less quickly. God calls us to do this, and gives us the graces needed for corresponding to his call.[18]

---

15. On Arndt's prayer literature, see above all Paul Althaus, d.A., *Forschungen zur Evangelischen Gebetsliteratur* (Gütersloh, 1927) and Hermann Beck, *Die Erbauungsliteratur der Evangelischen Kirche Deutschlands* (Erlangen, 1883).

16. Louis Bouyer, *The Spirituality of the New Testament and the Fathers*, trans. Mary P. Ryan (New York, 1963), pp. vi–ix.

17. R. Garrigou-Lagrange, *Les trois âges de la vie interieure, Prelude de celle de ciel* (Paris, 1939), I, pp. 16–19.

18. P. Pourrat, *Christian Spirituality*, trans. W.H. Mitchell and S.P. Jacques (London, 1922), I, p. v.

INTRODUCTION

Arndt's definition did include, of course, mystical theology proper, which has been outlined as dealing with "extraordinary states . . . such as mystical union with its concomitant manifestations—i.e. ecstasy, visions and revelations,"[19] although Arndt did not insist on the infused[20] nature of union.

Within the Lutheran tradition, the term "mystical union" (*unio mystica*) was, for the most part, understood in a radically different way than it was within Catholicism. As I have noted elsewhere, Luther taught of an ever-present mystical union of the believer with Christ; such a union is "not the end of the search for Christian perfection but rather the beginning, the incorporation of every believer into the body of Christ. The terminology of mystical theology was applied to this initial union; it was democratized as it were."[21] Among Luther's followers the various aspects of the application of saving grace to the believer, chief among which is the mystical union, tended to be formed into a progressive order of salvation (*ordo salutis*): election, vocation, illumination, conversion, regeneration, justification, mystical union, renovation, preservation, glorification.

The exact role played by Arndt in the development of the orthodox Lutheran doctrine on the mystical union and its place in the order of salvation has not yet been properly determined, but there is no doubt as to his significance in this,[22] nor to his continuing direct influence on theology and piety throughout the 17th century.

Arndt treats the doctrine of the mystical union in depth in his treatise on the topic included in his fifth book of *True Christianity* and translated below. In it he insists, with Luther, that God has freely intended the union from the beginning; that it is announced

---

19. Ibid.

20. "The mark of these states is their independence of those who experienced them. They are the privilege of the few to whom God unites Himself ineffably by flooding them with light and love. No one can effect these mystical phenomena within himself by any efforts or merits of his own. The soul of the ascetic with the help of grace makes an effort to rise towards God; but the soul of the mystic is suddenly and impetuously visited by God without exerting any activity beyond that of receiving and enjoying the Divine gift" (Ibid.). For details on modern studies relating to the infused nature of the mystic grace see Cuthbert Butler, *Western Mysticism* (London, 1922).

21. See my introduction to Jacob Boehme, *The Way to Christ* (New York, 1978), pp. 10–11.

22. Wilhelm Koepp, "Wurzel und Ursprung der orthodoxen Lehre von der *unio mystica*", *Zeitschrift für Theologie und Kirche*, 29 N.F. II (1921), pp. 46–71, 139–171.

The *ordo salutis* changed little in the 17th century. The similarities between Arndt

to the individual believer through God's word, externally in Scripture and internally in the heart; that it is totally a gift of grace; and that it is primarily union with Christ in his body, the Church. Like Luther, as well, he interprets it in close relationship with purification and repentance, describes it in nuptial and sacramental images, and sees it as the root of continuing love toward God and full renovation of life, finally completed in glory.

But there are differences between Arndt and Luther. Love, for Arndt, is the ultimate manifestation of a unitive life of faith in imitation of Christ. It is directed toward neighbor and God; its end is perfect patience and praise. The only object worthy of man's love or praise is the chief good, God, to whom man is directed throughout life. In all this there is little one cannot find in Luther, but in Arndt the emphasis on the life of love allows a much larger scope for a mystical interpretation of progressive perfection toward the completion of the renewal of the image of God, and of contemplative prayer, than exists in the thought of Luther.

Arndt agrees fully with Luther's accentuation of faith, but in his work the possibility for a perfected experience of the faith union is continually expressed in words that might well have sounded to Luther like those of the speculative mystics he so vehemently attacked. Arndt is no longer describing a union of the exact type

---

and David Hollatz are apparent in parallel chapters of Arndt's treatise on union in Book Five (translated below) with the respective sections on Hollatz's *Examen Theologicum*, as follows:

Arndt	Hollatz
I, II	electio
III	vocatio
IV	illuminatio
V	conversio
VI (Busse)	regeneratio
VI (Glaube)	justificatio
VII	unio
VII, IX	renovatio
X	conservatio
XIV	glorificatio

See David Hollatz, *Examinem theologicum acroamaticum universam theologiam theoretico-polemicam complectens* (Rostochii et Lipsiae, Apud Joh. Ruswormium, M. DCC XVIII). The pagination for the entries following election (which is considered by Hollatz within the article on vocation) are 233, 251, 292, 318, 337, 383, 402, 420, and 430 respectively. David Hollatz, *Evangelische Gnaden-Ordnung* (edition available for this study was a reprint of the 1745 edition, Philadelphia, Pa., 1810).

discussed by Luther. Rather, the believer is directed to explore the nature of his union with Christ; he is admonished to cast aside all love for the creaturely and to learn progressively to have, in fullness, the God who has united himself with the believer. Spiritual joy, Arndt believes, will crown the fulfillment of this unitive experience. When one considers such a position in the light of Arndt's extensive use of medieval texts, one can better understand why the antagonisms against him were so fierce.

The use of the *Theologia deutsch* in *True Christianity* is interesting, but its influence is not extensive. Verbal and theological similarities have been noted at only eight points.[23] Two of these are highly questionable,[24] and of the remaining six, the citations are extremely brief and of little significance for Arndt's theology as a whole.[25] In many cases Arndt, like Luther, deliberately ignored any statements in the original that referred to ecstatic mystical union at the end of a graduated progress toward the divine, and reshaped them according to his understanding of a union of all believers with Christ in faith. This intentional reshaping of medieval texts is especially apparent in his preface to the *Theologia deutsch*:

> The end of all theology and Christianity is union with God . . . marriage with the heavenly bridegroom Jesus Christ. . . . The life-giving faith, the new birth, Christ's dwelling in us, Christ's noble life in us, the fruits of the Holy Spirit in us, the enlightenment and sanctification, the kingdom of God in us. This is all one thing since where true faith is, there is Christ with all his justification, holiness . . . Christ and faith unite themselves with one another so that everything which is Christ's is ours through faith. Where Christ dwells in faith, he brings forth a holy life, and this is the noble life of Christ in us.[26]

As a guide for this "noble life of Christ" in the believer, the *Imitation of Christ* is of special value and might be easily read as a handbook directing man from repentance through conversion into the activities of a renovated life. This was the understanding Arndt had of the work. The only sections from it that he used directly were from Book One, 19–22, treating of Godly exercises, prayer,

---

23. See Weber, *Arndt*, pp. 53–63.
24. Ibid., pp. 53–56, 62–63, suggests parallels for *True Christianity*, I, pp. 2 and 31.
25. Ibid., pp. 56–63, notes *True Christianity*, I, pp. 11–12, 15, 16; II, pp. 6, 22, 23.
26. See below, Book Six, Part III.

compunction, and human misery[27] and, in their context in Arndt's work, they are perfectly consistent with his Lutheranism.

Nevertheless, unlike Luther, Arndt was willing to make use of medieval portrayals of ecstatic mystical transport to describe experiences of love for God possible for believers during intense prayer or devotion. In the second book of *True Christianity*, chapters 13ff., for example, Arndt made use of Angela of Foligno's writings to support his position. A parallel printing of Arndt's work and his source helps to indicate how important such an experience was for him and elucidates his thought in his expansion of the source.

Arndt	Angela
Since the living knowledge of God and the crucified Christ cannot be obtained unless without ceasing one reads daily in the book of the innocent and holy life of Christ Jesus our Lord, and since this contemplation and lifting of the mind to God cannot occur without a meditative faithful, humble, and earnest heart, which is not only a speech of the mouth but much more of the faithful heart and mind and is the uplifting of all the powers of the soul (Ps. 19:11 [Ps. 25:1]), it is necessary that one learn to understand the manner and virtue of prayer. Without prayer one does not find God. Prayer is the means by which one seeks and finds God (Mt. 7:7–8).	Forasmuch, therefore, as the knowledge of God uncreated and of Christ crucified is needful, and seeing that without it we cannot transform our minds in His love, it behoveth us to read diligently in that aforesaid Book of Life, that is to say, the life and death of Jesus Christ. And whereas this reading, or rather knowledge, cannot possibly be acquired without devout, pure, humble, fervent, attentive, and constant prayer (not with the lips alone, but with the heart and mind and all the strength), something must be said of prayer, as well as of the Book of Life.
2. Prayer is threefold: oral, internal, and supernatural as Paul says . . . (1 Cor. 14:15).	It is through prayer and in prayer that we find God. There are divers kinds of prayer, but in these three kinds alone is God to be found. The first is corporal, the second mental, and the third supernatural. Corporal prayer is that which is always accompanied by the sound of words and by bodily exercises, such as kneeling down, asking pardon, and bowing oneself. This kind do I continually perform; and the reason thereof is that, desiring to
3. Oral prayer is a careful, humble, external practice that leads to internal prayer, indeed that leads one into his own heart, particularly if one contemplates the words in faith and prays accordingly. Such prayer moves and lifts the spirit and the soul to God so that one holds a faithful conversation	

---

27. See Weber, *Arndt*, p. 45.

with God in childlike trust.

4. Internal prayer occurs without ceasing in faith, the spirit and mind as John 4:23 . . . Psalm 19:14 . . . Psalm 77:7 . . . Romans 8:15 . . . say. Through such internal prayer one is led to supernatural prayer, which occurs as Tauler says through true union with God by faith. [By it] our created spirit is melted and sunk into the uncreated spirit of God so that everything occurs in an instant (as happened to all the saints in words and deeds from the beginning of the world). This kind of prayer beside external prayer is as much better as is a small coin beside a thousand Mark gold piece. By it the mind is filled with God's love through true faith so that it can think of nothing other than God, and if no other thought fills its heart and mind it is sorrowful. The tongue cannot speak of such a mind (Ps. 37:7) or at least very little. It always weeps after God, it thirsts for God (Ps. 42:3, 63:2), it has its own pleasure and love in God and it closes the whole world and everything that is in the world out and it is ever filled more and more with God's knowledge, love and joy (Ps. 84:3) concerning which no tongue can speak. What the soul then knows is unspeakable and if in such high meditation it is asked, "What do you know?" it answers: "A good that is above all goods." "What do you see?" "A beauty that is above all beauty." "What do you experience?" "A joy above all joys." "What do you taste?" "A kindness above all kindness." Indeed it will say, "All words that I speak are only a shadow, for the precious thing I discover in my soul, I cannot describe." It is the voice and statement of the eternal word to the loving soul as John 14:21 says: "I will reveal myself to him who loves me." What one then sees and experiences is above nature. One hears unspeakable exercise myself in mental prayer, I was sometimes deceived and hindered therefrom by idleness and sleep, and did thus lose time. For this reason do I exercise myself in corporal prayer, and this corporal prayer leadeth me unto the mental. But this must be done very attentively. Therefore when thou sayest the Paternoster, thou must consider well that which thou sayest and not repeat it in haste in order to say it a certain number of times, as do those vain women who perform good deeds for a reward. Mental prayer is when the meditation of God filleth the mind so entirely that it thinketh on naught else save on God. But when some other reflection entereth into the mind it asketh not that it should be mental prayer because that prayer doth hinder the tongue from performing its office and it cannot speak. So completely is the mind filled with God that it can concern itself with naught else, neither think of anything save of God. Hence from this mental prayer proceedeth the supernatural.

Supernatural prayer is that during which the soul is so exalted by this knowledge, or meditation, or fulness of God that it is uplifted above its own nature and understandeth more of God than it otherwise could naturally. And understanding, it knoweth; but that which it knoweth it cannot explain, because all that it perceiveth and feeleth is above its own nature.

11

words and sounds, which are called words of the understanding and mind.

5. Then the soul learns to know and understand God properly. Insofar as it knows God it loves him and insofar as it loves him, it desires to have him for itself completely. This is the true mark of love, that it has the beloved completely, is united completely with the beloved, and changes itself completely into the beloved.

6. This is often discovered in the soul of man as in a blink that quickly goes. The soul eagerly searches [to see] if this blink and taste can come again so that it might be united with the beloved. It begins then to pray orally and unknowingly for it truly sees that one must seek such heavenly refreshment and pleasure again through prayer. Divine wisdom has ordained this, does nothing without the most beautiful order and gives order to all things.

7. Therefore it is ordered that no one can come to the prayer of the mind without oral prayer and without this, no one can come to supernatural prayer and union with the highest and loveliest good that only truly discovers but cannot describe.[28]

In these three degrees of prayer, therefore, man learneth to know God and himself. And knowing Him, he loveth Him, and loving Him he desireth to possess Him; and this is the sign of love, for he who loveth not only a part of himself, but the whole, transformeth himself in the thing beloved.

But because this transformation endureth not for ever, the soul seeketh and examineth all other means whereby it may transform itself in its Beloved, in order that this union may be repeated. Wherefore must it be known that the divine wisdom hath ordered all things and given unto each its appointed place.

For this reason hath the ineffable wisdom ordained that no man should attain unto mental prayer who hath not previously exercised himself in corporal prayer, neither doth it permit the supernatural to be vouchsafed unto any person who hath not first performed both corporal and mental prayer.[29]

Of greater interest to Arndt than Angela of Foligno, however, was Johann Tauler. Arndt wrote a foreword to the 1621 edition of Tauler's works printed at Hamburg.[30] The edition was a reprint of the sermons in the Basel 1522 edition of Tauler,[31] and contained

---

28. The edition of Angela used by Arndt has been unavailable for reference for this study. The translation is that of Mary G. Sheegman, *The Book of Divine Consolation of the Blessed Angela of Foligno* (New York, 1966), pp. 98–101.

29. *True Christianity*, II, 20:1–8.

30. Johann Tauler in *Postilla JOHANNIS TAULERI . . . Item/ zwey Geistreiche Büchlein. Das erste/ die Deutsche Theologia . . . Das ander/ die Nachfolgung Christi . . .* Mit einer Vorrede Johannis Arndtes (Gedruckt zu Hamburg/ durch Hans Moser, In Verlegung Michal Herings. ANNO MDC xxi).

31. Johann Tauler, *Johannis Tauleri des seligen lerers Predigt/ fast fruchtbar zu eim recht Christlichen leben. Deren Predigen garnab hie in diesem Buch des halbtheyls meer sind denn in andern vorgetruckten bucheren die man sidhar mit der hilff gottes funden hat . . .* (Gedruckt zu Basel Anno M.D. XXII).

many sermons not by that author. Tauler is quoted at numerous points in Books One and Two of *True Christianity* and is heavily relied upon in Book Three.[32]

> So that you may more fully and firmly understand at the beginning of this third book, which relates completely to the inward man how the children of God are to be drawn from the exterior to the interior man, that is to the true ground of the heart so that they may search, know, purify, and change it and clearly consider God and his kingdom in the inmost ground of the heart, I shall first of all generally and then particularly in this first chapter explain this, referring to the theology of that spiritual man Johann Tauler, quoting him in his own words insofar as our present adorned German speech will allow. On this I remark as follows: The whole of Holy Scripture looks upon and searches the heart of man and the whole of the theology of Tauler is likewise directed to the inward man, the ground of the heart or the soul. Therefore, he often speaks of the inner ground, that God and the kingdom of God are purely to be enjoyed sought and found there.[33]

The third book is, thus, only for those already united in the Lutheran sense, for those who have become one with Christ in faith. It is for these, for their continuance in renovation of character and love of God, Arndt believes, that Tauler's theology, despite its shortcomings, is particularly well suited.

Unlike Luther, Arndt saw little need to rethink his source radically. Tauler's emphasis on *Gelassenheit* worked easily into Arndt's order of salvation, and Tauler's statements on ecstatic mystical experience could be reinterpreted in terms of a developing progression in a believer's love for God.

> The true way to enter into the inner treasure and highest good is true inward faith. In the first two books it is clearly enough described in its power and characteristic how it clings to Christ alone and grounds itself only in him. There is yet one thing to be chiefly taken into regard, namely, that which serves for our purpose. It is the true living characteristic of faith, to cling to God truly with the whole heart, to place its whole trust in God, to trust in him with the heart, to give itself totally to him, to unite itself with God, to be and remain one with God, to rest in God alone, to keep his interior Sabbath, to allow God alone to be its highest desire, wish, hope, pleasure, and joy, to close out all creatures, to wish for nothing, to desire nothing except God alone, as the highest eternal, infinite, perfect Good, which is the good of all, without which there can be no good on heaven or on earth, in time and eternity, and [to receive] all this in and through Christ Jesus, our Lord, who is the beginner and ender of faith (Heb. 12:2). This faith leads us to our internal treasure and highest good. . . . This faith brings about and exacts

---

32. For a list of Arndt's use of Tauler quotations, see Weber, *Arndt*, pp. 77–100.
33. *True Christianity*, III, 1:3.

the proper Sabbath of the heart, rest in God. In the internal Sabbath God reveals himself. Therefore the Lord said . . . Mary has chosen the best part (Lk. 10:41–42). What is the best part? Without doubt, God alone in Christ Jesus. By this faith, which gives place and position in the heart to God alone, man has the best part. By this faith God possesses the human heart and Christ dwells in us together with the Holy Spirit and the Holy Trinity.[34]

In some cases the union of essences suggested in Arndt's sources was rejected,[35] but in others even this language is retained for Arndt's own purposes. Thus, under the influence of Eckhardt's sermon *Qui audit me*,[36] which Arndt understood to be by Tauler, he wrote:

Thus faith is the means by which [we] come to our internal treasure, namely faith that holds God [in] a quiet Sabbath and makes man turn in toward himself. The movement of the heavens is the noblest and the best. It continually turns into itself, into its source, out of which the movement took its beginning. Thus man's movement is the noblest and the best if man turns again into his source, which is God. Nothing other can occur if a man enters into himself with all his strength, and lifts his understanding, will, and memory from the world and from all carnal things, and turns his soul with all its desires to God through the Holy Spirit, and rests and rejoices away from the world by a quiet Sabbath, than that God begins to work in him. God waits upon this Sabbath of the heart, and it is his greatest joy to bring about his work in us. God desires us and searches after us and does nothing other than as if he wished to destroy his divine being and become nothing in himself so that he might reveal the abyss of his divinity to us and the fulness of his being and his nature. God is as eager to be our possession as he is his own possession. Man can do nothing better for God than to rest and keep this sabbath. For this work God only requires that man give him a humble and quiet heart. Then he brings about a work in the soul to which no man can come. The eternal wisdom of God is so delicate in its work that it can accept nothing that belongs to a creature. Insofar as the soul rests in God, God rests in it. If it rests completely in God, God rests completely in it. If you use your own will, memory and desire for your pleasure, God cannot use them nor have his work in them. If two are to be one, one must rest and suffer and the other must work. God is an infinite working power and pure movement. He does not rest, and works in you insofar as his work can be brought about and you do not hinder it. This can be better understood by the following example: If an eye is to see and receive an image, it must be naked and empty of all forms and images. Insofar as it has an image or form in it, it cannot see or grasp [another] image. So the soul with all its powers, understanding, will, memory, desires, is not able to grasp God if it is full of the world and earthly things. In a similar way, the ear must be emptied of all

---

34. *True Christianity*, III, 2:1.
35. Weber, *Arndt*, pp. 102ff.
36. For Arndt's source see Basel 1522 Tauler, 313.

sounds if it is to hear a harp properly and your soul must be emptied of the world if it is to hear God's kindness. The more the soul draws away from earthly things, the more heavenly it becomes and the more it destroys fleshly lusts, the more it participates in the divine nature (1 Pet. 1:4).[37]

Tauler's influence is strongest in Arndt's chapter that discusses the direction of a soul searching this union in love:

God is to be sought in two ways, an external and an internal. The first occurs in an active manner when man seeks God. The second occurs in a passive manner when man is sought by God. The external seeking occurs through the many practices of Christian works. . . . The other occurs when a man enters into the ground of his heart and there realizes the kingdom of God is in us (Lk. 17:21). If the kingdom of God is in us, God himself is in us with all his goodness. God is thus nearer to the soul and more internal than the soul is to itself. There the ground of the soul must be sought. This occurs if, in a passive way, a man allows God to deal with him in all external and internal ways as is pleasing to God, and leaves himself completely to God and allows himself to be satisfied only in God's will, [accepting] what God will have, whether he be rich or poor, happy or sad, spiritually joyous or without consolation. Thereby the heart is purified from all creatures and from all that which is brought in from the outside by the senses and reason. If the soul is thus emptied of all rational, sensual, creaturely things that are not God himself, one comes to the ground, where one finds God alone with his light and being.[38]

Tauler's sermon *Que mulier dragmas*, the source for this selection, outlines in general the same movement,[39] but, although following Tauler, Arndt is never unaware of his Lutheranism and immediately places his words in an eschatological context, insisting at the same time that no possibility exists for a man to work his way to such a union; even the experience of the union already granted is a gift of grace.[40] Similar protective measures are taken in a later chapter, possibly influenced by Eckhart's *Beati pauperi*.[41] There, too, Arndt's debt to his Lutheran tradition rises to the fore, and he insists on the Christocentric nature of the union:

Concerning this nobility of the soul many people know nothing, even those who are wise and intelligent in this world. Many have written of the soul and its powers but have not come to its proper ground. Christ is the true power

---

37. *True Christianity*, III, 2:3.
38. Ibid., III, 4:1.
39. For Arndt's source see the Basel 1522 Tauler, f. LXXIX[r].
40. See *True Christianity*, III, 4:2.
41. *True Christianity*, 6, 1:2. For Arndt's source see the Basel 1522 Tauler, f. CCXX[r].

15

of the soul, its understanding, its will, its memory, the light in its understanding, the pleasure in its will, the joy in its memory. Christ is the true
healing, adornment and treasure of the soul so that a man because of the love
of Christ that he experiences may no longer sin as is indicated in 1 John
3:6–9. . . . Indeed, out of this love of Christ arises a joy and desire. . . . It
arises in the ground of your soul from God, for God has sanctified a place for
himself in man . . . where neither nature, nor man nor any creature may
enter. The same is the noble pure being of the soul, a place that the eternal
God wishes to have for himself and wishes to share with no other.[42]

Arndt's use of late medieval mystics grew out of Luther's use
of them, and it differed from his predecessor's approach to the same
extent that his teaching on the mystical union did. Whereas
Luther's democratization of that principle shapes the way in which
Arndt sees medieval texts on the subject and his use of them, the
tensions inherent in Arndt's teaching—his desire to maintain orthodox Lutheranism and his attraction to the possibility of mystical
insight in this life—do manifest themselves in his use of medieval
mystical texts. Earlier Lutheran historiography has influenced, but
undergone a change in, Arndt's work. Whereas it had been concerned with establishing a tradition of witnesses to the truth (*Zeugen
der Wahrheit*) to uphold Lutheran teachings in the face of Roman
Catholic polemic, Arndt marks the beginning of a tradition in Lutheranism in which the medieval mystics are used as *Zeugen* in
support of a specific wing within Lutheranism. It is in this, above
all, that Arndt is followed later in the 17th century by Philipp Jacob
Spener and the Pietists in their use of late medieval mystical texts,
as he was by them (and their 19th-century Revivalist-Evangelical
descendants) in his theology.

A Note on the Text

In the translation that follows, Arndt's text has been reduced
by two-thirds. Such a reduction has its obvious difficulties, despite
the repetitiveness of Arndt's style and argument. All omitted passages have been indicated by brief paraphrases.

Book One has been translated from the first corrected edition
of 1606 published in Braunschweig by Andreas Duncker (Exemplar

---

42. *True Christianity*, III, 6:3.

in Schwenkfelder Library, Pennsburg, Pa.). Those selections from the second to sixth books follow the version accepted as definitive and continually reprinted after Arndt's death. All these translated sections have been checked against the first editions of the respective texts.

Book One was chosen to be translated because it is the least derivative of the books, because it reflects well his meditative style, and because it offers the fullest introduction to his thought as a whole. The sections on prayer in Book Two and on the mystical union in Book Three as well as the discussions of the microcosm-macrocosm in Book Four are of more immediate interest to readers of a series on "mysticism," but the extensive use of texts from Angela of Foligno (1248–1309) in Book Two, Valentine Weigel (1533–1588) in Book Two, Paracelsus (1493–1541) in Book Four, and the Tauleran sources in Book Three tend by themselves to mislead readers as to the orientation of Arndt's theology as a whole.

A previous English version of the first four books, by Anthony William Boehm, was printed in London in 1712. This version was revised by Charles F. Schaeffer in the mid-19th century and was printed in Philadelphia, Pennsylvania, in 1869. The revised version often gives way to loose paraphrase however, and for this reason a new translation has been done. Brackets indicate additions to the original, but references to Scripture verses have been silently entered. Scriptural passages have been regularized according to the Revised Standard Version. Passages that are clearly intended as "proof-texts" by Arndt are omitted but their deletion and locations are indicated.

Johann Arndt

TRUE CHRISTIANITY

THE CLASSICS OF WESTERN SPIRITUALITY

Foreword
To The Christian Reader

Dear Christian reader, that the holy Gospel is subjected, in our time, to a great and shameful abuse is fully proved by the impenitent life of the ungodly who praise Christ and his word with their mouths and yet lead an unchristian life that is like that of persons who dwell in heathendom, not in the Christian world. Such ungodly conduct gave me cause to write this book to show simple readers wherein true Christianity consists, namely, in the exhibition of a true, living faith, active in genuine godliness and the fruits of righteousness. [I wished to show as well] that we bear the name of Christ, not only because we ought to believe in Christ, but also because we are to live in Christ and he in us. [I also wished to show] how true repentance must proceed from the innermost source of the heart; how the heart, mind, and affections must be changed, so that we might be conformed to Christ and his holy Gospel; and how we must be renewed by the word of God to become new creatures. As every seed produces fruit of a like nature, so the word of God must daily produce in us new spiritual fruits. If we are to become new creatures by faith, we must live in accordance with the new birth. In a word, Adam must die, and Christ must live, in us. It is not enough to know God's word; one must also practice it in a living, active manner.

Many think that theology is a mere science, or rhetoric, whereas it is a living experience and practice. Everyone now endeavors to be eminent and distinguished in the world, but no one is willing to learn to be pious. Everyone now seeks out men of great learning, from whom one may learn the arts, languages, and wisdom, but no one is willing to learn, from our only teacher, Jesus Christ, meekness and sincere humility, although his holy, living example is the proper rule and directive for our life. Indeed, [he is] the highest wisdom and knowledge, so that we can clearly say: "Omnia nos Christi vita docere potest" [the pure life of Christ can give us all things]. Everyone wishes very much to be a servant of Christ, but no one wishes to be his follower. Yet he says in John 12:26: *"If any man serves me, he must follow me."* Hence, a true servant and lover of Christ must be Christ's follower. He who loves Christ will also love the example of his holy life, his humility, meekness, patience, suffering, shame, and contempt, even if the flesh suffers pain. And although we cannot, in our present weakness, perfectly imitate the holy and noble life of Christ (which, indeed, is not intended in my book), nevertheless, we ought to love it, and yearn to imitate it, for thus we live in Christ, and Christ lives in us, as John in the first Epistle 2:6 says: *He who says he abides in Him ought to walk in the same way in which he walked.* It is now the desire of the world to know all things, but that which is better than all knowledge, namely, *to know the love of Christ* (Eph. 3:19), no one desires to learn. No one can love Christ who does not follow the example of his holy life. There are many men in this world indeed who are ashamed of the holy example of Christ, namely, of his humility and lowliness, that is, they are ashamed of the Lord Jesus Christ. Of them the Lord says in Mark 8:38: *"Whoever is ashamed of me and of my words in this adulterous generation, of him also shall the Son of man be ashamed when He comes."* Christians now desire an imposing, magnificent, rich Christ, conformed to the world, but no one wishes to receive or to confess and to follow the poor, meek, humble, and despised Christ. He will, therefore, say: *I never knew you; you were not willing to know me in my humility, and therefore I do not know you in your pride* (Mt. 7:23).

Not only, however, is the ungodly life and existence completely opposed to Christ and true Christianity, it also daily heaps up the wrath and punishment of God, so that God fits all creatures to be avengers against us, and heaven and earth, fire and water, must contend against us. Indeed, all nature is distressed over this, and almost overwhelmed. Hence, a time of difficulty, war, famine, and pestilence must come. Indeed the last plagues are pressing in with such violence and power that one cannot be certain of any creature. Even as the terrible plagues of the Egyptians overtook them before the redemption and departure of the children of Israel from Egypt, so too before the final redemption of the children of God dreadful and unheard-of plagues will overtake the ungodly and impenitent. It is therefore high time to repent, to begin another course of life, to turn from the world to Christ, to believe truly in him, and to live as a Christian in him, so that we may securely *dwell in the shelter of the Most High, who abides in the shadow of the Almighty* (Ps. 91:1). Thus the Lord exhorts us in Luke 21:36: *"Watch therefore always, and pray that you may be worthy to escape all these things."* The same is also testified in Psalm 112:7.

Now, to this end, dear Christian, this book will serve as a guide, [showing you] not only how you may, through faith in Christ, obtain the forgiveness of your sins, but also how you may properly use the grace of God to lead a holy life, and how you may demonstrate and adorn your faith by a Christian way of life. True Christianity consists, not in words or in external show, but in living faith, from which arise righteous fruits, and all manner of Christian virtues, as from Christ himself. Since faith is hidden from human eyes and is invisible, it must be manifested by its fruits, inasmuch as faith creates from Christ all that is good, righteous, and holy.

Now, if faith waits the promised blessings, hope arises out of faith. What else is hope but a constant and persevering expectation, in faith, of promised blessings? But if faith shares with a neighbor the blessings that it has itself received, love arises out of faith, and imparts to the neighbor that which it has itself received from God. If faith endures the test of the cross, and submits itself to the will of God, patience grows out of faith. If it sighs under the cross, or offers thanks to God for mercies it has received, prayer is born. If it compares the power of God with the misery of man, and submits and bends to God, humility is born. If faith is concerned that it not lose the grace of God, or, as Saint Paul says, *worketh out its salvation with fear and trembling* (Phil. 2:12), then the fear of God is born.

Thus you see how all the Christian virtues are the children of faith, arise and grow from faith, and cannot be separated from faith as their source, if they are indeed genuine, living, and Christian virtues, arising from God, from Christ, and from the Holy Spirit. Hence no work can be pleasing to God without faith in Christ. How can true hope, proper love, constant patience, earnest prayer,

23

Christian humility, and a childlike fear of God exist without faith? All must be drawn from Christ, the wellspring, through faith, both righteousness and all the fruits of righteousness. You must take care that you do not connect your works and the virtues that you have begun, or the gifts of the new life, with your justification before God, for none of man's works, merit, gifts, or virtue, however lovely these may be, count for anything. [Our justification depends] on the exalted, perfect merit of Jesus Christ, received by faith, as it is sufficiently discussed in chapters 5, 19, 34, and 41 of this book, and in the first three chapters of Book II. Take great care, therefore, not to confound the righteousness of faith with the righteousness of a Christian life, but make a clear distinction [between them], for here is the whole foundation of our Christian religion. Your repentance must be no less, however, in righteous earnestness, for otherwise you have no less, however, in righteous earnestness, for otherwise you have no righteous faith, which daily purifies, changes, and amends the heart. You must also know that the consolations of the Gospel cannot be applied, unless preceded by a true righteous sorrow, by which the heart is broken and made contrite, for we read: *To the poor has the good news been preached* (Lk. 7:22). How can faith give life to the heart unless [the heart] has been previously mortified by earnest regret and sorrow and a thorough knowledge of sin? Do not, therefore, think that repentance is a slight and easy work. Remember the solemn and severe words of the Apostle Paul, when he commands us to mortify and crucify the flesh, with its lusts and desires, to offer the body as a sacrifice, to die to sin, to be crucified to the world (Col. 3:5; Rom. 6:6, 12:1; 1 Pet. 2:24; Gal. 5:24, 6:14). Truly, none of these things result from gratifying the flesh, nor do the holy prophets portray repentance in pleasant terms when they call for and demand a contrite and broken spirit and say: *Rend your heart —weep and lament* (Joel 2:13, 17; Jer. 4:8). Where is such repentance now found? The Lord Jesus Christ describes it, [saying that] one should hate oneself, deny oneself, and renounce all that one has if one desires to be his disciple (Lk. 9:23; Mt. 16:24). Truly, all this can never proceed from light words. Of all this you have a living example and portrait in the seven Penitential Psalms (Ps. 6, 32, 38, 51, 102, 130, 143). The Scriptures abound in [illustrations of] the jealousy of God, who demands both repentance and its fruits, without which eternal salvation is lost. Thereafter, the consolation of the Gospel can manifest its true natural power, but the Spirit of God, through the Word, must work both [repentance and consolation] in us.

This book that I have written treats such sincere and true, inner, deep repentance, the exhibition and practice of true faith and the love a Christian should have in all his acts, for what proceeds from Christian love proceeds from faith. It is true that I have quoted, especially in the Frankfurt edition, some earlier writers, such as [Johann] Tauler, [Thomas] à Kempis, and others, who may seem to ascribe more than is due to human ability and works, but my whole book strives against such [an error]. I would, therefore, kindly remind the Christian reader that he continually look to the great object and purpose for which I wrote this book. He will find that its main purpose is to teach the reader how to know the hidden and inherited abomination of original sin, to learn to see our misery and helplessness, to refuse to put any trust in ourselves or our abilities, to take away everything from ourselves, and to ascribe all to Christ, so that he alone may dwell in us, work all things in us, alone live in us, and do all things in us, because he is the beginning, middle, and end of our conversion and salvation. All this has been plainly and abundantly explained in many passages of this book, and, at the same time, the doctrines of the Papists, Syngerists, and Majorists have been expressly refuted and rejected. The doctrine, moreover, of justification by faith has been set forth in this book, and especially in Book II, in the most pointed and explicit manner possible. In order, however, to obviate all misapprehensions, I have subjected the present edition to a very careful revision, and I beg the faithful reader to understand and judge the Frankfurt edition and some few Braunschweig exemplars according to the present corrected edition. May he also take note of the explanation and corrections at the end of this edition, which I hope may be inserted in their proper place in future editions.

May God enlighten us all by his Holy Spirit, so that we may be pure and without offence, in faith and life, till the day of our Lord Jesus Christ (which is near at hand) is filled with the fruits of righteousness, to the homage and praise of God.

Amen.

Book One

LIBER
SCRIPTURAE

1

WHAT THE IMAGE OF GOD IN MAN IS

Be renewed in the spirit of your minds, and put on the new nature, created after the likeness of God in true righteousness and holiness (Eph. 4:23–24).

The image of God in man is the conformity of the human soul, understanding, spirit, mind, will, and all internal and external bodily and spiritual powers with God and the Holy Trinity and with all divine qualities, virtues, wills, and characteristics. This is indicated in the decision of the Holy Trinity: *Let us make man in our image after our likeness; and let him have dominion over the fish of the sea, and over the birds of the air, and over the cattle, and over all the earth* (Gen. 1:26).

From this it is clear that the Holy Trinity has placed its image in man so that in the whole life and walk of man pure divine holiness, righteousness, and goodness ought to appear and shine forth, just as divine love, power, and purity is found in the holy angels. In man God wished to have his joy and pleasure as in his children. Just as a father sees himself and rejoices in his child, so also God has his joy in men (Prov. 8:31). Although the Lord God has pleasure in all his works, yet he had a special joy in man, since in man his image shone forth in the highest innocence and clarity. There are three chief powers created in the human soul by God: understanding, will, and memory. These powers the Holy Trinity brings forth and protects, makes holy and illuminates, adorns and embellishes with its grace, works, and gifts.

An image is that in which one can see a similar likeness and form and there can be no image unless it is like that to which it is made as an image. No image can appear in a mirror unless it receive its likeness or a like form from something else, and the clearer the mirror, the purer the image shines forth. Thus the purer and cleaner the human soul, the clearer the image of God shines forth from it.

JOHANN ARNDT

To this end God created man unspotted, pure, and clean in all his bodily and spiritual powers so that God's image might be seen in him, not as a dead shadow in a mirror, but as a true, living portrait and likeness of the invisible God and of his superlatively beautiful inner and hidden form, that is as an image of divine wisdom in the understanding of man, an image of God's goodness, endurance, meekness, and patience in the mind of man, an image of God's love and mercy in the affections of the heart of man, an image of his righteousness, holiness, purity, and cleanness in the will of man, an image of his kindness, graciousness, love, and truth in all the actions and words of man, an image of power in the dominion given to man over the whole earth and over all animals, and an image of eternity in the immortality of man.

By this image, man is to know God his Creator and himself. [He is to know] his Creator, that is, that God is all, and the highest being out of which everything has its being, and that God is the essence of all things and that man bears God's image. Since man is the image of the goodness of God, God must be essentially the highest good and the good of all. He must be essentially love, essentially life, essentially holy. Therefore, to God belongs all honor, homage, acclaim, praise, glory, strength, power, and might. [These are to be given] to no creature but to God alone, who is himself essentially all of these. Thus, it is pointed out in Matthew 19:17 that a person asked the Lord who took him for a pure man: *"Good master what must I do to inherit eternal life?"* The Lord answered: *"Why do you call me good?" No one is good except God alone*, that is, God alone is essentially good and without him and outside of him there can be no true good.

Man is also to know himself from his image, [that is], that there is to be a distinction between man and God. Man is not to be God but the image, likeness, portrait, and imprint of God in which God wishes to allow himself to be seen. Thus, nothing other is to live, shine, act, will, love, think, speak, or rejoice in man except God himself. If anything other is noted in man that God himself does not act or do, God's image cannot be in man but rather the image of that which man allows to work in him and to be seen in him. Out of this resignation arises that which Tauler defines as a pure simple suffering of the divine will; man allows God to work all things in him and does not hinder God with his own will or strive against God. It is said that one is completely resigned to God when he is a simple, pure, clean, holy instrument of God and of God's holy will and of all divine acts. Thus, man does not act according to his self-will, but his will is God's will; man has no self-love, but God is his love; no self-honor, but God is to be his honor; no wealth, but God is his wealth and possession without any love of creature and the world. Thus, nothing is to act, live, and be in him except God purely alone. This is the highest innocence, purity, and holiness of man. This is indeed the highest innocence if a man does not bring about what is in his own self-will but allows God to work in him and to bring everything about. Indeed, this is the highest simplicity, if a man is like a simple child in whom there is no self-honor or self-love.

God is to completely possess man from within and without. We have an example of this in our Lord Jesus Christ, who is a perfect image of God in that he completely sacrificed his will to his heavenly Father's will in highest obedience, humility, and meekness without any self-honor, self-love, self-gain, or possessiveness and without any self-joy or pleasure, but he allowed God to work everything in and through him in whatever he thought, spoke, or did. In a word, his will was God's will and pleasure. Therefore, God called from heaven: *This is my beloved son in whom I am well pleased* (Mt. 3:17). This is the proper image of God out of which nothing other shines than that alone which is God himself, namely, pure love and mercy, long-suffering patience, meekness, kindness, holiness, comfort, life, and blessedness. Thus, the invisible God wished to become visible and revealed in Christ and to give himself to be known to man. According to his divinity, Christ is in a much higher way God's image, namely, God himself and God's essential image and the light of his glory (Heb. 1:3). Of this we will not speak at present but only of Christ's holy humanity in which he lived and walked.

The image of God in Adam was also such a holy innocence and Adam was to have acknowledged and protected this in true humility and obedience. [He was to have acknowledged] that he was not himself the highest good, but that he was an image of the highest good, which reflected itself in him. Since he wanted to become this, however—that is, God himself—he fell into the most abominable and frightful sin.

31

Second, man was also to know that through the image of God he was capable of divine loving, gracious love, joy, peace, life, rest, strength, might, and light so that God alone might be all things in man and live and work in him alone. In man there was to be no self-will, self-love, self-honor and acclaim but God alone was to be man's acclaim and honor and he alone was to have the praise. A likeness follows its pattern and not its opposite. A likeness rejoices in its similarity and finds pleasure in this. God wished to flow out completely into man with all his goodness, for God is a goodness that completely shares itself.

Finally, man was to know from the image of God that he was united with God by it and that in this union the highest rest, peace, joy, life, and blessedness of man consisted as, on the other hand, the greatest unrest and unhappiness of man arose out of nothing other than when he acted against God's image, turned himself from God, and was deprived of the highest eternal good.

2
WHAT THE FALL OF ADAM IS

For as by one man's disobedience many were made sinners, so by one man's obedience many will be made righteous (Rom. 5:19).

The fall of Adam is disobedience against God by which man turned from God to himself and robbed God of the honor in that he himself wished to be God. By this, he destroyed the holy image of God, namely, perfect, original righteousness and holiness. In his understanding he was blinded, in his will disobedient and antagonistic to God, in all the powers of his heart he was twisted and became God's enemy. This abomination was continued and passed on to all men through physical birth. By it, man dies and is spiritually dead, is a child of wrath and damnation, if he is not redeemed through Christ. Therefore, simple Christian, you must not consider the fall of Adam to be a slight or insignificant sin as if it were the mere bite of an apple, but it is the fall of man in that man wished to be God himself. This was also the fall of Satan. This is the most abominable and frightful sin.

The fall occurred first in man's heart and thereafter was revealed and made clear in the eating of the apple. It is also to be noted in various ways in the fall and sin of Absalon (2 Sam. 14:25). He was also (1) the son of a king, (2) a most beautiful man in whom there was no fault from head to toe, and (3) a son, dearly beloved by his father as is clear from the tears of David (2 Sam. 18:33). Absalon was not satisfied to remain with this glory, but he wished to be king himself, and he took for himself the royal honor. When he so decided this in his heart, he became his father's mortal enemy and sought after his life. Adam too was (1) God's son, (2) the most beautiful among the creatures; there was no flaw in him in body or soul, and he was (3) God's beloved child. Nor was he satisfied to remain in this glory but wished to be God himself and therefore became an enemy of God and if it were possible he would have killed God.

JOHANN ARNDT

How can there be a more abominable and grosser sin? Out of this abomination the following arose: first, man became like Satan in his heart in that they both began with similar sins and as a result man changed God's image into Satan's image, became Satan's instrument, and was capable of all the evil of Satan. Because of this, out of the divine, spiritual, heavenly image man became earthly, fleshly, animal and beastly. So that Satan might plant his devil image in man he first sowed in man by his crafty, poisonous, insidious words and treachery his serpent's seeds, which are called self-honor, self-love, self-will, and the desire to be God.

As a result, all those who are drunken in their self-love are called in the Scriptures "a generation of vipers" (Mt. 3:7) and a race of serpents, who have the devil's qualities. Genesis 3:15 reads: *I will put enmity between the seed of the serpent and the seed of the woman*.

Out of this serpent's seed grew nothing other than an abominable fruit among those who are called the children of Belial, the children of the Devil, the image of Satan (Jn. 8:44). A natural seed in a hidden manner contains within itself the whole quality of growth and characteristic [of the full plant], its height, width, length, and breadth, its twigs, leaves, flowers, and fruits. One is astonished how in so small a seed so great a tree can lie hidden with its many and manifold fruits. It is the same in the poisonous evil seed of the serpent, in the disobedience and self-love of Adam, which is passed on to all descendants according to physical birth. In this seed a poisonous tree lies hidden and innumerable evil fruits in which the whole image of Satan with all its evil qualities and harm appears.

Look at a small child. Evil qualities arise at the moment of birth, particularly self-will and disobedience, and when the child grows up a little, an inherited self-love, self-honor, self-praise, self-righteousness, lying, and other things of the same kind break forth. Soon pride, arrogance, pomposity, despising God, cursing, swearing, evil desires, lies and deceptions, despising God and his Word, despising parents and authority, break forth. There follow wrath, antagonism, hatred, envy, enmity, desire for vengeance, murder, and all kinds of abominations, particularly if external circumstances arise that awake the Adamic carnal qualities in man. These lead to impurity, uncleanliness, whorish fantasies and adulterous thoughts, unchaste speech, shameful actions, words, and works, pleasure in gluttony, over-indulgence in food and drink and clothing, light-mindedness, luxury, eating, and drinking. Then arise covetousness, profiteering, deception, envy, false judgment, antagonism, craft, cunning, and in a word all kinds of evils and vices, roguishness, and villainy in so many unheard-of and manifold ways that it is not possible to count them all as it is written in Jeremiah 17:9 *"Who can understand the heart of man?"* Indeed, there is yet more. Heretical spirits arise that lead astray. Then arise the rejection of God, idolatry, a flight of truth, the sin against the Holy Spirit, falsification of faith, the twisting of the Scriptures, and all the deceptions of the worst sort. These are all the fruits of the seed of the serpent in man and the image of Satan.

Who could have believed in the beginning that in so small, weak, and simple a child there could lie hidden such a waste of all kinds of vices, so undoubtedly evil a heart, so abominable a worm and basilisk. Man himself demonstrates it in his life and walk, in his evil thoughts and activities from his youth on (Gen. 6:5).

There is an evil root out of which so poisonous a tree grows, an evil seed of the serpent and of the vipers' generation out of which so despicable an image comes. Everything grows from the inside outward and is made much worse by external offences. For this reason, the Lord Christ sternly forbade the offences of youth because the seed of the serpent lies hidden in children. In it, much shame and evil rest and lie secretly hidden away, as poison in a serpent.

Therefore, man, learn of the fall of Adam and understand properly original sin, for one cannot finish speaking of or probing the depths of corruption. Learn to know yourself, what you have become through the fall of Adam. Out of God's image came forth Satan's image in which all false qualities, characteristics, and evils of Satan are contained. In God's image all true qualities, characteristics, and virtues are contained. Before the fall man carried the image of the divine, that is, he was completely heavenly, spiritual, divine, and angelic. Now, after the fall, he carries the image of the earth, that is, internally he is completely carnal and diseased.

Look then. Is not your wrath and anger that of a raging lion? Is not your envy and unsatisfiable covetousness that of a dog and wolf? Is not your impurity and intemperance that of a swine? Indeed, you will find in yourself a whole world full of evil beasts, and most of them in that small member your tongue, for it says in James

3:6: *The tongue is a fire full of evil serpents, a world full of impure spirits and full of impure birds.* Isaiah (13:21) and Revelation (18:2) give witness that there is no wild beast so wrathful as is man, no dog so envious, no wolf so rapacious and covetous, no fox so deceptive, no basilisk so poisonous, and no swine so filthy. Because of his bestial and animal qualities, Herod was called a fox by the Lord Jesus (Lk. 13:32). Such men are dogs and swine before whom one is not to place holiness nor to cast pearls (Mt. 7:6).

If a man does not turn from such evil qualities and is not renewed in Christ, but dies in such a state, he remains eternally proud, arrogant, haughty, and satanic, a wrathful lion, an envious dog, a rapacious wolf, a poisonous serpent and basilisk, and he can never ever be relieved of such abominations, but must eternally carry the image of Satan and remain in eternal darkness to testify that he did not live in Christ and was not renewed according to the image of God. Revelation (21:8, 22:15) notes that the idolators and magicians and all those who love and act in falsehood will be outside with the dogs.

3

HOW MAN IS ONCE AGAIN RENEWED
TO ETERNAL LIFE IN CHRIST

For neither circumcision counts for anything, nor uncircumcision, but a new creation (Gal. 6:15).

The new birth is a work of God the Holy Spirit, by which a man is made a child of grace and blessedness from a child of wrath and damnation, and from a sinner a righteous man through faith, word, and sacrament by which our heart, thoughts, mind, understanding, will, and affections are made holy, renewed, and enlightened as a new creature in and according to Jesus Christ. The new birth contains two chief aspects in itself: justification and sanctification or renewal (Tit. 3:5).

There is a twofold birth of a Christian man: the carnal, sinful, damnable, and accursed birth that comes from Adam, by which the seeds of the serpent, the image of Satan, and the earthly bestial quality of man is continued, and the spiritual, holy, blessed, gracious, new birth that comes out of Christ, by which the seed of God and the heavenly, godly man is perpetuated in a spiritual manner.

As a result, each Christian man has two birth lines in himself, the fleshly line of Adam and the spiritual line of Christ, which comes out of grace. Just as Adam's old birth is in us, so also must Christ's new birth be in us. This is the new and the old man, the old and the new birth, the old and the new Adam, the earthly and the heavenly image, the old and the new Jerusalem, flesh and spirit, Adam and Christ in us, the internal and the external man.

Note how we are newborn out of Christ. Just as the old birth in a fleshly manner was continued from Adam, so the new birth in a spiritual manner is continued from Christ and this occurs through the Word of God. The Word of God is the seed of the new birth (1 Pet. 1:23 . . .; Jas. 1:18 . . .). This Word awakens faith and faith clings to this Word and grasps in the Word Jesus Christ together with the Holy Spirit. Through the Holy Spirit's power and activity, man is newborn. The new birth occurs first through the Holy

Spirit (Jn. 3:4). This is what the Lord calls "to be born of the Spirit." Secondly, it occurs through faith (1 John 5:1 . . .). In the third place it occurs through holy baptism (Jn. 3:5 . . .). On this, note the following:

Out of Adam and from Adam man inherited the greatest evil as sin, curse, wrath, death, the Devil, hell, and damnation. These are the fruits of the old birth. Out of Christ, however, man inherited the highest good through faith, namely, righteousness, grace, blessing, life, and eternal blessedness. Out of Adam, man has a carnal spirit and inherited the dominion and tyranny of the evil spirit; out of Christ, however, man inherited the Holy Spirit with his gifts and a consolatory government. Whatever kind of spirit a man has, such a birth, quality, and characteristic he has in himself as the Lord says in Luke 9:55: *Do you not know what manner of spirit you are of?* Out of Adam man has received a proud, arrogant, haughty spirit through the fleshly birth. If he wishes to be born again, he must receive through faith out of Christ a humble, lowly, simple spirit. The Lord calls this in John 3:6 "to be born of the Spirit." Out of Adam man has inherited a faithless, unthankful soul opposed to God; out of Christ he must receive through faith a faithful, thankful soul giving thanks to God. Out of Adam man has received a disobedient, haughty, loose spirit; out of Christ he must receive an obedient, moral, kind spirit through faith. Out of Adam man inherited a wrathful, antagonistic, vengeful, murdering spirit by his fleshly birth; out of Christ he must inherit a loving, merciful, long-suffering spirit through faith. Out of Adam man received a covetous, unmerciful, self-oriented, thieving spirit; out of Christ he must receive a merciful, mild, helpful spirit through faith. Out of Adam man inherited an unchaste, unclean, intemperate spirit; out of Christ he must receive a pure, chaste, and temperate spirit. Out of Adam man received a lying, false, slandering spirit; out of Christ he must receive a true, upright, consistent spirit. Out of Adam man has received a bestial, earthly, animal spirit; out of Christ he must receive a heavenly, divine spirit.

For this reason, Christ had to become man and be grasped by the Holy Spirit, become sanctified with the Holy Spirit beyond all measure. *For indeed, the spirit of the Lord rested upon him, the spirit of wisdom and understanding, the spirit of counsel and might, the spirit of knowledge and the fear of the Lord* (Is. 11:2) so that in him and through him human nature might be renewed and we in him, out of him, and through him might be born again and become new creatures so that we might inherit from him the spirit of wisdom and of understanding for the spirit of foolishness, the spirit of knowledge for our inherited blindness, the spirit of the fear of God for the spirit of opposition to God. This is the new life and the new birth in us.

As we all died spiritually in Adam and are not able to do anything except the dead works of death and darkness, so we must all be made again living in Christ and do works of the light (1 Cor. 15:22). As we have inherited, through the physical birth, the sins from Adam, so we must inherit righteousness through faith from Christ. And as we inherited pride, covetousness, lust, and all impurity through the flesh of Adam, so we must be made holy, purified, and renewed in our nature by the Holy Spirit and all pride, covetousness, lust, and envy must die in us and we must receive, from Christ, a new spirit, a new heart, thoughts, and mind, just as we received sinful flesh out of Adam.

Because of this new birth Christ is called our eternal father (Is. 9:6). Thus, we are once again renewed to eternal life in Christ, born anew out of Christ, and become new creatures in Christ. All works that are to be pleasing to God must come from this new birth, out of Christ, out of the Holy Spirit, and out of faith.

Thus, we live in the new birth and the new birth in us. Thus, we live in Christ and Christ in us (Gal. 2:20). Thus, we live in the spirit and the spirit of Christ in us. This new birth and the fruits of this birth Saint Paul describes in Ephesians 4:23 . . . 2 Corinthians 3:17 . . . Colossians 3:10 . . . Titus 3:5 . . . Ezekiel 11:18. . . . The new birth thus arises from the incarnation of Christ. Since man was fallen and turned away from God, through his own honor, pride, and disobedience, this fall cannot be made better, or repented for, except through the deepest humility, obedience, and humbling of the Son of God. Since Christ walked his humble path on earth among men, so he must live in you, and renew the image of God in you.

Look now to the loving, humble, meek, obedient, patient Christ and learn from him, that is, live in him (Mt. 11:29). [In the first place], ask why he thus lived? [He lived so] that he might be an example, mirror, and rule for your life. He is the proper rule of life. The rule of our life is not the rule of Saint Benedict or the rule of some other men but Christ's example, which the apostles show us. Second, look to his suffering, death, and resurrection. Why did he suffer this? Why did he die and rise? [He did so] that you might die from your sins with him and in him, with him and through him you might again spiritually be resurrected and walk in newness of life (Rom. 6:4). See chapters 11 and 31 for more regarding this.

The new birth arises and springs from the wellspring of the suffering, death, and resurrection of Christ (1 Pet. 1:3). We have been born anew to the living hope through the resurrection of Jesus Christ. As a result, the holy apostles always laid as the foundation for repentance and the new life, the holy suffering of Christ (Rom. 6:3; 1 Pet. 1:18–19 . . .). Peter gives the reason why we should live in holy life, namely, because we were purchased with so great a price (1 Pet. 2:25 . . .). Our Lord Christ made a similar statement in Luke 24:47: *Thus it is written, that the Christ should suffer and on the third day rise from the dead, and that repentance and forgiveness of sins should be preached in his name to all nations.* Thus we hear that the Lord himself indicated that both things, preaching and repentance, were living streams flowing from the well of his suffering, death, and resurrection.

The suffering of Christ is, therefore, two things—namely, a payment for all our sins and a renewal of man through faith and true repentance. Both belong to man's renewal. They are the fear and the power of suffering of Christ, which work in us renewal and sanctification (1 Cor. 1:30), and thus the new birth arises from Christ in us. As a means to it, holy baptism is ordered by which we are baptized in the death of Christ so that we might die with Christ to our sins by the power of his death and once again arise from our sins through the power of his resurrection.

4

WHAT TRUE REPENTANCE AND THE PROPER YOKE AND CROSS OF CHRIST ARE

Those who belong to Christ Jesus have crucified the flesh with its passions and desires (Gal. 5:24).

Repentance or true conversion is a work of God the Holy Spirit, by which man understands his sins and the wrath of God against sins from the law. Out of this are awakened in his heart repentance and sorrow. From the Gospel, however, he understands God's grace and through faith he receives forgiveness for his sins in Christ. Through this repentance, the mortification and crucifixion of the flesh and all fleshly lusts and the evil qualities of the heart and the life-giving power of the spirit comes. By it, Adam and all his evil die in us through true sorrow and Christ lives in us through faith (Gal. 2:20). The two things are tied together. The new life and the renewal of the spirit follow upon the mortification of the flesh. When the old man dies the new comes to life and when the new comes to life the old dies (2 Cor. 4:16 . . . Col. 3:5 . . . Rom. 6:11 . . .).

The mortification of the flesh must occur through true repentance. Therefore take note [of the following]. We have earlier said that man by the fall of Adam became completely bestial, earthly, fleshly, ungodly, and loveless, that is, without God and without love, turned away from the love of God to the love of this world, and chiefly to himself and to his own self-love, so that in all things he sought, loved, and honored himself, and turned his energy so that he would be highly considered by every man. This all came about by the fall of Adam, in that he wished to become God. This abomination is born into all men.

This twisted, evil quality of man must now be changed or made better through true repentance, that is, through true, divine sorrow and through faith, grasping the forgiveness of sins, and through the mortification of self-love, pride, and the lust of the flesh. Repentance does not only occur when one ceases to give freedom to gross external sins and leave them, but when one enters oneself, changes and makes better the internal ground of one's heart, and turns oneself from self-love, from the world and all worldly lusts, to spiritual, heavenly life, and becomes a participant of the merits of Christ through faith.

It follows that a man must deny himself (Lk. 9:23); that is, break his own self-will; give himself completely to God's will; not love himself but hold himself as the most unworthy, miserable man; deny all that he has (Lk. 14:26); that is, reject the world and its honor and glory; consider his own wisdom and power as nothing; not depend on himself or on any creature but only and simply on God; hate his own life, that is, the fleshly lusts and desires such as pride, covetousness, lust, wrath, and envy; have no pleasure in himself, and consider all his acts as nothing; praise himself for nothing; ascribe no power to himself; attempt to attribute nothing to himself but mistrust himself; die to the world, that is, the lust of the eyes, the lust of the flesh, and the pride of life; be crucified to the world (Gal. 6:4). This is the true repentance and mortification of the flesh without which no one can be a disciple of Christ. *This is true conversion from darkness to light and from the power of Satan to God, that they may receive forgiveness of sins and a place among those who are sanctified by faith* (Acts 26:18).

This repentance and conversion is the denial of oneself, the true cross and the true yoke of Jesus Christ, of which the Lord spoke in Matthew 11:29. . . . You are, through deep, heartfelt, inner humility, to extinguish self-love and self-honor and, through meekness, your own wrath and desire for vengeance. *For the new man, this is indeed an easy yoke and a light burden but for the flesh it is a bitter cross, for it is the crucifixion of the flesh with all its lusts and desires* (Gal. 5:24).

They are in error who consider only worldly troubles and oppositions as the cross. They do not know that inner repentance and mortification of the flesh are the true cross that we are daily to bear after Christ, that is, by it we are to love our enemies in great patience and those who slander us in holy meekness, and to conquer in deep humility our pride and haughtiness, which stand against us, just as Christ went before us in great meekness and denied the world and everything that is in the world and died to the world.

This yoke of Christ is our cross, which we are to carry and which is to die to the world. This does not mean that we are to walk about in a cloister or to take on a certain order or rule and yet at the same time in our heart remain nothing other than the world, filled with spiritual pride, pharisaic contempt of other people, full of lust, full of secret hate and envy.

Dying to the world is the mortification of the flesh and all those things that are associated with the lust of the flesh. By continual, internal, hidden sorrow and regret one turns inwardly to God and away from the world, dies daily in one's heart to the world, and lives in faith in Christ, in deep humility and meekness. The grace of God consoles such a person in Christ.

Christ called us to this repentance. After it follow the forgiveness of sins and the imputation of his righteousness and his holy obedience in the power of faith. Without such inner faith Christ is of no use to man, that is, man does not participate in his grace and the fruit of his merit, which must be received with a sorrowful, broken, repentant, faithful, and humble heart. The fruit of the death of Christ in us is that we die to our sins through repentance, and the fruit of the resurrection of Christ is that Christ lives in us and we in him (Gal. 2:20).

This is the new creature in Christ and the new birth that alone counts before God (Gal. 6:15). On this see chapter 14.

Therefore, learn to understand repentance in a proper manner. Many people err concerning it who believe that true repentance is to leave external idolatry, rejection of God, murder, adultery, unchastity, theft, and other gross external sins. This is, indeed, external repentance, of which many passages in the prophets speak (Is. 55:7 . . . Ezek. 18:28, 33:14). But the prophets looked much deeper, namely into the heart, and taught us of a much higher, inner repentance in which one is to die to pride, covetousness, and lust, to deny oneself, to hate and reject the world and all that which man has, to give oneself to God, to crucify the flesh, to bring a proper offering to God daily, [namely] a broken, contrite, and trembling heart, and to carry a sorrowful soul in one's body. This internal repentance of the heart is described in the seven Penitential Psalms.

This is true repentance when the heart internally through sorrow and regret is broken down, destroyed, laid low, and by faith and forgiveness of sins is made holy, consoled, purified, changed, and made better so that an external improvement in life follows.

If a man only repents externally and leaves the gross vices out of fear of punishment, and the heart remains unchanged and does not begin an inner new life in Christ, he can still be damned. Even if he cries, "Lord, Lord" it will not help, but he will hear the words, "I do not know you." *For not all who say Lord, Lord, will come into the kingdom of Heaven but those who do the will of my father in Heaven* (Mt. 7:21). Among these are all those persons who stand in high position whether they be learned or unlearned, for those who do not truly repent in their hearts and become new creatures in Christ, Christ will not accept as his.

5
WHAT TRUE FAITH IS

He who believes that Jesus is the Christ is a child of God (1 John 5:1).

Faith is a deep assent and unhesitating trust in God's grace promised in Christ and in the forgiveness of sins and eternal life. It is ignited by the Word of God and the Holy Spirit. Through this faith we receive forgiveness of sins, in no other way than through pure grace without any of our own merits (Eph. 2:8) but only by the merits of Christ. For this reason, our faith has a certain ground and is not unsteady. This forgiveness of sins is our righteousness, which is true, continual, and eternal before God. It is not the righteousness of an angel but of the obedience, merit, and blood of Christ and becomes ours through faith. Even if it is weak and we are still hemmed around with many sins, these are covered over out of grace for Christ's sake (Ps. 32:2).

By this deep trust and heartfelt assent, man gives his heart completely and utterly to God, rests in God alone, gives himself over to God, clings to God alone, unites himself with God, is a participant of all that which is God and Christ, becomes one spirit with God, receives from him new power, new life, new consolation, peace and joy, rest of soul, righteousness and holiness, and also, from God through faith, man is newborn. Where new faith is, there is Christ with all his righteousness, holiness, redemption, merit, grace, forgiveness of sins, childhood of God, inheritance of eternal life. This is the new birth that comes from faith in Christ. Therefore, the Epistle to the Hebrews in chapter 11:1 calls faith a substance or a certain true assurance of things on which man hopes and a conviction concerning things man does not see. The consolation of living faith becomes powerful in the heart; it convinces the heart, in that one finds in one's soul heavenly goodness, namely, rest and peace in God, so certain and true that one might then die with a happy heart. This is strength in the spirit, in the internal man and the joyousness of faith, or *parrhisia* (Eph. 3:12; Phil. 1:20; 1 John 2:28, 3:21), that is, joyousness in God (I Thess. 2:2) and *plerophoria*, a completely unhesitant certainty (I Thess. 1:5).

When I am to die this faith must strengthen me in my soul and must assure me internally by the Holy Spirit. It must be an inner, living, eternal consolation; it must hold me and strengthen me also as a supernatural, divine, heavenly power to conquer death and the world in me, and there must be such an assurance and union with Christ that is able to stand in either death or life [2 Tim. 1:12; Rom. 8:38]. Therefore, John [in 1 John 5:4] says: *"Everything which is born of God conquers the world."*

Everything that is born of God is truly no shadowy work, but a true life work. God will not bring forth a dead fruit, a lifeless and powerless work, but a living, new man must be born from the living God. Our faith is the victory that conquers the world.

That which man is to conquer must be a mighty power. If faith is to be victorious over the world, it must be a living, victorious, active, working, divine power; indeed Christ must do everything through faith.

Through this power of God we are once again drawn into God, inclined toward God, transplanted and set in God, taken out of Adam and as a cursed vine placed in Christ the blessed and living line (Jn. 15:4). Thus, in Christ we possess all his goods and are made righteous in him.

Just as a graft is set in a good stem and grows, blossoms, and brings forth fruit in it, but out of it dies, so a man outside of Christ is nothing but a cursed vine and all his works are sins (Deut. 32:32 – 33): *Their grapes are grapes of poison.* In Christ, however, he is righteous and holy. Therefore, Paul in 2 Corinthians 5:21 says: *"For our sake he made him to be sin who knew no sin, so that in him we might become the righteousness of God."*

From this you now see that works cannot make you righteous. First, you must be established in Christ through faith and be righteous in him before you can do any good work. See to it indeed that your righteousness is the grace and gift of God that comes before all your merit. How can a dead man walk, stand, or do anything good if someone does not first make him living? Thus, since you are dead in sins and dead before God you can do no work pleasing to God unless you are first made living in Christ.

Righteousness comes alone from Christ through faith, for faith is in man as a newborn, small, naked, and simple child that stands unclothed simply before his Redeemer and Sanctifier, and receives all from him who begot it, namely, righteousness, piety, holiness, grace, and the Holy Spirit.

Thus, if this naked, simple child is to be clothed with God's mercy, it must lift both its hands up and receive everything from God, grace together with all holiness and piety. Receiving this, it is made pious, holy, and blessed.

Therefore, righteousness comes only from faith and not from works. Indeed, faith receives Christ and makes him its own with all those things which he is and has. You must turn from sin, death, the Devil and hell. If you have all of the sin of the world upon yourself, it cannot harm you, for so strong, mighty and living is Christ in you with his merits through faith.

Since Christ now lives and dwells in you through faith, his indwelling is not a dead work but a living work. As a result, the renewal from Christ through faith comes about. Grace brings about two things in you: first, faith places Christ in you and makes you his possession; second, it renews you in Christ so that you grow, blossom, and live in him. What is the use of a graft in a stem if it does not grow and bring forth fruit? Just as once through Adam's fall, through the deception and treachery of the Devil, the seed of the serpent was sowed in man—that is, the evil, satanic pattern of life out of which an evil, poisonous fruit grew—so by God's word and the Holy Spirit faith was sowed in man as a seed of God in which all divine virtues, qualities, and characteristics, in a hidden manner, were contained and grew out to a beautiful and new image of God, to a beautiful and new tree on which the fruits are love, patience, humility, meekness, peace, chastity, righteousness, the new man, and the whole kingdom of God. The true sanctifying faith renews the whole man, purifies the heart, unites with God, makes the heart free from earthly things, hungers and thirsts after righteousness, works love, gives peace, joy, patience, consolation in all suffering, conquers the world, makes children heirs of God and of all heavenly eternal goods and co-heirs of Christ. If you find someone who does not have the joy of faith but is weak of faith and seeks comfort, do not reject him because of this but comfort him in the promised grace in Christ. This always remains firm, certain, and eternal. If we fall in weakness and stumble, God's grace does not fall away if we arise again through true repentance. Christ remains always Christ and the Sanctifier. He may be grasped with weak or with strong faith. Weak faith belongs as much to Christ as strong. Whether a man is weak or strong of faith, he is Christ's own just the same. The grace that is promised is common to all Christians and is eternal. On this, faith must rest, whether it be weak or strong. In his time, God will allow you to come to refreshing, joyous consolation, whether he bring it to your heart in a short time or in a longer period (Ps. 32:2–5, 77:8–11). On this see Book II.

6

GOD'S WORD MUST DEMONSTRATE ITS POWER IN MAN THROUGH FAITH AND BECOME LIVING

Lo, the kingdom of God is in the midst of you (Lk. 17:21).

Since everything is based on the rebirth and renewal of man, God included everything that must occur spiritually in man in faith in the external Scriptures, and in them described the whole new man. Since God's Word is the seed of God in us, it must bring forth spiritual fruit and it must do so through faith in the manner taught and testified externally in the Scriptures or it is a dead seed and a dead birth. What the Scripture teaches I must experience for my comfort in spirit and faith.

God did not reveal the Holy Scriptures so that they might externally on paper remain a dead letter, but that they might become living in us in spirit and faith and that a completely new inner man might arise. [If this does not occur], the Scriptures are of no use to us. This must occur in men through Christ in the spirit and faith as the Scriptures externally teach, as, for example, in the history of Cain and Abel. In their manner of life and qualities you can discover what is in you, namely, the old and the new man with all their works. These two are opposed to each other in you. Cain always wishes to overcome and drive out Abel. This is nothing other than a battle between flesh and spirit and the enmity of the seed of the serpent and the seed of a woman. The flood must occur in you and this quality of the flesh must be drowned. The faithful Noah must remain in you, God must make a new covenant with you and you with him. The confusion of Babel must not be built up in its pomposity in you. You must leave with Adam and all his family, giving up everything, even your body and life, and travel alone in the will of God, so that you might achieve blessing in the promised land and come into the kingdom of God. This is nothing other than what the Lord said [in Luke 14:26]: *He who does not leave father, mother, child, sister, house, field, goods, indeed life, cannot be called my disciple, that is, before he would deny Christ.* You must strive with

Abraham against the five kings that are in you, namely, the flesh, the world, death, the Devil, and sin. You must leave Sodom and Gomorrah with Lot, that is, the ungodly life of the world must be denied and you must not look back with Lot's wife as the Lord said in Luke 17:32.

In a word, God gave the whole of the Holy Scriptures in spirit and in faith and everything in them must happen in you spiritually. This is true as well of the battles of the Israelites against the pagan peoples. What is this other than the battle between the flesh and the spirit? The same is true of the whole, external, mosaic priesthood with the tabernacle, with the ark of the covenant, and with the seat of grace. This must all be in you spiritually through faith with offerings, sacrifices, and prayers. The Lord Christ must be all this in you. He has brought this all together in the new man and in the spirit and will perfect everything in faith, indeed, often in tears, for the whole Bible flows together in one center or central point in man, just as all of nature does.

In the New Testament as well, the letters are nothing other than an external witness to that which must occur in faith in all men. The whole New Testament must be completely and totally in us and stir also with power in us, for the kingdom of God is in us. Just as Christ was conceived and born physically by the Holy Spirit in the faith of Mary, so he must be spiritually conceived and born in me. He must grow and come to life spiritually in me. Since I am created a new creature out of Christ, I must also live and walk in him. I must be with him and in him in exile and misery. I must walk with him in humility and the rejection of the world, in patience and meekness, in love. I must forgive my enemies with him, be merciful, love my enemies, do the will of the Father. I must be tempted with him by Satan and I must also conquer. I must, for the sake of truth, which is in me, be slandered, rejected, despised, attacked, and if it is necessary I must suffer death for his sake as have all his saints, as a witness to him and all the elect that he was in me and I in him and that I have lived through faith.

To be properly conformed to the image of God is to be born in him and with him, to put on Christ properly, to grow and mature with him and in him, to live in misery with him, to be baptized with his baptism, to be despised with him, to be crucified with him, to die and rise again with him, to rule and have dominion with him, and to do all this not only by bearing a holy cross but also by daily repentance and inner regret and sorrow for sin.

You must daily die with Christ and crucify the flesh or you can not remain united with Christ as your head. Otherwise, you will not have him in you except in an external way, outside of your faith, heart, and spirit. This will not help you for he wishes to be in you, to be living, to comfort and to make you blessed.

Note that faith does everything that makes the holy Word of God alive in you and it is a living witness of all that of which the Scriptures testify. Faith is a substance and essence (Heb. 11:1).

Thus, it is clear enough from this how all sermons and statements of Christ—indeed, the whole Holy Scripture—are directed to all men and to each man. All the prophecies and all the parables of Christ relate to me and each man in particular as well as do all the miracles.

Therefore, it is also written that it is to occur spiritually within us. Since Christ has helped others he will help me for he is in me and he lives in me. He has made the blind to see. I am spiritually blind; therefore, he will make me also to see. Thus it is with all the miracles. Therefore, acknowledge yourself as a blind person, a lame person, a cripple, a deaf person, as one exposed, and he will help you. He made the dead live again. *I* am dead in my sins and, therefore, he must make me live again, so that I have a part in the first resurrection.

In a word, faith does all that in man of which the Scripture testifies externally. It describes the image of God externally and that image must come to be in me through faith. It describes the kingdom of God externally in letters and it must come to be in me through faith. It describes Christ externally and he must come to be in me through faith. The Scripture describes Adam, his fall and renewal, and all these things must be in me. The Scripture describes the New Jerusalem, which must be in me and I must be it. The Scripture testifies externally concerning the new birth, the new creature, and this all must be in me and I must be it through faith or the Scripture is of no use. This is all faith and the work of faith in us, indeed God's work and the kingdom of God in our hearts.

7

HOW THE LAW OF GOD IS WRITTEN IN THE HEARTS OF ALL MEN AND CONVINCES THEM EACH DAY THAT THEY HAVE NO EXCUSE BEFORE HIM

When the Gentiles do what the law requires, they show that the law is written on their hearts (Rom. 2:14–15).

When God, the Lord, created man according to his image in perfect righteousness and holiness and adorned and beautified him with great divine virtues and gifts, brought him forth as a perfect, beautiful masterpiece, as a high, noble work and piece of art, he planted three chief properties in the human conscience so deeply that they were never able to be rooted out, indeed, not even in eternity. First, he gave a natural testimony that there is a God, second, that there is a final judgment (Rom. 2:15), and third, the law of nature or natural righteousness by which honor and shame might be distinguished and joy and sorrow might be discovered.

There has never been a people so wild and barbaric that has denied that there is a God, for nature has witnessed this to them internally and externally. Indeed, they have discovered in their consciences that there is not only a God but that he is also a righteous God who punishes evil and rewards good, since in their consciences they found fear or joy. From this they deduced further that the soul must be immortal as Plato clearly insisted. Finally, from the law of nature, that is, from their inherited natural love, they saw clearly that God is the source of all good in nature. Further, they understood that this God must be served with virtue and a pure heart. Therefore, they placed the highest good in virtue and out of this the schools of virtue of Socrates and other wise philosophers arose.

From this we can see now how God allowed to remain, even after the fall, a spark of natural life or a track and sign of the natural testimony of God so that man might learn to know his beginning, from whence he came, and to pursue the same, as many pagans have remarked, particularly the poet Aratus whom Saint Paul quoted (Acts 17:28): *We are God's race and Mani* [sic]: *An dubium est habitare Deum sub pectore nostro In caelum redire animas, caeloque venire* [There is no doubt God lives in our hearts and our souls come from heaven and go again to heaven].

Because the pagans despised the natural witness of God against their consciences and therefore despised the Creator himself, they were damned through their own fault and had no excuse. Saint Paul gives witness of this (. . . Rom. 1:21 . . . Rom. 1:32; 2:15–16 . . .). Thus, the pagans have no excuse because they not only know by nature that there is a God but also against their consciences they have not sought God. Much less do those who have an excuse to whom God revealed his word and whom he called through Jesus Christ, his son, to repentance, that is, to arise from their sins to turn from the ungodly way of life so that through faith they might be participants and able to receive the merits of Christ and be eternally blessed.

Therefore, each man who is called Christian and is not converted will have two powerful witnesses against him at the final judgment: first, his own heart, conscience, and the law of nature; second, God's revealed word, which will be directed toward him on that day. Therefore, a frightful judgment and damnation will follow as the Lord said [in Mt. 11:24 . . .; 12:42 . . .].

Out of this eternal torment and pain will arise, for God has created this soul immortal and the conscience in the soul, which is always and internally directed to God, can nevermore come to God. This is the greatest and eternal pain of the soul.

Such an inner and externally enduring pain of the soul will become the greater, the more God's wrath will be heaped up against it through unrepentance on the day of wrath (Rom. 2:5). God the Lord, according to his righteous law, gave pagans over to a twisted mind because they cast out and accounted as nothing the inner law of nature and their own consciences written as God's righteousness in their hearts and they strove against this as against God himself. Through this blindness of their thoughts they were given over into the most abominable, horrible sins and abominations by which they heaped up God's righteous wrath upon themselves. Because those who wished to be Christians have cast out both the internal and the external word and witness of God and have not wished to be repentant but have stood against the Holy

Spirit and sinned against God, God has given them over to their own twisted thoughts so that they become worse than the pagans and the Turks and, therefore, *God sends upon them a strong dillusion to make them believe what is false so that all may be condemned who did not believe the truth but had pleasure in unrighteousness* (2 Thess. 2:11–12).

As a result, the most horrid sins are in motion among Christians as have never been heard of: devilish pride and pomp, unsatisfiable covetousness, shameful lust, bestial unchastity, inhuman deeds that arise out of blindness and the hardness of a twisted mind. In their lives, Christians do not wish to follow the lowly, poor, meek, and humble Christ but they are enraged against him, mock his holy life even though God has given him as a light to the world . . .(Jn. 8:12). Thus, God allows them to follow Satan and to take on his devilish life with all abominations, lies, unmercifulness; to perfect the works of darkness, for they do not walk in the light as the Lord says in John 12:35. . . .

Finally, God punishes the pagans with so frightful a blindness and a twisted mind because they have not followed the small, inner light that is in them from nature, and their own consciences, and the law of nature, or as Paul said in Romans 1:28, they have not seriously considered that they know God and, thus, that they have lost eternal blessedness through their own fault. How much more will those persons be robbed of eternal blessedness who have not only the law of nature written in their hearts but God's Word in their hearts written through a new covenant and through the revealed Word of God and who still do not value this great grace and blessedness. On this see Jeremiah 31:33. . . .

Hebrews 19:26ff. . . . is written against those who have sinned against known truth not out of weakness but openly and have remained impenitent.

8

WITHOUT TRUE REPENTANCE NO ONE WILL HAVE CONSOLATION IN CHRIST AND HIS MERITS

No unclean person dare eat the passover (Ex. 12:48).

The Lord Jesus says in Matthew 9:12–13: *"Those who are well have no need of a physician, but those who are sick. I came not to call the righteous, but sinners to repentance."*

In this the Lord tells us that he calls the sinner but [he calls him] to repentance. It follows, therefore, that no one can come to the Lord without true repentance and conversion from sins and without true faith.

Repentance is nothing other than to die through true regret and sorrow for sins and to receive forgiveness of sins through faith, and to live righteously in Christ. True, divine regret must precede repentance. By it, the heart is broken and the flesh is crucified. The Epistle to the Hebrews (6:1) calls this repentance of dead works, that is, the leaving of works that bring about death.

If these are not left, Christ with all his merits is of no use to a man. Christ our Lord placed himself before us as a physician and his holy blood as the precious, sanctifying medicine for sins.

This most costly medicine cannot help and will not work if the patient will not give up what is bad for him. Christ's blood and death will help no man who does not leave his sins. On this, Paul speaks in Galatians 5:21: *"Those who do this* (understand, the works of the flesh), *they will not inherit the kingdom of God, that is, they will have no part in Christ."*

Furthermore, if Christ and his holy blood are to be our medicine we must first be ill. Those who are well have no need of a physician, but those who are sick do (Mt. 9:12). Now all those who are not spiritually sick, who are without true repentance, who are without heartfelt sorrow for their sins, who have no broken, contrite heart and are not in dread before God's wrath, who do not wish to flee worldly pleasures, who search after vain honor, wealth, and pleasure, and who do not sorrow for sin, these, I say, are not ill and therefore they do not need the physician, that is, Christ is of no use to them.

Mark this well. Why is it said that Christ has come to call sinners, but to call them to repentance? [It is so said] because only a repentant, broken, contrite, faithful heart is capable of receiving the precious merit, blood, and death of Jesus Christ.

Blessed is the man who finds this holy calling in his heart, that is, the godly grief for sin brings about a regret of the blessed which no one regrets (2 Cor. 7:10). This godly sorrow the Holy Spirit brings about through the Law and through earnest meditation and the holy suffering of Christ. The suffering of Christ is likewise a sermon of repentance and the most frightful mirror of the wrath of God is also a sermon of grace. Consider the cause why our dear Lord suffered his bitter death, namely, because of our sins. Consider also the love of God, that he gave his Son. In this we see God's righteousness and mercy.

How can a person who believes on Christ at the same time have a desire to sin, not wish to leave sin, for which Christ had to pay with his blood and death, with his life? Consider how he had to pay for our pride and desire for honor with so much humility and rejection. Do you still have a desire for pride and can you not be satisfied enough with the honor of this world? How greatly did Christ have to pay for your covetousness with his great poverty, and do you still not have enough of the riches of this world? How greatly did Christ have to pay for the lust of your flesh with his great dread and pain of death. Do you still have joy in this mortal fleshly lust? How can you have joy in that which caused the Lord Christ the highest pain? How can you have joy in that which was in your Lord Christ the highest sorrow even unto death? With what deep meekness and great patience your Lord paid for your wrath, hate, enmity, bitterness, desire for revenge, and unforgiving spirit. Are you still so easily enraged and is your desire for revenge so sweet, sweeter than your life? Is that for which the Lord had to drink so bitter a cup of death, sweet to you?

Therefore, all those who call themselves Christians and do not leave their sins crucify Christ again and hold him up to contempt as it is written in Hebrews 6:6. They cannot partake of the sufferings of Christ for they have tread on the blood of Christ with their feet. As it is written in Hebrews 10:29: *They have profaned the blood of the covenant*, that is, they do not consider it a purification of sin, they do not hold that it is a payment poured out for their sins, they despise the spirit of grace, that is, they stand against, cast out, make fun of, and sin against the high, precious, offered grace with their ungodly lives. Since the blood of Christ was also poured out for them, revenge cries over them; they must experience the righteous judgment of God of which we are easily to be in dread . . . (Heb. 10:31). Our God is not a weak, dead idol, who will always allow himself to be mocked and his grace to be made fun of, but he is a living God.

Indeed, our own heart convinces us that a great vengeance and wrath of God will follow upon the person who does not leave his sins and does not hear how the eternal Son of God had to suffer so frightful a death for sin.

This is the reason why repentance was preached throughout the whole world immediately following the holy death of Christ, namely, because in the first place this occurred for the sins of the whole world, and secondly all men throughout the earth are to be repentant as Acts 17:30 states. This medicine is to be taken up by faithful, sorrowing, repentant hearts so that the precious gift of grace of God to man will not be lost.

Upon such a deep repentance the forgiveness of sins follows, for how can sins be forgiven in a person who was never sorrowful and in one who still has pleasure in sins and will not give them up? Is it not a foolish, twisted affair to wish forgiveness of sins and not to wish to give up sins? [It is foolish] to seek comfort in the sufferings of Christ and yet not to leave sins for which Christ had to die.

There are many people who throughout their life have not done true repentance and yet wish to have forgiveness of sins. They have not left their covetousness, pride, wrath, hatefulness, envy, falsity, unrighteousness; indeed, they have continued them and yet they wish to have Christ's merits ascribed to them. They have convinced themselves that they are good Christians since they know and believe that Christ died for sins. They think that thus all are made holy. Ah, you deluded, false Christian. God's Word has not taught you that thus you will become holy. No apostle or prophet preached so, but they preach so. If you wish to have forgiveness of sins you must be repentant and leave your sins, have sorrow for your sins and believe in Christ.

How shall one, however, be sorrowful for sins that he does not intend to leave? How shall he leave sins for which he does not have sorrow? Christ, his prophets and apostles teach that: You must die to the sins and the world, that is, your own pride, covetousness, pleasure, wrath, enmity, and you must turn to the Lord and seek grace. Then you will have forgiveness of sins, then the physician will come who binds up broken hearts and heals their pain (Ps. 147:3). Otherwise, Christ is of no use and does not help even if you say much about your faith. True faith renews man and mortifies the sins in man, makes a man living in Christ, that is, he lives in Christ, in his love, humility, meekness, patience.

Note that Christ is thus in you the way to life; in him you are a new creature. If you remain in your sins, however, you will not die from them but allow yourself to do what you wish, what your old Adam does. How can you be a new creature? How can you belong to Christ since you do not mortify the flesh together with its lusts and desires (Gal. 5:24)?

Even if you heard ten sermons every day, went to confession every month, went to receive the Lord's supper, none of this would help you unless you had forgiveness of sins. This is because there would be present no repentant, contrite, faithful heart that would be capable of receiving the healing medicine. God's Word and sacraments are indeed healing medicines, but they do not help any unrepentant person who does not have a continually sorrowful, faithful heart. If you poured costly balm over a stone, what would it help? It would do nothing for the stone. If you sowed your best wheat among many thorns it would not bring forth fruit unless the thorns had first been taken out (Lk. 8:7). Finally, Christ is of no use to the person who remains in his sins. His birth is of no use to the person who will not be newborn in Christ. His death is of no use to the person who will not die with Christ from his sins (Rom. 6:11). His resurrection is of no use to the person who will not arise with Christ from his sins. His ascension is of no use to the person who will not live in a heavenly manner of life and walk.

If a man turns with the prodigal son (Lk. 15:18), weeps and is sorrowful for his sins, hates and shuns them, asks God for grace, and looks in faith to the crucified Christ and his bloody wounds (as the Israelites looked to the snake in Numbers 21:8), and says: *God be gracious to me a poor sinner* (Lk. 18:13), everything will be forgiven and forgotten, even if that man has committed the greatest sin in the world.

The holy blood of Christ and his holy death pays for this much. *Tanta est perfectio in redemtione, parta sanguine Christi et tanta est perfectio applicationis gratiae et imputationis totius meriti Christi per fidem.* His redemption, which came through the blood of Christ, is so perfect and all the merits of Christ will be perfectly ascribed to the repentant heart through faith. God accepts repentance for sins (Wisd. 12:19), that is, God completely forgives the repentant person out of pure grace for Christ's sake. Indeed, it is God's pleasure and joy to be merciful and to forgive the sins out of grace . . . (Jer. 31:20). This is because the death of Christ comes to its power and fruit and as a result there is joy in heaven and before the angels of God that a poor sinner for whom Christ's blood was shed has not lost this precious blood (Lk. 15:7).

9

BY PRESENT UNCHRISTIAN ACTIVITY CHRIST AND TRUE FAITH IS DENIED

They have the form of godliness but deny the power thereof (2 Tim. 3:5).

Because men call themselves Christians and yet do not act as Christians, Christ is denied, mocked, despised, insulted, beaten, crucified, cut off, and killed as the Epistle to Hebrews 6:6 states that some men crucify and mock the Son of God again. The holy prophet Daniel foresaw that in the last days Christ would be cut off (Dan. 9:26).

This prophecy was fulfilled at the crucifixion in Jerusalem when the Jews cried: *Crucify him, crucify him*. Indeed, Christ is daily crucified and cut off with the result that one is hardly able to see him, that is, his holy noble life any longer. Where Christ's life is not, Christ is not, even if one speaks many words concerning faith and doctrine. What is Christian faith without a Christian life? A tree without fruits, as the Apostle Jude calls the false apostle (Jude 12). One finds the whole world filled with these now. Therefore the Lord says in Luke 18:8: *When the Son of Man comes, will he find faith on earth?*

Truly, the Lord did not understand such faith as is now discussed with the mouth but denied by deed. Men now love Christ with their tongues but not in deed and truth. Christ understood the whole newborn man, the tree with its fruits, renewed through faith, in which Christ lives and dwells through faith. Such faith he will find in few. Where true faith is, there Christ and his holy life are. Where one does not follow Christ in his life through faith, there is neither faith nor Christ, but that one is cast out and denied.

In Luke 12:9, the Lord says: *He who denies me before men will be denied before the angels of God*. This denial occurs not only when one denies the faith and Christ with his lips, but much more when by his deeds and life he strives openly against Christ and the Holy Spirit as Saint Paul says: By their deeds they deny him. Indeed,

Christ is as much denied by an ungodly devilish life as with the mouth, indeed, also with hypocrisy and pretense as the parable of the two sons in Matthew 21 indicates. . . .

False Christians are those who say "Yes, yes, Lord, Lord" and are internally evil men and do not do what the Father has commanded. Saint Paul says of these in 2 Timothy 3:5: [*They*] *hold the form of religion but deny the power of it*. What is it to deny the power of godliness other than to deny the faith and Christ, to be a pagan with a Christian name, a son of disobedience, who has no faith, as Paul says in Ephesians 2:2? Therefore, to those who have the name of Christian but do not act in a Christian manner he will deny and say: *I never knew you; depart from me you evildoers* (Mt. 7:23).

10

THE LIFE OF THE PRESENT CHILDREN OF THIS WORLD IS COMPLETELY SET AGAINST CHRIST AND THEREFORE IT IS A FALSE LIFE AND A FALSE CHRISTIANITY

He who is not with me is against me (Mt. 12:30).

If one compares the life of the present world with Christ's teaching and life, one discovers immediately that the greater part of the world is completely opposed to Christ. What is the life of man now other than covetousness, concern over food, search for wealth, the lust of the flesh, the lust of the eye, and the pride of life, that is, the most and best that is in the world, great honor in the world, a great appearance, a great name, disobedience, wrath, enmity, war, disunity, contention, a desire for revenge in words and deeds, secret envy, an unforgiving spirit, unrighteousness, impurity, deception, falsity, slander? In a word, the whole life of the children of this world at this time is nothing other than worldly love, self-love, self-honor and [the desire for] self-gain.

Christ and his life, on the other hand, are nothing other than pure, simple, clean love for God and man, kindness, meekness, humility, patience, obedience to death, mercy, righteousness, truth, purity, holiness, rejection of the world and all worldly honor, wealth, and pleasure, denial of oneself, a continual cross, suffering, tribulation, a continual desire and groaning for the kingdom of God and a ready desire to do the will of God.

Christ says: *He who is not with me is against me* (Mt. 12:30). The life of this world is not with Christ. It does not agree in any way with him. There is almost no one of one heart, thought, mind, and spirit with Christ in the way one ought to be. Saint Paul testifies that this should be so (. . . 1 Cor. 2:16 and Phil. 2:5 . . .). Therefore, all the children of this world are against Christ. He who is against Christ, however, is the Antichrist. If he is not so in doctrine, he is so in his life.

Where is one to find true Christians? They are a small number

[as is noted in] Luke 12: . . . , Isaiah 1:8 . . . , Micah 7:1 . . . ,
Psalm 74:19 . . . , Psalm 102:7. . . .

God knows where and who his children are. Christ is with
them, indeed in them at all times even to the end of the world. He
will not leave them as orphans. *God's firm foundation stands bearing
this seal: "The Lord knows those who are his"* and *"Let everyone who names
the name of the Lord depart from iniquity"* (2 Tim. 2:19). Let him who
does not wish to do this give up the name of Christ and call himself
what he will.

11

HE WHO DOES NOT FOLLOW CHRIST IN HIS LIFE IS NOT TRULY REPENTANT, IS NO CHRISTIAN, AND IS NOT THE CHILD OF GOD. WHAT THE NEW BIRTH IS, AND WHAT THE YOKE OF CHRIST IS

Christ has left us an example that we should follow in his footsteps (1 Pet. 2:21).

God gave us his beloved Son as a prophet, doctor, and teacher, affirmed his calling through a voice from heaven, and ordered us to hear him. The Son of God fulfilled his teaching capacity not only with words but also with actions and with the beautiful examples of his most holy life as was fitting for a righteous teacher. Saint Luke speaks of this in Acts 1:1. *In the first book, O Theophilus, I have dealt with all that Jesus began to do and teach until the day when he was taken up.* In this verse, the evangelist puts the word "do" before the word "teach" to point out that doing and teaching belong together. Indeed a perfect teacher must first do and then teach. Thus, Christ's life is the true teaching and the true Book of Life.

God's Son became man and walked among men upon this earth so that he might give us a clear, living example of a godly, innocent, perfect, holy life, so that we might follow him as a light in the darkness. Therefore, he is called the light of the world and he who follows him walks not in darkness (Jn. 8:12).

From this it is clear that a person must remain in darkness who does not follow Christ in faith and holy life, and that such a person can nevermore have the light of life. What is darkness, however? It is nothing other than an unrepentant life, which Paul calls "the works of darkness," which we must cast off and we must put on the armor of light (Rom. 13:12). In a word this means to be repentant.

It was earlier said fully enough that godly sorrow and true faith changes the whole man, crucifies the flesh, and brings about a new life through the Holy Spirit, so that there are not only words that tell us of this. So that we might have a living, visual example of the Spirit that makes one alive or makes a new man, God placed before us his beloved Son, not only as a Savior but as a mirror of godliness, with his holy life, as the true new man in whom nothing of the Adamic, sinful flesh rules and lives except God himself, to the end that we also might be daily renewed according to his image. Concerning this, we must note the following account:

We know and experience, unfortunately daily, how our sinful nature, flesh and blood, body and soul, is wrapped around with so many impurities, evils, sins, and vices. These are all the works, qualities, and characteristics of the Devil in the fleshly, natural man. Above all there is the evil will of man. Out of an evil will all sin arises. If there were no evil will, sin would nevermore occur. An evil will turns itself from God. Everything that turns itself from God as from the eternal good is and must necessarily be evil. This turning away is the fall of man and of the Devil and for this reason sin came, which is inherited by all men and continued through man.

From this it is clear that our flesh and blood are poisoned in nature by the Devil's quality and our fleshly will is poisoned by Satan's evil, as by lies, pride, evil desire, and all kinds of vice that stand against God. Because of such evil qualities, the Lord Christ named the Pharisees "children of the Devil" (Jn. 8:44) and gave one of his apostles over to the Devil (Jn. 13:2). He gave him over to the Devil as if he were covetousness, lies, pride, and all the evil lusts of the Devil himself by which the natural, carnal man is ensnared.

From this it follows that all those who live in unrepentance, in pride, covetousness, lust, and envy, live in the Devil and are ensnared with the Devil's life-style. They may adorn themselves externally as beautifully as they please; they still remain devils in their hearts, as our Lord said to the Jews. Although this is very frightful, it is nevertheless the truth.

Although our miserable, greatly corrupted human nature is ensnared in so unspeakable and frightful a sorrow, it may be made better and renewed. How? Since it is corrupted with the most abominable evil, it must be made better and renewed by the highest good, namely, by God himself and, therefore, God had to become man.

God's Son did not become man for his own sake but for ours, so that he might unite us once again with God through himself, and make us participants of the highest good, and purify and make us holy once again. That which is to be made holy must be made holy through God and with God. As God is personally in Christ, so God must be united with us through faith and man must live in God and God in him; man must live in Christ and Christ in him. God's will must be in man and man must live in God's will. Christ Jesus must be the medicine for our corrupted nature. The more Christ lives in man, the more is human nature made better.

Would not that man be more noble in whom Christ brings about all things, whose will is Christ's will, whose thoughts are Christ's thoughts, whose mind is Christ's mind (as Saint Paul said, "*We have the mind of Christ*" [in 1 Cor. 2:16]) and whose speech and word is Christ's word? Indeed, we must thus be free. Christ's life is the new life in man and the new man is the man in whom Christ lives in the spirit. Christ's meekness must be the meekness of the new man; Christ's humility, the humility of the new man; Christ's patience is the patience of the new man, and so forth. The whole life of Christ must be in the life of the new man. This is a new creature and the noble life of Christ in us as Saint Paul says: "*It is no longer I who live, but Christ who lives in me*" (Gal. 2:20). To repent properly is to properly follow Christ. By this, the old man dies and the carnal life dies and the new spiritual life begins. There is then a true Christian not only according to title and name, but according to act and truth. Indeed, he is a true child of God, born out of God and Christ, renewed in Christ and made living through faith.

Although we are not able in our present weakness to come to perfection, yet we must strive after it. We must weep and hope in our hearts that Christ and not Satan will live in us and have his reign in us. Indeed, we are to strive for this and, through daily sorrow, mortify the old man. Insofar as the old man dies, Christ will live in us. Insofar as the evil nature through the Spirit of God is taken off, grace is placed in man. Insofar as the flesh is crucified, the spirit is made living. Insofar as the work of darkness is extinguished in man, man is more and more enlightened. Insofar as the external man is cast off and mortified, the internal man is renewed (2 Cor. 4:16). Insofar as one's own affectations and the whole carnal life in man dies—such as self-love, self-honor, wrath, covetousness, lust—insofar Christ lives in him. The more the world leaves man in the lust of the eyes, the lust of the flesh, and the pride of life, the more do God, Christ, and the Holy Spirit enter man and possess him. Thus, the more nature, flesh, darkness, and the world rule in man, the less grace, spirit, light, God, and Christ exist in man.

If this is to happen it will be a bitter cross for the flesh, for by it the flesh will be extinguished, crucified with its lusts and desires, and this is the true power and fruit of repentance. Flesh and blood wish for themselves a free, dissolute, certain life, according to their own lusts and wills. That is, for the flesh, the sweetest and most pleasant life. Christ's life is for the flesh and the old man a bitter cross, however. For the new, spiritual man, nevertheless, it is an easy yoke and a light burden and a lovely rest. In what does loving peace consist other than in faith in Christ in his meekness, humility, patience, and in the love of Christ (Mt. 11:29)? Thus you will find peace for your soul. Indeed, for the person who properly loves Christ, death for Christ's sake is the highest joy. This is the easy yoke of Christ, which we are to take upon ourselves and in which the true peace of the soul consists.

If we are to take the yoke of Christ upon ourselves as it is, that is, his holy, noble life, we must cast off the Devil's yoke, that is, the carnal, seeking, dissolute life, and we must not allow the flesh to rule over the spirit but everything that is in man, the will, understanding, reason, desires, and all Adamic fleshly lusts must come under the yoke of Christ and under his obedience.

The flesh is pleased to be honored, highly considered, and praised. It wishes to gain wealth, good days, and pleasure, but all this must be brought under the yoke of Christ, that is, under Christ's rejection, poverty, and shame. One is to consider pleasures as worthless, to draw oneself away from all that is high, glorious, pompous, powerful, and beautiful in the world. This is the true humility of Christ and his noble life and his easy yoke, which is a light burden. He did not come to be served but to serve us and he gave his life as a payment for our sins (Mt. 20:28). What is Christ's life other than holy poverty, external rejection, and the highest pain?

A carnal man seeks after honor and wishes to gain things for himself; the spiritual man loves humility in Christ and wishes nothing for himself. All men endeavor to be something, but no one wishes to learn to be nothing. The first is the life of Adam, the second is the life of Christ. A carnal man who does not yet know what Christ is, namely, pure humility, meekness, and love, thinks the life of Christ is great foolishness and believes that the free, seeking, carnal life is great wisdom. Out of his great blindness he believes that he has the best and most joyous life. He does not know that he lives in the Devil. Such people are deceived by this false light of their fleshly wisdom and deceive others with it. Those who are enlightened by the eternal, true life are afraid of the false life, if they see pomp, pride, arrogance, lust, wrath, vengefulness, and similar fruits of the carnal life. Then they think: "Ah, Dear God, how far are we yet from Christ and his knowledge, from true repentance, from true Christianity, and from the fruit of the new birth of the true children of God. Indeed, [the man who lives in such sins] lives in Adam, and in the old birth, indeed, in the Devil himself. To live openly and essentially in sin is nothing other than to live in the Devil. The life of Christ is not in such a man; in him there is no repentance, he is not a true Christian, and much less a child of God. He does not understand Christ in the proper fashion. The person who does properly understand Christ as a Savior and Sanctifier and as an Example of life must know that he is pure love, meekness, patience, and humility. This love and meekness of Christ he must have in himself; indeed, he must have and discover it in his heart and love it just as a man must know the smell and taste of food. Thus, you must know Christ in yourself as the most noble food in which is discovered your soul's life, power, consolation, and rest. When one tastes how gracious the Lord is (Ps. 34:8), and knows the truth, then one discovers the highest and eternal good. Then he knows that the life of Christ is the best, noblest, and most lovely life and that no life is so good, so precious, so soft, so restful, so peaceful, so joyous, so gracious and so similar to the eternal life as the life of Christ.

Since it is the best life, it is also the dearest for us. In the man, however, in whom the life of Christ does not exist, the peace and rest of eternal life is not properly understood, nor is the highest good, the eternal truth, the proper peace and joy, the proper light, the true love, all of which is Christ. Therefore, John says in 1 John 4:7–8: *"He who loves is born of God and knows God. He who does not love does not know God for God is love."*

From this it is clear that the new birth is from God and that its fruits and the new life do not consist in words alone or in external appearance but in the highest virtue, which is God himself, namely, in love. One must have the quality, characteristics, and likeness of the person out of which one was born. If one is born out of God, he must have love, for God is love.

It is also so with the true knowledge of God. This does not consist in words or in mere learning but in a living, loving, gracious, powerful consolation in which through grace one tastes the sweetness, joyousness, loveliness, and graciousness of God in his heart. This is the living knowledge of God, which is found in the heart and lives in it. This is what Psalm 84:2 speaks of: *"My heart and flesh sing for joy to the living God,"* and Psalm 63:3: *"Your steadfast love is better than life."* In these Psalms the joy and sweetness of God in the faithful heart is described. Thus, a man lives in God and God in him; he knows God in truth and is known by him.

12

A TRUE CHRISTIAN MUST DIE TO HIMSELF AND THE WORLD AND LIVE IN CHRIST

Christ died for all, that those who lived might live no longer for themselves but for him who for their sake died and was raised (2 Cor. 5:15).

This verse is an excellent verse of consolation, for it clearly says that Christ died for all. It is also a beautiful guide to the holy life, in that it tells us we are not to live for ourselves but for him who died for us. If we are so to live we must first die to ourselves and the world. It cannot be otherwise; the person who wishes to live in Christ must die to worldly lusts and he who wishes to live for himself and the evil world must let Christ go.

There is a threefold death. First, there is a spiritual death, by which man daily dies to himself, that is, to his fleshly lusts, to covetousness, pride, pleasure, wrath, and so forth. The second is the natural death and the third is the eternal death.

Concerning the natural death, Saint Paul spoke in Philippians 1:21: *To live is Christ and to die is gain*. This indicates that when a Christian experiences the natural death, Christ is his life, and death is victory, that is, he receives a better life and wealth, an eternal for a physical life, and this is his victory.

It is also proper to interpret this passage as referring to the spiritual dying to sin. The soul whose life is Christ is blessed, that is, if Christ lives in the soul or if the soul takes the life of Christ to itself, that is, his humility and meekness. Most people have the Devil's life in themselves, and the Devil with covetousness, pride, pleasure, wrath, and sinfulness, that is, the whole of the Devil's life, is their life.

Therefore, take note who lives in you. Blessed is the man who can say in his heart: Christ is my life, not only following this life but also now. While you live here Christ must be your life, that is, he must live in you and to die must be gain, that is, if pride, covetousness, pleasure, wrath, and enmity die in you, if you die to yourself and the world. How great a gain, for by this Christ lives in you. The more you die to the world the more Christ lives in you. Is not this a great gain? Live then so that Christ lives in you in time, so that you might live with him in eternity.

Where the desires of this world are, there can be no peace and rest. To these, man must completely die before Christ can live in him. This is indicated to us in the dear, old Sarah who in her old age, after all womanly desires had died, became pregnant and bore Isaac, that is, one who laughs. Following the mortification of her body she bore the son of the free man (Gen. 18:12). Thus, if the worldly desires do not die in you, you cannot conceive and bear the joy of the spirit.

This is also exemplified in Abraham, for he did not receive the promise of Christ and the circumcision before he left his fatherland and had left his earth. Thus, so long as a man clings to the world firmly with his heart, he cannot discover or taste Christ in his heart.

As soon as Herod died, Christ came back to Judah (Mt. 2:19–20). So long as the fox Herod is in your heart, with his earthly, worldly desires, Christ will not come. If he dies in you however, Christ will come. If Adam rules in you, Christ cannot live in you. Therefore, Saint Paul says in Galatians 2:20: *"I live, yet not I but Christ lives in me"* (Col. 3:3 . . .).

You are truly dead if you cease to be what you were, that is, if your sins die in you (Rom. 6:1–18). *If we live in the spirit, let us also walk in the spirit*, that is, if we praised ourselves in faith and the spirit, let us also show forth the fruits of the spirit (Gal. 5:25 . . . Rom. 8:13).

In 1 Samuel 15:8, Saul cast Agag, the Amalekite king, into prison, although according to God's commandment he was to have killed him. In the same way, many people secretly conceal their desires that they should kill. It is not enough that you hide away your lusts; you must kill them or you will be cast out of the kingdom as Saul was, that is, out of eternal life. The whole of the Holy Scripture with its histories, images, and figures looks toward Christ whom we are to follow in a holy life. Indeed, the great world-book of nature gives witness to God and his love.

Many men are as trees in the winter who at that time have no leaves but put forth leaves again in the spring. Many of them, if the cold winter of misfortune comes upon them, subdue their evil lusts but as soon as the sun shines again and it goes better with them again they begin their evil lusts in a greater way. They are hypocrites. A Christian, however, is pious, both in good and evil times, and loves God at both times in fortune and misfortune, in ownership and loss, in need and superfluity.

In 1 Kings 20:42 we read of Ahab. God gave the King of Syria into his hands and he was to keep him in prison. This indicates that God is stronger than all enemies and overcomes those who sin against him. When a battle arose, Ahab called him his brother and let him go, but a prophet came to Ahab and said: *Because you have let go out of your hand the man whom I had devoted to your destruction, your life shall go for his life*. In a like manner, many people call evil lusts their brothers and let them live. They ought to kill them and because they do not, they must give up their life for them.

Without the mortification of the flesh, nothing spiritual can be in man, neither true prayer nor meditation. Therefore, the Lord God commanded in Exodus 19:20 that no animal was to come near to the holy mountain Sinai or it would be killed. Thus, you must kill bestial lusts if you wish to draw near to the holy mountain of God, to pray and to meditate on God's word, or you will die eternally.

In Genesis 32:28 we read that Jacob received another name, Israel, that is, one who fought with God or God's prince, since in a battle with the angel he saw the face of God. Therefore, he called the place "Peniel," that is, God's face. One must first be a Jacob, that is, a victor. You must first be a Jacob, that is a victor through the Holy Spirit over your evil lusts, if you wish to be an Israel, that is God's prince, and if you wish to come to the place Peniel, that is to God's presence.

In Genesis 29:17–25 we read that Jacob wishes to have the woman Rachel as his beautiful wife, but he had to take Leah first. Leah was physically ugly; Rachel was pretty and beautiful. Therefore, if you wish to have the beautiful Rachel, that is, if your soul is to be the wife of Jacob, that is, of Christ, you must first take to yourself Leah, that is, you must not be pleasing to yourself, you must be hateful to yourself, ugly, you must hate yourself and deny yourself. How many are led astray, as was Jacob, from their own lives, that is, from themselves, who think they have the beautiful and pretty Rachel, that is, they think they have a Christian life that will be pleasing to God. Yet when they look at it, it is Leah. Their life is hateful and unformed before God's eyes. If you are first unworthy in your own eyes as a Leah, the most unworthy in her father's house, learn first humility, meekness, and patience. Then you will become the beautiful Rachel.

Note how loyally Jacob served seven years for Rachel and yet it seemed to him it was one single day, so much love did he have for her. So also your Lord Christ served your soul thirty-three years in this world and endured difficult service for you, as Jacob said: *These twenty years have I been with you; by day the heat consumed me and the cold by night, and my sleep fled from my eyes* (Gen. 31:38–40). Note that the Lord Christ also served you in a similar way as he said in Matthew 20:28: *"The Son of Man is not come to be served but that he might serve and give his life a payment for many."* Therefore, will you then not love Christ and deny the world, his enemy?

13

FOR THE LOVE OF CHRIST AND FOR THE ETERNAL FUTURE GLORY FOR WHICH WE ARE CREATED AND REDEEMED EACH CHRISTIAN IS TO WILLINGLY DIE TO HIMSELF AND THE WORLD

For you know the grace of our Lord Jesus Christ, that though he was rich, yet for your sake he became poor, so that by his poverty you might become rich (2 Cor. 8:9).

For the sake of your Lord Christ, you are to die to yourself, your sins and the world, to do good and to lead a godly, holy life. [You are not to do this so] that you will earn something by it, (Christ has earned everything for you) but only out of pure love for Christ, since he died for you.

If you love Christ, do not love him with your tongue but with deed and truth. If you love him keep his words (. . . Jn. 14:23 . . . 1 John 3:3). The Lord said in Matthew 11:30: *My yoke is easy and my burden is light*, that is, for a true lover of Christ it is a pleasure and true joy to do good deeds. Love makes all things easy. He who does not properly love Christ does everything with hesitation and unwillingly and doing good is difficult for him. For a true lover of Christ, dying for Christ's sake is a joy (Phil. 1:29 . . .).

Note the example of Moses as it is explained in Hebrews 11:24–26: *By faith Moses, when he was grown up, refused to be called the Son of Pharoah's Daughter, choosing rather to share ill treatment with the people of God than to enjoy the fleeting pleasures of sin. He considered abuse suffered for the Christ greater wealth than the treasures of Egypt, for he looked to the reward.*

Note the example of Daniel in Daniel 1:8. The King of Babylon chose him with his friends from those imprisoned in Babylon that they might serve him and he allowed them to eat from his table and gave them the wine that he drank, and trained them until they were prepared to serve a king. Daniel and his companions felt that the king would corrupt them with expensive food from his dish and they requested him to give them vegetables to eat and water to drink. This they did out of love for wisdom and as a result wisdom came from above into their souls. In a like manner you must destroy the pleasure of the flesh that is expensive food if Christ the Eternal Wisdom is to come into your soul. Like the young men who became beautiful because they lived temperately, ate vegetables, and drank water, so your soul will be beautiful before God, indeed it will become a partaker of divine nature if you cast off sins and shun fleshly lusts (2 Pet. 1:4).

Saint Paul says in Galatians 6:14: *"Through Christ the world has been crucified to me and I to the world,"* that is, I have died to the world and the world has died again in me. A Christian is truly in the world but not of the world. He lives indeed in the world but he does not love it. The world's pomp, honor, pretense, glory, lust of the eyes, lust of the flesh, pride of life, is for a Christian as a dead thing, a shadow to which he pays no attention. Thus, the world is crucified and dies for Christians and they are dead and crucified to the world, that is, they do not desire any worldly honor, wealth, lust, and joy.

A heart to which God gives his grace so that it does not desire any worldly honor, wealth, and pleasure is a holy heart. For this every Christian should daily pray, that God will give him this grace so that he might not desire worldly honor, wealth, and pleasure.

Solomon the wise king said in Proverbs 30:7–8: *Two things I ask of thee; deny them not to me before I die; remove far from me falsehood and lying; give me neither poverty nor riches; feed me with the food that is needful for me.* A Christian however, should thus also pray and say: "Two things I request from you, that I might die to myself and the world." Without these two he can be no true Christian but is a false work to whom as a hypocrite the Lord will say: *I do not know you* [Mt. 7:23, 25:12].

This is a bitter cross for the flesh, namely, to die to itself and the world, to drive the world from itself, so that it can inherit heaven. Yet the spirit and the love of Christ conquer all things. It is an easy yoke and a light burden for the spirit. Although the world hates those people who have died to the world, nevertheless God loves them, for the enmity of this world is the friendship of Christ and the friendship of the world is the enmity of God. He who wishes to be a friend of the world will be an enemy of God (Jas. 4:4 . . . Jn. 15:18 . . .).

The world is like the sea, containing within itself only living things and casting out everything that is dead and dying. Thus, the person who has died to the world is thrown and cast out by the world. The others, who lead a glorified, pompous life of pretense, are the beloved children of the world.

In a word, he who has brought it about that all pride, covetousness, lust, wrath, and search for vengeance have died in his heart has died to the world and the world to him and he begins to live in Christ and Christ in him. Such a person Christ acknowledges as his own. To the others he says: I do not know, because you do not know me, you have shamed me by your life, that is, you have shamed my humility, meekness, and patience and therefore I am ashamed before you (Mk. 8:38). In a word, he who does not live here in time with Christ will not live with him there in eternity. Christ will not live in that person there, in whom he has not lived here. That person will not be blessed there who has not had Christ's life in him here.

Note with whom you have most conformed and unified your life here, with Christ or with the Devil. With whomever you have done so you will remain united after death in eternity.

The person who has died to himself can easily die to the world. To die to the world means not to love the world or anything that is in the world as 1 John (2:15) states. . . . What is the world to one who has died to the world in his heart? He who loves the world will easily be overcome by the world as Samson was by Delilah (Judg. 16:6) and he must suffer all that the world brings upon him.

The love of the world thus belongs to the old creature and not to the new birth. The world has nothing except honor, wealth, and pleasure, or the lust of the flesh, the lust of the eye, and the pride of life in which the old man rejoices. The new man, however, has his joy in Christ alone; he is his honor, wealth, and pleasure.

God's image renewed through Christ is the greatest adornment and honor for man after which we should chiefly strive. Tauler says: "Cannot dear God give you more joy than a corrupted creature?"

God's Word says that man was not created for the world but that the world was created for man. Indeed, man was created to a much higher life and dwelling not for the sake of costly eating and drinking, not for great wealth, for many cities and villages, for lands and pastures, not for pomp, and costly clothing, not for gold and silver, not for any temporal passing thing regardless of how good and costly it seems; nor was he created to be a possessor and inheritor of this earth on which he could have his lust, idolatry, joy, and paradise and not know or hope for more than what he could see with his bestial eyes. No, for these things man was truly not created and therefore he must not remain in the world but must go out of it again. Even if we were born with great wealth in this world, death takes us away again with our wealth and drives us out. It does not let us take a littlest piece with us in spite of our wealth.

This is a great and clear example that we are not created for this life and that this world is not the *principalis finis nostrae creationis* [chief end of our creation] or we would remain in it. There must then be another more glorious end of our creation. To this, our beginning, which is God himself and the divine image that we bear in Christ and to which we are renewed, gives witness. It gives witness that we are chiefly created for the kingdom of God and for eternal life and to that as well we are redeemed by Christ and born again through the Holy Spirit.

Should a man now cling with his heart on this world and weigh down his noble soul with temporal things even though his soul is much nobler and better than the whole world? Man is the most noble of creatures since he carries the image of God in Christ. Therefore, as was earlier said, man was not created for the sake of the world but the world for the sake of man because he carries the image of God in Christ, which is so noble that the whole world with all its wealth is not able to bring a soul into being or to raise up the image of God. For this reason, Christ had to die so that the corrupted and dying image of God in man might once again be renewed through the Holy Spirit and so that man might once again be the house and the dwelling place of God in eternity.

Ought I now to give up my soul, which Christ paid for so dearly, for a handful of gold and silver, for the wealth of this world, its honor and lust? It is truly a pearl in filth and cast before swine (Mt. 7:6). This is what the Lord means when he says: *"What does it gain a man if he gain the world and lose his soul, that is, himself "* [Mt. 16:26]? The whole world with all its glory cannot help a soul for the soul is immortal but the world is passing.

14

A TRUE CHRISTIAN MUST HATE HIS OWN LIFE
IN THIS WORLD AND LEARN TO DESPISE
THE WORLD ACCORDING TO THE
EXAMPLE OF CHRIST

If anyone comes to me and does not hate himself, indeed his own life, he cannot be my disciple (Lk. 14:26). *He who loves his life loses it, and he who hates his life in this world will keep it for eternal life* (Jn. 12:25).

If a man is to hate himself he must first not love himself. Second, he must daily die to sin. Third, he must daily battle with himself, that is, with his flesh.

First, there is nothing upon earth more harmful to man's holiness than the love of self, which is not a natural love and preservation of self, but is to be understood throughout this book as a carnal, inordinate love and self-seeking. Nothing is to be loved except God alone. If a man loves himself he makes himself to God and is a God himself. What a man loves, on that his heart rests, on that his heart hangs; indeed, that takes man captive and makes him its slave and robs him of his noble freedom. You have as many servants and prison guards as you have earthly things that you love. If your love is pure, clean, and simple and directed toward God, you will not be trapped by anything and will maintain all your freedom. You must desire nothing that will hinder you from the love of God. If you wish to have God completely, you must give yourself completely up. If you love yourself and have most pleasure in yourself, you will have for yourself much sorrow, dread, unrest, and sadness. However, if you love God and have pleasure in him and give yourself completely to him, God will concern himself for you and no fear and sorrow will fall upon you. A person who loves himself and seeks himself in all things, his own gain, homage, honor, will not have peace. He will always find something that is opposed to him and because of this he will be uneasy. Therefore, nothing is good for you that is directed to your gain, homage, and honor, but if it shames you and roots out your evil roots that hinder you from the love of God it is good for you.

Your own gain, homage, and honor will pass with everything in the world, but God's love is eternal. The peace and rest that arise out of love of self and temporal things will not remain long. Very small things can arise that disturb this rest. If your heart rests alone in God and in his love, there is eternal peace. Everything that does not come from God must pass and is vain. Therefore, note this short rule: Leave all things and you will find all things through faith. God is not found by those who love themselves or the world.

Inordinate self-love is earthly and not from God. Self-love hinders heavenly wisdom, for true heavenly wisdom does not hold itself high and does not seek to be praised upon the earth. Therefore, it is a poor and small thing and is almost forgotten. Although much is preached about it, nevertheless, because man is far from it in life, this noble pearl remains hidden from many. If you wish to have it, however, you must give up human wisdom, your own pleasure, and inordinate self-love. Thus, you can gain heavenly wisdom for the haughty, costly, earthly, human wisdom. For the wisdom of this world you will receive a small and poor thing in the eyes of this world, but it is heavenly and eternal.

No one can love God unless he hates himself, that is, he must not have pleasure in himself and in his sins, he must set aside his own will and mortify it. The more a man loves God, the more he hates his evil will and affectations, the more he crucifies his flesh with its lusts and desires. The more a man leaves himself and his own love through the power of the Holy Spirit, the more he enters into God and his love through faith. For just as the refusal to desire something external brings internal peace, so man comes to God if he leaves everything internally and clings to no creature with his heart but to God alone.

He who will deny himself must not follow himself and his own will but Christ. *"I am the way, the truth and the life"* says the Lord in John 14:6. Without a way man cannot travel, without truth he cannot know, and without life he cannot live. I am the way on which you must go. I am the truth that you must believe, and the life that you must hope in and live. I am the way that does not pass away, the truth that does not deceive, and the life that does not end.

I am the right way of eternal life in my merit, the highest truth in my word, and the eternal life in the power of my death. If you wish to remain on this way, truth must lead you to eternal life. If you do not wish to err, follow me. If you wish to know the truth, trust me. If you wish to possess eternal life, be consoled in my death.

However, what is this certain correct way, this truth that does not deceive, this noblest and best life? The way is the holy and precious merit of Christ; the truth is Christ's eternal word; the life is the eternal blessedness. If you wish to ascend into heaven, believe in Christ and humble yourself on earth according to his example; this is the way. If you do not wish to be deceived by this world, cling to his word in faith and follow it in his holy life; this is truth. If you wish to live with Christ, you must die with him, in him, and through him to sin, and become a new creature; this is life. Thus, Christ is the way, the truth, and the life, both in his merit and in his example.

Be imitators of Christ as dear children, says Saint Paul in Ephesians 5:1. All our energy should be directed so that our life will be similar to the life of Christ. If false Christians who only have the name of Christ suggest anything else to you, the example of Christ will be enough for you. A Christian ought to be ashamed to live in pleasure and joy since our Lord Jesus lived his life in sorrow and misery. No true warrior can see his leader fight to the death unless the leader has forgotten his own pleasure. If you see your prince bearing abuse and you search for honor, is it not a sign that you are not under his standard?

We all wish to be Christians and yet there are few who follow Christ's life. If following after wealth and vain honor would make good Christians, Christ would not have commanded us to consider this of so little use against eternal good. Look at his life and teaching and you will see how different he was to this wretched world. His crib, the stall, the swaddling clothes, are all a mirror of the disdain of this world. Christ did not come to lead you astray by his example. No, he came to lead you on the right path with his example and by his teaching. Therefore, he said he was the way and the truth. Since he chose to go to glory through insult and suffering, so you without a doubt must choose to go to hell by honor and great pomp. Therefore, turn away from your broad way and go on the way that cannot err. Follow the truth that cannot deceive and live in him who is himself life. This way is truth and this truth is life. O great blindness, that a poor worm upon the earth wishes to be so great and a Lord of glory upon the earth was so small! Therefore, you faithful soul, if you see your Bridegroom, the heavenly Isaac, come to your feet, you should be ashamed to ride upon a great camel. When Rebecca, riding upon her camel, saw her bridegroom, Isaac, come, she covered her face, got quickly down and went to his feet (Gen. 24:64). You dismount also from the high camel of your heart and go on foot in deep humility to your Bridegroom. He will then love you and take you with joy.

Leave your father's land and your father's house, said the Lord to Abraham, and go into a land which I will show you [Gen. 12:1]. Leave the lustful house of your self-love and your own will. Self-love makes twisted judgments, overshadows reason, darkens the understanding, leads the will astray, sullies the conscience, and closes the gate of life. It does not know God and neighbor, casts out all virtue, searches for honor, wealth, and pleasure, loves the world more than heaven. *He who loves his life will lose it* (Jn. 12:25). However, he who loses his life, that is, who denies his own self-love, will come to eternal life. Inordinate self-love is a root of unrepentance and eternal corruption. Those who have self-love and self-honor are without humility and a knowledge of sin. Therefore, they can gain no forgiveness of their sins even if they seek it with tears. They concern themselves more and bear sorrow for their own troubles than they do because they had troubled God. *Non fuerunt lacrimae offensi Dei sed proprij damni* [Tears came, not because God had been sorrowed but because of their own trouble].

In Matthew 13:45–46 it stands: *"The kingdom of Heaven is like a pearl for which a merchant sold all that he had and bought the pearl,"* that is, a man must leave everything in his heart and leave himself if he wishes this noble pearl, that is, God himself and eternal life. Look at the Lord Christ who came down from heaven not to seek himself or to love himself or to hold himself up but to seek you. Why, therefore, do you not seek only him who forgot himself and gave himself for you?

The righteous bride wishes to please no one except her bridegroom. Why do you wish to please the world, you who are Christ's bride? The soul is a pure bride of Christ who loves nothing else in the world except Christ. Therefore, you must count as nothing everything that is in the world and despise it in your heart so that you will be worthy to be loved by your bridegroom. The love that does not love Christ alone and consider him in all things is an adulterous love and not that of a pure virgin. The love of Christ must be that of a pure virgin.

In the law of Moses it is commanded that a priest shall take a virgin to wife (Lev. 21:14). Christ is the true High Priest who will have the soul that is virginal and that will love nothing else in the world other than him alone. Indeed, it is not even to love itself, for the Lord said: *He who comes to me and does not hate himself, indeed, even his own life, cannot be my disciple* (Lk. 14:26).

Note now what to hate oneself means. We carry the old man near us and we are, ourselves, the old man. The old man's activity and nature is nothing other than to sin, to love himself, to seek his own gain and honor, to fulfill his pleasure in the flesh. Flesh and blood does not leave its own evil quality; it loves itself, it honors itself, it esteems itself, it seeks itself in all things, it allows itself quickly to become angry, is envious, wrathful, and seeks vengeance. You do all this, indeed, you yourself are all this. This comes out of your own heart and is your own life, the life of the old man. Therefore you must hate yourself, indeed your own life, if you wish to be Christ's disciple. He who loves himself loves his own vice, his own pride, covetousness, wrath, hate, envy, his own lies, falsity, unrighteousness, and evil lusts. These things you must not love, excuse, or defend. You must hate them, reject them, and die if you wish to be a Christian.

15

IN A TRUE CHRISTIAN THE OLD MAN MUST DAILY DIE AND THE NEW MAN DAILY BE RENEWED.
WHAT IT MEANS TO DENY ONESELF.
WHAT THE TRUE CROSS OF A CHRISTIAN IS

If any man would come after me, let him deny himself and take up his cross and follow me (Lk. 9:23).

Saint Paul speaks of the old and the new man in Ephesians 4:22–24 . . . and 1 Corinthians 6:19–20. . . .

The old man is nothing but pride, covetousness, lust of the flesh, unrighteousness, wrath, enmity, hate, envy, and so forth. These things must die in a true Christian if the new man is to arise and daily be renewed.

If this old man dies, the new man will be living. If pride dies in you, humility will be awakened through the Spirit of God. If wrath dies, meekness will be planted in its place. If covetousness dies, trust in God will be increased in you. If the love of the world dies in you, God's love will be raised up in its place. This is the new inner man with his members; these are the fruits of the Holy Spirit; this is living active faith. This is Christ in us and his noble life; it is the new obedience, the new commandment of Christ, it is the fruit of the new birth in us, in which you must live if you wish to be a child of God. Only those who live in this new birth are the children of God.

As a result, a man must deny himself, that is, he must take himself away from his honor, his will, his self-love and his pleasure, his own gain and homage and what is more, indeed, he must give up his own rights and consider himself worthless in all things and give up his life. A true Christian, in whom the humility of Christ is, knows well that a man has no right to anything that comes down from above since he has it all by grace. Therefore, he makes use of everything with fear and trembling as if it were a foreign good, only for what is necessary and not for pleasure, not for his own gain, homage, and honor.

As an example, let us set against one another the true Christian who denies himself with the false Christian who is possessed with his own inordinate love. If the false Christian is rejected, the insult causes him great pain; he becomes angry, impatient; he curses and he slanders, is anxious to defend himself with his words and deeds and often swears an oath. This is the old man who is such a boar; he becomes easily angered; he is antagonistic and seeks revenge. On the other hand the person who denies himself is meek and patient and gives up all revenge; he considers himself responsible and worthy to suffer all things, that is, he denies himself.

In such great patience, meekness, and humility, the Lord Jesus went before you. He denied himself (Mt. 8:20 . . . Lk. 22:27 . . . Lk. 9:58 . . . Ps. 22:7). David too, denied himself, when Shimei cursed him and he said [in 2 Samuel 16:11]: *The Lord has bidden him.* Thus, he wished to say: "Before God you are a poor worm and worthy of suffering all things." Thus, the dear saints and prophets denied themselves, considered themselves unworthy of everything that might happen that is good for a man, and therefore they endured all things. If anyone cursed them, they blessed him from afar. If anyone persecuted them, they thanked God for it (Acts 5:40–41). If anyone killed them, they prayed for him (Acts 7:59). Thus, they went through many tribulations into the kingdom of God (Acts 14:22).

Note that to deny oneself one is not to be concerned with what happens, whether good or bad, or to hold oneself worthy of suffering everything that comes to him.

This denial is the cross of Christ, which we must take upon ourselves as the Lord said [in Luke 9:23]: *"He who wishes to be my disciple must deny himself and to take up his cross and follow me."* This is for the flesh a bitter cross, for the flesh wishes to be sure, free, and dissolute, to live according to its own lusts when it ought to live in humility, meekness, and the patience of Christ, and to take the life of Christ to itself. This life of Christ is for the flesh a bitter cross, indeed, it is his death, since the old man must die.

Everything that was born in man from Adam must die in a true Christian. If a man will take the humility of Christ upon himself, pride must die. If a man will take the poverty of Christ upon himself, covetousness must die. If he wishes to bear the insult of Christ, his search for honor must die. If he wishes to take the meekness of Christ upon himself, his search for revenge must die. If he wishes to take the patience of Christ upon himself, his wrath must die.

Note that all this is to deny oneself, to take up one's cross and follow Christ. All this is to be done not for one's own merit, reward, gain, acclaim, and honor, but for the love of Christ alone, because he did it and this is his noble life and he has commanded us to follow him. This is the image of God in Christ and in us, which is for man the highest honor. A man is to allow himself to have enough with this and to strive eagerly for it.

Why is it that a man so eagerly strives after the honors of this world by which he becomes no better before God than other people? This is proven from the moment of our birth and of our death. The greatest person in the world has the same body, flesh, and blood as does the poorest man. No man is one hair's breadth wider than another. One is born as another, and one dies as another. Yet the search for honor plagues us. All search for self-love, which is forbidden because we are to hate ourselves.

Now it is certain that the person who loves himself, that is, who seeks his own pleasure, is proud and arrogant, seeks his own acclaim and honor, turns his soul away from God and Christ to himself and to the world. Christ comes now and says: If you wish to be holy, you must hate yourself and deny yourself and not love yourself so much or you will lose your soul. The old Adam will not do this but always wishes to be something in the world.

How few of you there are who understand this Adamic quality [of life] and strive against it. Since we are born into it and since it is born with us, we must die to it. Ah, how few of you there are who do this! Everything that is inherited from Adam must die in Christ. In the humility of Christ our pride must die. In the poverty of Christ our covetousness must die. In the bitter suffering of death our lust must die. In the insult to Christ our honor must die. In the patience of Christ our wrath must die.

The person who now dies thus to himself can thereafter easily die to the world, and despise all its riches and glory. He can do so, so that he desires no worldly honor, wealth, or pleasure but has his honor, wealth, and pleasure in God alone. God is his honor, wealth, and pleasure. He is truly a stranger and guest in this world. He is God's guest and God will lift up in his heart the joyous Sabbath year and make him full of spiritual joy and hold the *jubilaeum aeternum*, the joyous Sabbath year, with him.

16

IN A TRUE CHRISTIAN THERE MUST AT ALL TIMES BE A BATTLE BETWEEN THE SPIRIT AND THE FLESH

I see in my members another law at war with the law of my mind (Rom. 7:23).

In each true Christian are two men, an inner man and an outer man. These two live together but they oppose one another. The life of the one is the death of the other. If the external man lives and rules, the internal man dies. If the internal man lives the external man must die, as Saint Paul says in 2 Corinthians 4:16. . . .

These two are referred to by Saint Paul in Romans 7:23 as a law of the mind and a law of the members. In Galatians 5:17, he calls the two spirit and flesh. . . .

If the spirit conquers, the man lives in Christ and in God and is called spiritual and lives in a new birth. If the flesh conquers, the man lives in the Devil in the old birth and does not belong to the kingdom of God and is called carnal. To set the mind on the flesh is death (Rom. 8:6). A man is named in the Scriptures according to that which has dominion over him, either carnal or spiritual.

If in this battle one conquers his evil lusts, it is the power of the spirit of the inner man that conquers. Where this does not happen there is a weakness of faith and of spirit, for faith and spirit are one thing as is written in 2 Corinthians 4:13: *"Since we have the same spirit of faith so speak we."*

That man is much stronger who conquers himself and his evil desires than the man who conquers his enemies, as it is written in Proverbs 16:32: *He who is slow to anger is better than the mighty, and he who rules his spirit and he who takes his city.* If you wish to have a great victory, conquer yourself, your wrath, pride, covetousness, and evil desires, and you will conquer the kingdom of Satan. In all these vices Satan has his kingdom. There are many warriors who have helped to conquer a city but have never conquered themselves.

If you cling to evil or to the flesh you destroy your soul. It is now better, however, that the soul conquer so that the body be preserved than that the body conquer and body and soul together be lost. And therefore it says *he who loves his life will lose it, and he who hates his life in this world will keep it for eternal life* (Jn. 12:25).

This is indeed a difficult battle but it results in a glorious victory and gains a beautiful crown: *Be faithful unto death and I will give you the crown of life* (Rev. 2:10). Our faith is the victory that conquers the world. The world, however, is in your heart. Conquer yourself and you have conquered the world.

Someone might say, "What should I do if sin in the meantime conquers my will once again; will I then be damned and not be a child of God as John says: *He who sins is from the Devil* (1 John 3:8)? The answer is this: If you discover a battle of flesh against the spirit in yourself and you often do what you do not wish to do, as Saint Paul says, this is a witness of a faithful heart, since faith and spirit battle against the flesh. Saint Paul teaches us by his example that there is such a battle in the pious and faithful as he states [in Romans 7:23]. . . . Thus he complains: *"How wretched the man that I am, who will deliver me from this body of death? That is, from the body in which sin and death adhere which plague me so greatly."* The Lord himself says: *The spirit is willing but the flesh is weak* (Mt. 26:41; Mk. 14:38).

Sin does not rule in man as long as this battle goes on. That against which a man strives cannot rule. If it does not rule in man because the spirit strives against it, it does not damn man. The saints, Saint Paul (Rom. 7:18) . . . and John (1 John 1:8) state . . . all had sin. Indwelling sin does not damn but ruling sin does. Since a man strives against sin and does not willingly do it, sin is not accounted him as Saint Paul says in Romans 8:1: *There is therefore now no condemnation for those who are in Christ Jesus, for the law of the spirit of life in Christ Jesus has set me free from the law of sin and death, that is, it does not allow the flesh to rule.* In those in whom there is not such a battle, who do not feel such a striving within them, who are not *renati* [reborn], they have ruling sin, are conquered, and they are the slaves of sin and of Satan and are thus damned as long as they allow sin to rule in them.

God described it to us through the *typum* [image] of the Canaanites who lived in the Promised Land but were not allowed to rule it. God allowed the Canaanites to live under Israel (Josh. 16:10), but they were not able to rule. Rather, Israel was the lord and not the Canaanites who remained there. In a like manner, sins remain in the saints but those sins do not rule. The new man is called Israel, God's warrior (Gen. 32:34), and must rule, but the old man must be extinguished.

This demonstrates to the new man, strengthens him, and affirms to him that there must be a continuous struggle against the old man. The victory and the might of the spirit are the true Israelite, a new man. *Militia probat Christianum: terra Canaan bellando occupatur et retinetur* [The striving one is the Christian. The land of Canaan is to be taken and held by battle]. If the Canaanites come to power for a short time and flesh has dominion and control, Israel and the new man must not remain long under their rule and sin and the Canaanites must not be allowed to rule for long, but the [new] man must strengthen himself through the grace of God in Christ, through true repentance and the forgiveness of sins rise again and call on the true Joshua, the prince of the people, so that he strengthen him, be victorious in him. Thus, the earlier fall is covered over, forgotten, and forgiven, and man is renewed once again to life and established in Christ. If you still feel weakness of the flesh in yourself and cannot do everything you eagerly wish to do, the merit of Christ is ascribed to you as it is to a repentant man and with his perfect obedience your sins are covered. At this point the imputation of Christ's merits takes place and not before. Thus, the payment of the merits of Christ is given to the repentant man. That man is a godless, unrepentant man who allows sin to freely reign in him and his lusts freely to serve his flesh. The merit of Christ is not imputed to him, and is useless for him. How shall the blood of Christ be useful to such a man who treads upon it with his feet (Heb. 10:29)?

17

A CHRISTIAN'S INHERITANCE AND GOODS ARE NOT IN THIS WORLD. THEREFORE, CHRISTIANS ARE TO USE TEMPORAL THINGS AS IF THEY WERE GUESTS HERE

We brought nothing into the world, and we cannot take anything out of the world; that if we have food and clothing, with these let us be content (1 Tim. 6:7–8).

All temporal goods that God has created and given to man were created by God for the use [of the body]. For this we are to use them and we are to take everything from God with thanks and fear and trembling. If there is anything superfluous in gold and silver, food and drink, clothing, and so forth, it is all given to man to test him, [to see] how he will use it, what he will do with it, whether he will cling to God and look only to the invisible, heavenly goods, and rejoice in God, or if he will fall away from God and give himself over to temporal lusts and the earthly world, if he will love the earthly paradise more than the heavenly one.

Therefore, in regard to temporal things, God gave man a free will and tests him through wealth, high gifts, honor, and favor [to see] if he will hold fast to God or if he will allow himself to turn from God because of them, if he will live in God or out of God, with God or against God. Thus, he will be judged according to his own choice and he has no excuse as Moses points out in Deuteronomy 30:19. . . .

Therefore, all things in this world stand before our eyes, not for the sake of pleasure and amusement, but as a prescribed test of which we can easily conceive if we let go of the highest good to willingly accept this world in which our hearts' pleasure and joy is the forbidden tree with its fruits from which we are not to eat. The whole world is now doing this. It seeks its pleasure in temporal things, amusing the flesh with costly food and drink, with costly clothing, and with other earthly joys that turn most people away from God.

Christians, on the other hand, are to remember that they are here pilgrims and guests of God and they are therefore to use things only for their need and not for temporal pleasure. God alone is to be our pleasure and joy and not the world. If it is otherwise, we sin, and we eat daily with Eve from the forbidden tree through evil lusts. Christians do not have their lusts in earthly food, but their internal eye is directed to the eternal food. Christians do not strut about with earthly clothes, but look to their heavenly clothing of the glory of God, and their glorified bodies. In this world, everything is a cross for Christians, a temptation, an attraction to evil, a poison and gall. Whatever stirs up lust in man and brings him to please the flesh without the fear of God, that is poison for the soul, even if it seems to be a medicine for the body and looks as if it is good. But no one will learn to understand the forbidden tree with its fruits. Each man grasps with great desire for the forbidden lust of the flesh, that is, the forbidden tree.

If one is a true Christian and makes use of everything with fear, as a guest, and sees to it that he does not enrage God as the head of the household, in his eating and drinking, in his clothes and dwellings, or in his use of temporal things, and does not mistreat his fellow guests, he protects himself from false practice and with faith he looks always toward the eternal coming and invisible being where true goods are. What help is the body if it is long practiced in the lusts of this world and then is eaten by worms? Think on the Job who said: *Naked came I from my mother's womb and naked must I go again* (Job 1:21). We bring nothing with us except a naked, needy, weak, and empty body. We cannot take anything from this world. We must leave our body and life behind. We can take nothing along.

Everything that we have received from the moment of birth to the moment of death in this world in regard to food, drink clothing, and dwelling places is all *panis misericordiae et doloris* [the bread of mercy and pain], simple necessity for the body. We must leave everything behind at the moment of death and depart poorer than when we came, for a man dies poorer than when he came into the world. If he comes into this world, he brings with him a body and life and is then a roof, food, and a dwelling place for himself, but when he dies, he must not only leave this, but his body and life as well. Who is then poorer when he dies than a man? But if he is rich in God, how can he be a poor creature?

Since we are now strangers and guests, and temporal things lead only to the preservation of the mortal body, why do we trouble and weigh down our poor soul with it? After death, it is indeed no use to us. See how great a foolishness it is to gather so many goods for a poor mortal body that you must, nevertheless, leave behind in the world (Lk. 12:20–21). Do you not know that there is another better world, that there is another better body and life than this mortal body and than this miserable, temporal life? Do you not know that you are a stranger and a guest of God's (Ps. 39:12)—before me, the Lord says, before my eyes—although you do not think or consider it (Lev. 25:23)?

Since the Lord says that we are guests and strangers, it is necessary that our fatherland must be elsewhere. This can be seen when we consider time and eternity, the visible and the invisible world, the earthly and heavenly dwelling place, the mortal and the immortal way of life, that which passes and that which does not pass, the temporal and the eternal being. If we set these against one another and consider them, our soul will be illuminated and by faith we will see many things that remain unknown to those who do not have such a vision. They fill themselves with the earthly filth of this world, dance in it, immerse themselves in worldly sorrows, covetousness, and search for profit. They are blind in their souls, although in temporal things they are still clever. They think there is no nobler and better joy, no nobler and better life and way of life than that of this world. For true Christians, nevertheless, this is an exile, a veil of tears, indeed, a dark grave and a deep prison.

Therefore, those who love this world and have their paradise in it do not rise above the bestial understanding. They leave it as a beast (Ps. 49:20), they are blind in the inner man, they have no heavenly thoughts, they cannot rejoice in God, they rejoice only in the filth of this world. If they have this, they are happy. These are truly bestial men. Ah, miserable, blind people. They sit in darkness and the shadow of death (Lk. 1:79) and go into eternal darkness.

So that we might learn that we are guests and strangers in this world, we are to look to the example of Christ and to follow him, his life and teaching. He is our leader, our exemplar and image, whom Christians are to desire to be conformed to. Look to the life and teaching of Christ and see that he was the noblest man in this world. But what was his life? Nothing other than pure poverty and the rejection of worldly honor, pride, and goods? *Quae tria pro trino numine mundus habet*. These three, the world holds for a triune God. He himself said: *The son of man has nothing on which to lay his head* (Mt. 8:20).

Look at David, how poor, despised, and persecuted he was before he became king. When he was king he did not uphold all his royal honor and worth as high as the joy of the eternal life, as he said in Psalm 84:2 . . . *"I have land and people and a kingly dwelling place, the mountain of Zion, but it is nothing compared to your lovely dwelling place."* Job acted in a like manner when he trusted in his redeemer (Job 19:25).

Take the examples of Peter, Paul, and all the apostles. They sought their goods and their riches, not in this, but in the coming world. They took the noble life of Christ unto themselves, changed into his love, meekness, humility, and patience. This world rejected them. If one cursed them, they blessed him for it; if one insulted them, they thanked him for it; if someone persecuted them, they served God for it; if someone beat them, they suffered it with patience and said, *Through many tribulations we must enter the kingdom of God* [Acts 14:22]; and if anyone killed them, they prayed for them and said with their Redeemer: *Father, forgive them; do not hold this sin against them* [Acts 7:60]. Thus, they died to wrath, vengeance, bitterness, pride, arrogance, the love of this world and their own life, and lived in Christ, that is, in his love, meekness, patience, and humility. They became truly alive in Christ and, thus, they lived.

The children of this world cannot know much about this noble life of Christ. They are dead in sins, in their wrath, hate, envy, covetousness, usury, pride, and search for vengeance, and so long as a man remains in these and does not repent, he can never be made living in Christ even if things go as well for him as he could ever wish. The true Christians know, however, that they must walk in the footsteps of their Redeemer (1 Pet. 2:22) and they have his life as an example and their book is Christ himself. They learn his life and teaching from him, that is, *omnia nos Christi vita docere potest* [the life of Christ can teach us all things] (2 Cor. 4:18 . . . Heb. 13:14).

Since we are strangers and guests in this world, who have no abiding place, it must follow that we were not created for this miserable world. Therefore, this world is not our true fatherland and possession. We know a better and nobler land for which we would rather lose two worlds, indeed, body and life, so that we might gain that one. Therefore, a Christian rejoices in the knowledge that he can be rich in Christ and that he is created to eternal life. See how wretched blind people, the foolish of this world, are, how much foolishness they have in this world that they weigh down their own soul for temporal things and, indeed, lose it.

18

GOD IS HIGHLY INCENSED IF ONE PLACES TEMPORAL THINGS BEFORE ETERNAL THINGS. HOW AND WHY WE ARE NOT TO CLING TO CREATURES WITH OUR HEARTS

The fire of the Lord burned among them and consumed some outlying parts and the camp (Num. 11:1).

The children of Israel murmured against Moses and said: Who will give us meat to eat? We remember the fish and the cucumbers we ate in Egypt.

In this incident, as in the Gospel, there is pictured for us the people who seek only worldly and fleshly things, who turn with more eagerness to wealth, honor, and pleasure so that they might be wealthy, rather than that they might be holy, who love the honor of man rather than the honor of God (Jn. 12:43), who seek the lust of the flesh rather than the poverty and lowliness of the spirit. It is a test for a true Christian that he sorrows more for his own soul than for his body, that he looks to the coming honor and glory more than to temporal honor, that he looks more to the invisible, which is eternal, than to the visible, which will pass away, that he mortifies and crucifies his flesh so that the spirit might live.

In a word, this is the whole of Christianity, to follow Christ, our Lord. "Summa religionis est, imitari eum, quem colis" [Religion consists chiefly in this, that you follow him whom you honor] says Augustine. And Plato, understanding things out of the light of nature, said "Perfectio hominis consistit in imitatio Dei" [The perfection of man stands in the imitation of God]. So, Christ our Lord must be our mirror and the guide of our whole life, so that our heart, thought, and mind is turned to [the question of] how we come to him, how through him we become holy, and how we might eternally live with him, so that we can await our end with joy.

It must also come about that all our work, occupation, walk, and vocation is done in faith, in the love and hope of eternal life, or to make it clearer that in all things, whatever a man does, the eternal life and eternal blessedness is not forgotten.

Through the fear of God there grows up in a man a holy desire for the eternal, and the great unsatisfiable desire for temporal things is subdued. Thus, Saint Paul teaches well in his comment in Colossians 3:17: *Whatever you do, in word or deed, do everything in the name of the Lord Jesus, giving thanks to God and the Father through him.*

God's name is called God's honor, acclaim, homage, and praise (Ps. 48:10). *As thy name, Oh, God, so thy praise reaches to the ends of the earth.* If we direct all our acts and life to this, they are directed into the eternal and they are works that are done for God (Jn. 3:21) and follow us after our death (Rev. 14:13).

In a word, we must seek God in all things, as the highest Good and the eternal Life, if we do not wish to lose God and eternal life. This Paul teaches us in 1 Timothy 6:11, where he warns us about covetousness and says: *Man of God, flee this.* He calls the Christian a man of God because he is born of God, lives in and according to God, is God's child and heir. A man is a worldly man who loves the world, whose portion in life is of the world, whose belly God fills with the world's goods (Ps. 17:14). A Christian man is to flee this and to search after faith and love, and to grasp eternal life to which he is called.

For if this does not occur, a great sin is done, which God will punish with eternal, hellish fire. History gives us an example of this. When the children of Israel sought to fill their bellies, God's wrath was ignited against them and their camp was destroyed (Num. 11:1ff.). This was a miraculous fire, a fire of vengeance, and it was the wrath of God and his passion.

When we see such punishments, whether it be fire, water, war, hunger, or pestilence, we are not to think otherwise than that it is the wrath of God that has been caused by the fact that man seeks only the temporal and forgets the eternal, that he places the temporal before the eternal, that he concerns himself more with his body than with his soul, which is the highest unthankfulness and rejection of God. For this, he is both temporally and eternally punished. Each man himself ought to consider if that is not the greatest unthankfulness to place the eternal, almighty God, from whom we have body and soul, in a lower position than the weak creatures we make as idols. Is it not the greatest insult to God to love creatures more than the Creator, to cling to that which passes more than to that which is eternal?

God, the Lord, created all creatures and all temporal things for our need, not for us to cling to with our love, but that we might seek and know God in temporal creatures and cling to the Creator with our love and hearts, that is, the creatures are only the footprints of God, signs of God that are to lead us to God. Thus, we are not to cling to them.

What will finally come from this love of the world in which God does not exist? Nothing other than fire and hell, as the example of Sodom and Gomorrah indicates (Gen. 19:24). The Lord ignited a fire against them. That fire was a mirror of the eternal fire and damnation.

All the creatures of God as God created them are good, but if man's heart clings to them and makes them into idols, they come under the curse and are an abomination before God as golden and silver idols are. Gold and silver are good, but the abomination involved in clinging to them makes them a curse and out of this eternal fire and eternal pain result.

In a word, a Christian is to have his heart, love, pleasure, wealth, and honor in eternal things and, from this, eternal life follows, *for where your treasure is, there is your heart also* (Lk. 12:34; Mt. 6:21). Out of the love and pleasure of this world, nothing other can come than eternal damnation. *The world passes away, and the lust of it; but he who does the will of God abides forever* (1 John 2:17). Therefore, John says in 1 John 2:15, *"Dear children, do not love the world or the things in the world."* He thus teaches us that God does not wish us to love any creature because:

1. Love is the whole heart of man and the most noble force. It is to be given to God alone as the noblest and highest Good.

2. It is the greatest foolishness to love that which cannot love us in return. The temporal, weak, dead thing has no love for us and, therefore, it is useless for us to love it. Much more, we are with our hearts to love God above all creatures, for he loves us so much that he created us for eternal life, redeemed us, and made us holy.

3. It is natural that each person should love that which he is like. Therefore, God created you to his image and likeness so that you might love him and your neighbor.

4. Our soul is like wax. Whatever a man impresses upon it, it holds that image. Thus, a man is to see God's image in his soul as in a mirror. That to which a man turns himself will be seen in him. Turn a mirror toward heaven and you will see heaven; turn it toward earth and you will see earth. Thus, your soul will show the image of that to which you turn it.

5. When the Patriarch Jacob was in a foreign land, in Mesopotamia, and served fourteen years for his wives and six years for his payment, he served twenty years. In his heart, he always planned to return to his native land. This he finally did. Thus, although we truly are to be and live in this world in our occupation and calling, yet our heart is always to be directed to the heavenly, eternal fatherland.

6. Everything a man has, be it bad or good, he has from that which he loves. If he loves God he has all virtues and all goodness from God. If he loves the world, he has all the vices and all evil from the world.

7. The King Nebuchadnezzar loved the world far too much. He lost the image of man and was changed into a beast, for the text says clearly, *"He returned to his earlier form"* (Dan. 4:33). He must, thus, have lost it or have had an inhuman form in himself. Thus, all those lose the image of God from their hearts who love the world far too much, and they become internally dogs, lions, and bears and also cattle.

8. In a word, what a man has in his heart, that becomes revealed in it, and to that he will cling, whether it be God or the world. If he clings to the world, fire will arise out of it as this example indicates.

19

THE PERSON WHO IS MOST WRETCHED IN HIS HEART
IS MOST BELOVED OF GOD.
A MAN SEEKS THE GRACE OF GOD
THROUGH CHRISTIAN KNOWLEDGE

This is the man to whom I will look, he that is humble and contrite in spirit, and trembles at my word (Is. 66:2).

This verse the gracious and merciful God himself spoke through his prophets to console our troubled heart by his gracious appearance. If God is to be gracious to you, you must be in misery in your heart and consider yourself worth no divine or human consolation, but see yourself as completely nothing and look only to Christ in faith.

The man who considers himself something is not miserable in his heart and he does not look to God. Therefore, Paul says in Galatians 6:3: *If anyone thinks he is something, when he is nothing, he deceives himself.* The reason for this is that God alone is everything. If you wish to learn to know God, you must not only know that he alone is everything, but you must cling to this in your heart and demonstrate it in yourself.

If you wish to demonstrate in your deeds that God alone is everything, you must become nothing in your heart; [you must be] so small and so paltry as if you were nothing. You must be as David when Michal despised him and he danced before the seat of grace and said: *"I will make myself yet more contemptible than this before the Lord"* (2 Sam. 6:22).

The man who wishes to be something is the material out of which God makes nothing, indeed, he makes a fool out of it. However, a man who wishes to be nothing and considers himself as nothing is the material out of which God makes something; he thus makes for himself glorious, wise people. A man who considers himself before God as the most paltry creature, as the most miserable, is in God's eyes the greatest and most glorious. The man who considers himself the greatest sinner is the greatest saint before God.

Note, this is the lowliness that God lifts up, the misery that God looks upon, and the nothingness of man out of which God makes something, for just as God made the heaven and earth out of nothing as a glorious and miraculous creation, so he will make man, who is nothing, in his heart, into something glorious.

Notice the example of David. God looked upon his misery, took up his lowliness, and made a glorious work out of it. Likewise, Jacob said: *I am not worthy of the least of all the steadfast love and all the faithfulness which you have shown to me* (Gen. 32:10).

Look to the Lord Jesus. Out of his lowliness and out of his misery, indeed, out of his nothingness, by which he became a curse and serpent for us (Ps. 22:7), the smallest and most despised among men (Is. 53:3), God made a great glory.

Look at the artist. If he wishes to create a work of art he must have completely new material out of which he makes it. It dare not have been tampered with by any other person. God does the same. If he wishes to make something out of man, man must be nothing. The person who makes himself into something and believes that he is something is not material with which God can enjoy working. Indeed, such a man is nothing and God looks upon him as nothing. Therefore, the Virgin Mary said: *"The Lord has regarded the low estate of his handmaiden. For behold, henceforth all generations will call me blessed"* (Lk. 1:48).

That person is miserable in his heart who considers himself as nothing and who believes that he can be no pleasure for God, either in a spiritual or physical way. The person who considers himself worth something and believes that he is something, although he is nothing, does not find God's grace but loses it. God's grace stays with no man who considers himself to be something. The person who considers himself worthy of something does not receive everything from God in grace. It is grace and not worthiness that you are through and through. A man has nothing that is his own except his sin, his misery, his nothingness, and his weakness; the rest is all of God.

A man is nothing other than a shadow. Look at the shadow of a tree. What is it? Nothing. If a tree moves, the shadow moves also. Whose movement is it? It is not the shadow's but the tree's. Thus, what is your life? It is not yours but God's, as it is written in Acts 17:28: *In him we live and move and have our being.* The apple of a tree also appears in the shadow; it does not belong to the shadow, but to the tree. If you carry good fruits they are not yours, although they indeed appear in you, but they are as a shadow. They come from the eternal source, which is God. An apple does not grow from the wood, as the foolish believe, even though it hangs on the wood as a child hangs to its mother's breast, but it comes out of the power of growth [in the wood], *ex centro seminis*, out of the inner seed. Otherwise, dead wood would also bring forth apples.

By nature, however, man is a dead tree and God is the power of growth, as Psalm 27:1 says, *The Lord is the power of my life*. The Lord says in Luke 23:31, *"If they do this when the wood is green, what will happen when it is dry?"* Therefore, all men are dead wood and God is the power of growth (Hos. 14:9; Jn. 15:5).

If a man is miserable, nothing, and poor in his heart, God looks upon him. But God does not look upon a man as one man looks upon another. In such an act, no power is found, but God's act is power, life, and consolation. A miserable, faithful heart is capable of being viewed in such a way and the poorer and more unworthy it sees itself, the more does it discover God's consolation. An image of this is presented to us in Jacob, who considered himself too poor for all the pleasures of God and physical blessing (Gen. 32:10). In a like manner, a truly miserable heart considers itself not worthy of eternal, heavenly blessing and consolation, and thus says to God: "I am too poor for your great love and mercy, which you have shown to me in Christ; I have now become two armies in that you have given me your son and everything with him, *bona gratiae, et gloriae* [the goods of grace and glory]."

If a man weep as many tears as there is water in the sea, it would not make him worthy of heavenly consolation, for such consolation is pure, undeserved grace. A man is not worthy of this but only of punishment and eternal damnation.

Note that he who properly understands this in faith knows his misery, and God appears to him. Without this misery God does not appear to man and without the knowledge of such misery man does not find God's grace. Therefore, Saint Paul says in 2 Corinthians 12:9, *I will boast of my weaknesses that the power of Christ may rest upon me*. God is so good and merciful that he will not allow his work to

101

be corrupted, but the weaker a man is in himself the stronger is God's power in him, as the Lord said to Paul: *My power is made perfect in weakness* (2 Cor. 12:9).

The more wretched a Christian man is in his heart, the more does God look upon him, point out the riches of his goodness to the person who receives his mercy. He gives grace to a man beyond all his merit with heavenly consolation beyond all human possibility. God's consolation is not to be compared with human consolation. Thus, God looks upon the wretched man with his consolation.

A man is not miserable and ought not to consider himself miserable because he is poor and has no consolation in the world, but because he is a sinner. If there were no sin, there would not be any misery. A man cannot oppose so great a misery; he deserves much greater. He is not, therefore, to sorrow that great pleasures do not come to him; he is not in the least way worthy of them, nor is his own body. Although flesh and blood will not eagerly hear of it, nevertheless for the sake of truth each person must himself punish his sins so that the grace of God might live in him.

Of what shall a man esteem himself, or why shall he open his mouth? The best that a man can say with his mouth is to speak two words: I have sinned, be merciful to me. God does not command more from man than these two statements, that a man regret his sins and be sorrowful for them and ask for grace. He who neglects this has neglected the best thing in his life. Do not be sorry for your body, that it is naked and empty, hungry and thirsty, persecuted and imprisoned, poor and sick, but be sorry for your soul, that it must dwell in a sinful and mortal body. *"Wretched man that I am,"* says Paul, *"who will deliver me from this body of death"* (Rom. 7:24)? Look to this Christian knowledge of your inner misery, this regret seeking grace, and the faith that clings to God alone will open the doors of grace in faith by which God can enter you. Repent. *Behold I stand at the door and knock; if any one hears my voice and opens the door, I will come into him and eat with him, and he with me* (Rev. 3:20). This meal is the forgiveness of sins, consolation, life, and holiness. In this door of grace, gracious God meets the miserable soul at the proper time (Ps. 85:11–12). The poor sinner Mary Magdalen, the weeping soul of man, came to the Lord and anointed his feet and washed them with tears and dried them with the hair of deep humility and lowliness (Lk. 7:37). The spiritual priest (Rev. 1:6) came in his holy adornment of faith and brought the proper offering, a broken and contrite heart (Ps. 51:19), and the best sacrifice, deep regret. This is the proper, holy, sacrificial water, the tears for sin, by which in faith and in the power of the blood of Christ the spiritual Israelites are washed and made clean.

Look thus, dear Christian, and you will find God's grace through Christian knowledge of your misery and through the faith. The more miserable you are in your heart, the dearer you are to God and the more graciously God will look upon you.

20

BY TRUE CHRISTIAN SORROW LIFE IS DAILY MADE BETTER, MAN IS DIRECTED TOWARD THE KINGDOM OF GOD AND PROMOTED TO ETERNAL LIFE

For godly grief produces a repentance that leads to salvation and brings no regret, but worldly grief produces death (2 Cor. 7:10).

True Christianity consists only in pure faith, and a holy life. Holiness of life, however, arises out of true repentance and regret and of the knowledge of oneself. As a result, a man learns to understand his wrongdoings daily and to improve daily. By faith, he becomes a participant of the righteousness and holiness of Christ (1 Cor. 1:30).

If this is to occur, dear Christian, you must continually live in childlike, subservient fear of God and not be so free in your mind to do what gives the flesh pleasure. We all have strength, says Saint Paul, but we do not all use it (1 Cor. 6:12), that is, not everyone improves (1 Cor. 10:23). A child at home dares not do everything he wishes to do in his own freedom, but stands in fear of his father and has one eye on his father's pleasure. In a similar way, a true Christian and child of God must keep his thoughts in Christian chastity and not speak or act without the fear of God. He must do so as a well-reared and respectful child acts before his father if he wishes to do or say anything; he does everything in fear.

Most people give themselves over to temporal joy without any fear of God. It is better to have continual fear of God in your heart than continual joy of the world. This fear of God is the source of great meditation and great wisdom, but through the superficial joy of this world one loses divine wisdom, all meditation, and all fear of God.

By daily regret and the mortification of the flesh a man is daily renewed (2 Cor. 4:16). If our external man dies, the internal is daily renewed and brings forth divine joy with itself. On the other hand, the joy of the world brings sorrow and the evil serpent into one's heart. If a man knows that he has a great fault in his soul and has lost heavenly gifts, so that he strives against the pleasure of the flesh and the joy of this world, he stands in dread and is frightened because of all the world's joy.

If a man wishes to consider this properly, two things must be contemplated in his heart. Thus, he will not be pleased with the joys of this world and will never be sorrowful because of temporal misfortune. The first is the eternal pain of the damned. If he properly considers this eternal pain in his heart, he will no longer be happy in it because it is eternal. The second is the eternal joy of eternal life. If the heart properly grasps this concept, it will not allow the thoughtful man ever to be troubled by the misfortune of this world, because this joy is eternal. But the superficiality of our heart does not let us think properly about this. Therefore, few of us come thereby to a sanctifying sorrow or regret or to a sanctifying, heavenly joy in our hearts.

A Christian is not to rejoice too much in temporal things but only in God and in eternal life. He is not to be too greatly concerned over any temporal things. A lost soul that is eternally lost will sorrow throughout the days of its life. The temporal goods of a Christian cannot be lost; one will find them a thousand-fold once again in eternal life (Mt. 19:20), but a lost soul will not find them either here nor there.

Blessed is the man who is thus able to be properly sorrowful in a godly way and who is able to be properly joyous in a spiritual and heavenly way. We often laugh in superficiality and pride when we ought to weep. There is no true freedom and joy except in the fear of God experienced by a good conscience. A good conscience cannot be without faith or without a holy life. Faith and godly sorrow through the Holy Spirit improve upon the errors of man daily. The man who does not daily improve upon his errors loses the very best in this life, strives against the new birth, and hinders the kingdom of God from coming into himself, and cannot be redeemed from the blindness of his heart.

That man is a wise and intelligent man who in earnestness shuns and flees everything that hinders the improvement of his errors and the acceptance of heavenly gifts. Blessed is the man who learns to shun not only what is bad for his body and physical goods, but what is much worse for his soul and weighs his soul down.

Learn to strive in a manly fashion, for long and evil habit can be conquered by good habit (Rom. 12:21 . . .). A man can improve if he turns his eyes and thoughts to himself and his own errors and does not look upon other people (Prov. 18:21). Always look to yourself before you judge someone else and admonish yourself before you punish another person, your best friend.

If you now live in godly sorrow and continual regret, you will be despised because of it, and you will not have much favor among people. Do not be sorry because of this, but be sorry if you are called a Christian and cannot live the Christian life you ought to live, if you bear the name of Christian and do not do many Christian works. It is good and healthy for you if the world troubles you, for in such a case God will bring you joy (. . . Is. 57:15).

God's joy and the world's joy are completely opposed to each other and can hardly be born together at one time in one heart. Indeed, it is impossible, for they have different sources. The world's joy is born in good days and heavenly joy in sorrow.

It is not natural that a man is able to rejoice in sorrow, as Saint Paul says in 2 Corinthians 6:9–10 . . . , but the grace of God improves upon nature so that the apostles rejoiced that they were worthy of suffering something for the name of Jesus (Acts 5:41).

A Christian is a new creature whose sorrow is joy . . . (Rom. 5:3). The old man is troubled by sorrow, but the new man rejoices in it. Heavenly joy is much nobler than earthly joy. The rejection and insult received by Christ are a joy for a Christian. We, however, are ourselves responsible that we seldom find this heavenly joy, because we cling so eagerly to the joys of this world.

A properly humble man considers himself worthy of great suffering and troubles, but does not consider himself worthy of God's consolation. The more he considers himself unworthy of this with a humble and contrite heart, the more is he worthy of God's consolation. The more a man regrets his sins, the less consolation does he have in this world; indeed, the more bitter and heavier is the whole world to him.

If a man looks at himself, he finds more reason to sorrow than to be joyous. If he properly looks upon other people's lives, he finds more reason to weep for them than to envy them. Why did the Lord weep over Jerusalem, which persecuted him and killed him? Your sin and blindness were the cause of his weeping (Lk. 19:42).

Thus, the greatest reason for weeping should be our sins and other people's unrepentance.

If a person thinks of his death and how he must come before judgment, and if he considers the life he bears, he will become more sorrowful and will yet more earnestly improve himself. Let a man consider the pains of hell and he will leave all the lust of this world and will change it into great bitterness, and the greatest suffering in this world will be sweet compared with eternal pain. If we love to coddle the flesh, we will not be ignited with such burning meditation.

In a word, a Christian must learn this: If his body is well and lives in joy, this is the death of the spirit; however, if he mortifies the body together with the lusts and desires, the spirit lives. The first is here a second death. If the spirit is to live, the body must die spiritually and be offered as a living sacrifice (Rom. 12:1).

All the saints lived thus from the beginning. They ate their tearful bread with thanksgiving and drank their tearful drink with joy (. . . Ps. 80:6 . . . Ps. 42:4 . . . [Ps. 102:5]).

This tearful bread makes faith sweet and this tearful drink is prized through the true repentance of the meditative heart above all sweet wine. This is regret, which leads to holiness, which brings no one regret.

The sorrow of this world, on the other hand, brings about death, as Saint Paul says [in II Corinthians 7:10]: *The sorrow of this world comes from the loss of temporal honor and temporal goods.* Such loss brought many people into such sorrow that they hanged themselves or drowned themselves. There are many examples of this that occurred among the pagans. Christians must know better, however. How shall the loss of temporal goods bring about the death of a man since life is better than all the goods of the world?

Do not sorrow over the loss of temporal goods but over the loss of eternal goods. We possess temporal goods only for a short time and in death we are robbed of these once again. In death, we are all alike poor, and our glory does not follow after us (Ps. 49:18). The abuse of death we all carry next to ourselves. A king's body must be corrupted and die just as a poor beggar's body. *A living dog is better than a dead lion*, says Solomon in Ecclesiastes 9:4. But God will take away the insult of death from his people and will destroy the cover that is cast over all peoples and will swallow up death forever and wipe away all tears from our eyes (Is. 25:7–8; [Rev. 7:17]).

Therefore, do not trouble yourself over temporal things. The whole world is not worth as much as your soul, for which Christ died. Do not love temporal things so much that they will not trouble you unto death if you lose them. What a man loves too much troubles him too much if he loses it. You must finally lose these things in death. "Labor stultorum affliget eos"—*the toil of a fool wearies him*, says Solomon (Eccles. 10:15).

The child of this world gives up his goods with great trouble. He possesses them with great fear and leaves them with great pain. This is the sorrow of the world, which brings about death.

Revelations 14:11 says that those who prayed to the beast had no rest, and those who pray to the great and beautiful animal of worldly wealth and to their bestial, animal covetousness cannot have rest but have, rather, many plagues. They are like the camels and beasts of burden with which one takes costly raiment, precious gems and objects, and costly wine over the high mountain. Much attention is given to them by those who wait on them and by those who walk with them because they bear the treasure, but, when they come over the mountains the beautiful blankets and the costly things are taken from them and they have nothing more, except the marks of whips and welts, and they are tired and are left alone in their stables. It is the same with a person in this world who has born clothing and crowns. On the evening of his departure he has them no longer but has only the welts and marks of his sins that he has committed by the misuse of his wealth. This is the same even if he remains a glorious man of this world.

Therefore, learn to give up the world before it gives you up. Otherwise you will be frightfully troubled. The person who in this life gives up the world in his soul before he must leave his body dies happily and temporal things cannot trouble him. When the children of Israel wished to leave Egypt, Pharoah placed greater and greater unbearable burdens upon them and demanded that they carry them out (Ex. 5:9). Thus, the hellish pharoah, the Devil, burdens our hearts with temporal things, the nearer our end is, so that he may eternally overcome it and destroy it.

One can take nothing from this earthly kingdom with him into the heavenly kingdom, and we must even leave our own bodies behind. It is a narrow way to eternal life on which the soul must strive against everything that is earthly (Mt. 7:14 . . .). The separation of the wheat and the chaff occurs in death. The wheat of the faithful soul has all the chaff of this world beaten off by death and the temporal goods and honor are as chaff that the wind blows away (Ps. 1:4).

Consider the words of St. Paul: *"Godly grief produces a repentance that leads to salvation and brings no regret, but worldly grief produces death"* (2 Cor. 7:10).

21

CONCERNING TRUE, PROPER WORSHIP

The sons of Aaron offered unholy fire before the Lord and fire came forth from the presence of the Lord and devoured them (Lev. 10:1–2).

The unholy fire signifies false worship, for it was not of that fire which continually burned before the altar, which God had commanded to be used to burn the sacrifice. Since the sons of Aaron acted against God's commandment, God punished them with the fire of vengeance, which consumed them.

In this, we see the sternness of God, which he manifested because of the unholy fire. This fire is to signify to us false worship, worship done out of one's own meditation and self-established holiness and spirituality, which God has not ordered or commanded and which, therefore, does not serve him, but raises his wrath, vengeance, and zeal, which is a consuming fire (Deut. 6:15).

It is now necessary that we know what proper worship is, so that this fire might not oppose us. The temporal fire, which in the Old Testament punished false worship, signifies in the New Testament that God will punish false worship with eternal fire and that, in time, murders and the devastation of land and people, which is a frightful fire, will be ignited through the wrath of God.

If we wish to understand properly what true worship is, we must set the Old and the New Testament against one another and discover what it is in the comparison or collation. The external worship of the Old Testament offered an image and witness of the Messiah in the external ceremonies that had to be established according to the clear letter of the Law. In these marvelous images and figures, faithful Jews saw from afar the Messiah, believed in him, and were made holy through him by the promise. Our worship in the New Testament is no longer external, in typological ceremonies, rubrics, and commandments, but is internal in spirit and in truth, that is in the faith of a Christian, because through faith the whole moral and ceremonial law is filled, the temple, altar, sacrifice, seat of grace, and priesthood. Since we are placed in Christian freedom, we are redeemed from the curse of the law (Gal. 3:13), from all Judaic ceremonies (Gal. 5:1), so that by the indwelling of the Holy Spirit we are able to serve God with free heart and spirit (Jer. 31:33; Rom. 8:15) and our conscience and faith are bound to no human directives.

Three things belong to true, spiritual, inner, and Christian worship: first, true knowledge of God; second, true knowledge of sin and repentance; third, knowledge of grace and the forgiveness of sins. These three are one just as God is one and three. Thus, true worship also consists in one and three or in three parts that are one, for in the one knowledge of God exist repentance and forgiveness of sins.

The knowledge of God consists in faith that grasps Christ and knows God, God's power, God's love and mercy, God's righteousness, truth, and wisdom, and everything that God is himself in Christ and through him. What is God? Nothing other than pure power, nothing other than pure love and mercy, nothing other than pure righteousness, truth, and wisdom, and this is from Christ and the Holy Spirit.

God does not exist, however, for himself alone, but in his gracious will in Christ he exists for me. He is my almighty God, he is my merciful God, he is my eternal righteousness in his grace toward me, and in the forgiveness of my sins, he is my eternal truth and wisdom. Thus, Christ, my Lord, is for me eternal power, my almighty head, and the prince of my life. He is my merciful Savior and is eternal love for me. He is my eternal righteousness, truth, and wisdom. *God made Christ Jesus, our wisdom, our righteousness, and sanctification and redemption* (1 Cor. 1:30). This is also true of the Holy Spirit; he is my eternal love, righteousness, truth, and wisdom.

This is the knowledge of God. It consists in faith and not in an empty knowledge but in a joyous, happy, and living trust, by which I discover in myself, in a strong and consoling way, God's power, how he holds me and bears me, and how I live, move and have my being in him (Acts 17:28). I also feel in myself and discover his love and mercy. Is it not simple love that God the Father, Christ, and the Holy Spirit bring about in you, me, and all of us? Is

111

it not righteousness alone that God shows to us, in that he has redeemed us from sin, death, hell, and the Devil? Is this not simple truth and wisdom?

Note that faith consists in living, consoling trust and not in empty sounds and words. In this knowledge of God, or in this faith, we must daily grow as the children of God, so that we become ever more perfect in it (1 Thess. 4:1). Therefore, Saint Paul expressed the wish that we might know the love of Christ that exceeds all knowledge (Eph. 3:19). In other words, he said, "In this one thing, in the love of Christ, we have to learn throughout our life, not that we are to see in it empty knowledge of the love of Christ, which goes over the whole world, but that we are to discover, feel, and taste in word and faith its sweetness, power, and life in our hearts." Who can truly know the love of Christ who has not tasted it? Who can know what it is who has not experienced it, as Hebrews 6:4–5 says: *They have tasted the heavenly gift, the good word, and the power of the coming world*. All this occurs through the Word in faith. This is the appearance of the love of God in our heart through the Holy Spirit (Rom. 5:5), which is the fruit and power of the Word of God. This is the true knowledge of God, which arises out of experience and consists in living faith. Therefore, the Epistle to the Hebrews calls faith a substance, a being, and an undeniable witness (Heb. 11:1). This is a piece of the inner, spiritual worship, the knowledge of God, which consists in living faith, and faith is a spiritual, living, heavenly gift, light and power of God.

If by this true knowledge of God, God gives himself to our soul to taste and touch, as Psalm 34:9 says: *Taste and see how good the Lord is*, true repentance must necessarily follow, that is, a change and renewal of the mind and an improvement of life. If one knows and feels the power of God truly in his heart, humility follows, so that he humbles himself before the mighty hand of God. If he knows and senses God's mercy properly, love for neighbor follows. No one can be merciful who has not understood God's mercy. Who can deny something to his neighbor that God himself has given him in mercy? Out of God's mercy, great patience for neighbor results, so that if a true Christian would be murdered seven times in one day, and brought seven times to life again, he would still forgive his enemies for the sake of the great mercy of God. From God's righteousness flows forth knowledge of sins (. . . Dan. 9:7 . . . [Ps. 143:2] . . . [Ps. 130:3]). Out of a knowledge of truth flows faithfulness toward neighbor and this drives out all falsity, deception, and lies, so that a Christian thinks: If you treat your neighbor improperly you will lose the eternal truth of God, which is God himself. Therefore, since God deals with you truly and faithfully, deal with your neighbor in the same way. Out of the knowledge of the eternal wisdom of God, the fear of God flows forth. Since you know that God knows the heart of each man, and sees hidden things, tremble to stand before his eyes and his Holy Majesty . . . ([Ps. 94:9] . . . [Is. 29:15–16] . . . [Jer. 23:24, 32:19]).

This is the true knowledge of God in which repentance consists, and repentance consists in a change of mind and the renewal of the mind for the improvement of life. This is the other aspect of inner, true worship and it is the proper fire that man is to bring to the sacrifice. Without it, the wrath of God and the fire of vengeance will come over us.

Priests were not to drink wine or strong drink when they went into the tabernacle (Lev. 10:9). This signifies that if a man wishes to go into the eternal tabernacle of God, that is, to eternal life, he must give up the pleasure and lusts of the flesh of this world and everything by which the flesh conquers the spirit, so that the flesh will not be stronger than the spirit and conquer it. The love of this world, pleasure, and pride is a strong sweet wine by which the soul and the spirit are conquered. Noah and Lot were overcome by wine and lay in nakedness. Great honor, pleasure, and wealth are a strong wine that conquers soul and spirit. Because of it, one cannot come into the dwelling place of God, to a knowledge of God and holiness, and because of it one cannot distinguish what is holy or unholy, pure or impure; that is, one does not understand divine, heavenly things and one's people cannot learn properly from that one, that is, one's understanding and thoughts are not illuminated by the eternal light but are conquered by the wine of this world, and one goes into darkness. Following this repentance, that is following deep regret and sorrow for sins and following the true faith in Christ, forgiveness of sins results from the merits of Jesus Christ alone. His merits no one can enjoy without repentance. Therefore, without repentance no forgiveness of sins results. Note the thief on the cross. If he wanted to have forgiveness of sins and be with

113

Christ in Paradise he had to do penance on the cross and this occurs by a sorrowful and faithful heart, as is clear from his words to his companion: *"Do you not dread God's wrath? We receive what we deserve."* And he said to Jesus: *"Lord think on me when you come into your kingdom"* (Lk. 23:40–42). In him we see a heart of regret and faith.

The gracious forgiveness of faith that the sorrowing heart grasps and receives in true faith is established by God. We are not able nor is it possible for us to bring it about. Christ establishes everything by his death and blood. By it, everything is so perfectly forgiven that it is as if it had never happened. Indeed, the payment is greater than the guilt; therefore, David in Psalm 51:7 says: *"Cleanse me, not only from my sins, so that I might be snow white, indeed whiter than snow."* Thus, Christ's payment is greater than all your sins.

As a result of this, God no longer thinks on my sins, if as a sinner I turn away from my sins (Ezek. 18:22). Whatever is perfectly paid and more than paid is completely and totally done away with, as it is stated in Isaiah 43:25. This must also be then forgotten. But conversion must first occur as the prophet says [in Isaiah 1:16–18]: *"Wash yourselves, make yourselves clean and come let us reason together. Though your sins are like scarlet, they shall be as white as snow."* What does he wish to say? You wish to have forgiveness of sins. You can, I have said, but "Come here," he says, "we wish to reason together." Have I not preached repentance to you out of which forgiveness comes? Where is your repentance? Where is the true, living faith? Where is the renewal of your mind, the change of life? It is there where forgiveness of sins is. If your sins are as scarlet, that is, so deeply colored and so great that neither heaven nor earth can wipe them out, nevertheless, they will be white as snow. Repentance, repentance is the true confession. If you have it in your heart, namely, true regret and faith, Christ's blood and death will absolve you from all your sins. True absolution is the blood of Jesus Christ, which is poured out and cries to God in heaven.

This is the true flight to the free city where one is safe from vengeance. Moses set up three special free cities for the children of Israel (Deut. 4:41–43)—Bezer, Ramoth, and Golan. *To these cities, one might flee who had unintentionally killed his neighbor and if he arrived in these cities he was safe from blood vengeance.*

Oh God, how often we have slain our neighbors unintentionally with our tongues, with our thoughts, with hate and envy, with wrath, with a desire for vengeance, and with unmercifulness. Let us flee through the flight of divine sorrow and of faith to the free cities of the grace and mercy of God and to the holy cross of the Lord and to his precious merit. There, we will find the true free city where no blood vengeance will take us and which will measure us according to the measure by which we measured. Christ is signified by the free city. "Bezer" means a firm tower, *turris munita*. Christ is a true Bezer, a firm tower. *The name of the Lord is a strong castle, the righteous man who walks into it and is protected* (Prov. 18:10). This is the name of Jesus. "Ramoth" means to be held high. Christ is also the true Ramoth, to be held high (Is. 52:13, 57:15), the highest. *Before his name every knee should bow, in heaven and on earth and under the earth* (Phil. 2:10). "Golan" means a mass or group. Christ is the true Golan. He exceeds with much grace and forgiveness (Ps. 103:7), is merciful and rich to all who call on his name (Rom. 10:12).

The third aspect of true, inner, spiritual, proper worship is the forgiveness of sins. It flows from repentance as repentance flows from the true knowledge of God. These are three but are one in truth, for this is the one true knowledge of God.

This third aspect is foreshadowed in the fact that priests were to eat from the sacrifice, that is, to appropriate the death and blood of Christ through faith. They were to eat in the holy cities, that is, in repentance. Faith in the power of the blood of Christ makes you holy before God. It is as if you had never done a sin. This is the holy city . . . (Ezek. 18:22, 33:16).

Note that Moses' law is now given in spirit and is changed into an inner, holy, new life and Moses' sacrifice is changed into the true repentance by which we offer to God our bodies and souls and bring to him a needful thank-offering and give to him alone the honor, reveal knowledge of him, conversion, justification, the forgiveness of sins, so that God might remain alone all things, that his grace might be properly praised and honored with a thankful heart and voice into eternity. This is true worship (Mic. 6:8): *He has showed you, oh, man, what is good; and what does the Lord require of you but to do justice, and to love kindness, and to walk humbly with your God?* Ah, when do we wish to do repentance, so that we might come to forgiveness of sins? No man can come to forgiveness of sins except through repentance. How can sins be forgiven unless there is divine regret for sin that hungers after grace? How can there be such regret for sins in a person who does not wish to leave his sins and change his life? God converts us all for Christ's sake.

Understand now that true worship stands in the heart, in the knowledge of God, in true repentance by which the flesh is mortified and man is renewed once again to the image of God. By it, man is renewed once again to the image of God. By it, man is made into a holy temple of God in which the inner worship is established through the Holy Spirit, faith, love, hope, patience, prayer, thanksgiving, praise, and the honor of God.

It is not called worship [divine service] in that God needs our service or that he has use of it, but that he is so merciful and good that he eagerly, with all his goods, wishes to share himself with us, to live, act, and dwell in us if we will take him to ourselves by knowledge of him in faith and true repentance, so that he might have a place to work in us.

No works are pleasing to him unless he brings them about himself in us. Therefore, he has commanded us to be repentant, to believe, to pray, and to fast so that we and not he have benefit from it. No one can give or take from God, make him pious or harm him. If we are pious the benefit is ours; if we are evil the harm is ours. If you sin, how can you harm God by doing so?

God does not call us to serve him for his sake but for ours. Since God is himself love, man serves him and pleases him as often as he finds he can enjoy God's love and share it, just as a child serves a mother if it sucks her milk. All this occurs out of love. Much more does God give grace to those who love him.

22

A TRUE CHRISTIAN CAN BE KNOWN IN NO WAY BETTER THAN BY LOVE AND THE DAILY RENEWAL OF HIS LIFE. HE IS AS THE BRANCH OF A TREE

The righteous flourish like the palm tree, and grow like a cedar in Lebanon. They are planted in the house of the Lord, and flourish in the courts of our God. They will bring forth fruit in old age, they are ever full of sap and green, to show that the Lord is upright; "He is my rock, and there is no unrighteousness in him" (Ps. 92:12–15).

A true Christian is known by a Christian life and not by the name Christian. He who wishes to be a true Christian must endeavor to let one see Christ in him, in his love, humility, and graciousness, for no one can be a Christian in whom Christ does not live. Such a life must be given internally in the heart and by the spirit as an apple gains its strength of growth from the inner power of the tree. The spirit of Christ must rule a Christian's life and make him conformed to Christ, as Paul says in Romans 8:14: *All who are led by the Spirit of God are the sons of God. Anyone who does not have the Spirit of God does not belong to him* (Rom. 8:9).

The kind of spirit that motivates and moves a man internally lives in him externally. Therefore, the Holy Spirit is highly necessary for a true Christian life. Every life comes from the spirit whether it is good or bad. Therefore, the Lord commanded us to pray for the Holy Spirit and he promised us the Holy Spirit (Lk. 11:13), and he is the spirit of the new birth that makes Christ alive in us for a new, spiritual, heavenly life (Tit. 3:5). Out of every growing, living spirit of God the Christian virtues must blossom so that the righteous may blossom as a palm tree and as a cedar in Lebanon that the Lord has planted.

Therefore, man must first be renewed inwardly in the spirit of his mind after God's image and his inner desires and affections must be conformed to Christ, which Saint Paul says is done according to God's image (Eph. 4:23), so that his external life develops from the ground of his heart and that he is internally the same as he

117

is externally before men. This will be much more internally present in man than it is noted externally. God looks on the hidden things and tests a man's heart and kidneys (Ps. 7:10).

Although we are not internally as pure as the angels, we are to weep for this. This faithful weeping is accepted by God for our purification, for the Holy Spirit helps our weakness and comes before God *with sighs too deep for words* (Rom. 8:26). Indeed, the blood of Christ cleanses us thus, through faith, so that no spot or blemish remains in us (Eph. 5:27), and what is more, our purity, holiness, righteousness, are not the purity of the angel, but Christ's righteousness, indeed, Christ himself (1 Cor. 1:30).

Indeed, by our purity we are far above the purity and holiness of angels. It is Christ himself (Jer. 23:6), and this undeserved righteousness, purity, and holiness, given and received out of grace, are to renew our body, soul, and spirit and to bring about a holy life.

Therefore, in our Christianity, we are to be as a young palm tree that is ever green and continually grows and becomes greater. We are to grow and become mature in Christ. A person grows in Christ insofar as he takes to himself in faith, virtues, and a Christian life, and daily renews himself, and insofar as Christ lives in him and this is what it means to flourish as does a palm tree.

A Christian must daily renew himself and grow as a palm tree and intend to do enough as befits his name as if he just became a Christian today. Daily he is to groan that he might not be a false Christian. As each man is to endeavor according to his occupation to fulfill in the best way his calling, so we are called to Christ with a holy calling. Where there is no such holy intention there is no improvement and no growth and maturity in Christ; indeed, the life-giving spirit of Christ is not there. Such an intention to do good comes from the Holy Spirit and is the prevenient grace of God that attracts, draws, and drives all men. You have been given, truly, room and place, and you hear the voice of the wisdom of God that calls throughout all the streets (Prov. 1:29). Everything that a man looks upon is the remembrance of his Creator by which God calls him and wishes to draw him to himself.

As often as we note that we are called and attracted to him, we are immediately to begin to do good, for it is then the right time during which we will not be hindered. If another time comes, we may be hindered to think, hear, speak, and do good. Therefore the eternal wisdom of God looks ahead and calls us in all places so that we might not miss the opportunity.

Look upon the tree that stands continually and waits for the sunshine and for the good influences of the heavens and is always prepared to receive these. Thus, the grace of God and heavenly influences shine upon you, if you are not hindered by the world from receiving them.

Think on the short span of this life, how much you have avoided the practice of Christian virtues. For half your life you have slept and for the other half you have eaten and drunk and if you now die, you have hardly begun to live properly and to do good.

As a man desires to die, so ought he also to live. You do not wish to die as an ungodly man; therefore you ought not to live as an ungodly man. If you wish to die as a Christian you must live as a Christian. That person lives as a Christian who lives as if he would die today. A servant must always be prepared to appear before his master if his master calls him. God calls each man through death.

Blessed is the servant whose Lord finds him awake when he comes; he will set him over all his goods (Lk. 12:37, 44). Who is it who is awake? The person who does not let himself be led astray by the world and those who live according to the world. Those evil shoots are a scandal that often damages the whole tree so that it cannot grow and flourish.

23

A MAN WHO WISHES TO GROW AND MATURE
IN CHRIST MUST REJECT ALL WORLDLY COMPANY

How lovely is thy dwelling place, O Lord of hosts! My heart and flesh sing for joy to the living God (Ps. 84:1–2).

Far too often you must draw yourself away from and remain outside of worldly community, for just as there is nothing better for human love than to be its own house, so there is nothing better for the soul than to be in its own house, that is, to rest in God from which it has flown forth and to which it must flow back again if it is to be whole.

A creature does not rest in anything better than in that out of which it is come, a fish from the water, a bird from the air, and a tree from the earth. So it is with the soul in God, as Psalm 84:3 says: *"The birds have found a house and the swallow its nest."* As it is not good for a young man and a young woman to go walking together (Gen. 34:1), so it is not good if you allow your thoughts and words to walk much with other people. Hold them in the house of your heart so they will not raise up anger among other people.

In the forecourts of our God, the plants of the Lord grow green as cedars in Lebanon (Ps. 92:12). What are the forecourts of our God? They are the inner, spiritual feast days of the heart, the inner, spiritual Sabbath, and the growing Lebanon in the wilderness, in the solitariness of the spirit. Seek this and you will discover for yourself and will see God's wonder and pleasure.

Many desire to study and read of bright and witty things by which the heart is more stirred up than made better. Whatever does not bring rest for the heart and improvement ought not to be heard, spoken of, read about, or thought over. The trees of the Lord must continually grow and be mature in Christ. Saint Paul considered himself as a person who did not know anything except Jesus Christ the crucified (1 Cor. 2:2).

Therefore, the saints of God have always endeavored to live in the wilderness with inner, godly meditation and to be like heavenly minds and to rest in God. This is the highest rest of the soul. One of them said: "As often as I am among men, I return to home less than a man." Humanity consists in likeness to God and therefore God described man by saying that a man was an image that was like him (Gen. 1:26). The more unlike God the less he is a man; the more a man turns himself to God, however, the more he is like God. If a man turns himself to God he must turn away from the world. Every seed brings forth a fruit that is like it. Thus, the seed of God in you, the Holy Spirit and the Word of God, will become a tree of righteousness, a plant bringing forth the praise and honor of God (Is. 61:3).

Many times a word is spoken or a man speaks a word himself that is a thorn in the heart and that wounds the soul. No one is more certain or more at rest than when he is at home and when he keeps his thoughts, words, and meditation in the house of his heart. The story is told of Diogenes, the philosopher, that someone vexed him with the following syllogism: "What I am, you are not; I am a man, therefore, you are no man." Diogenes answered: "The statement is not right; you must begin with me and then it will be right."

If a person wishes to speak well he must first learn to be silent. To speak much is not to speak well. If anyone wishes to rule well, he must first learn to be a servant, for no one can rule well who is not obedient and a servant to God. If anyone wishes to have rest and peace in his heart he must guard his mouth and endeavor to maintain a good conscience. An evil conscience is the greatest unrest. But even an evil conscience finds rest in Christ through conversion and repentance. Noah's dove did not find rest where it wished it except in the ark, and, therefore, it returned to the ark (Gen. 8:9). The ark is Christ and his Christianity, which has only one door and window and that is repentance by which one enters into Christ. As the dove had to return again to the ark, so you must return into your heart to Christ from the many waters of this world or you will not find any rest.

If you are among people and must work in the world, do it with fear and humility, without [great] confidence, and be as a young tree, bound to the stake of humility and the fear of God, so that if the winds of a storm rise up, they will not break you. How often are many deceived who work with too much certainty in the world. The world is no more to be trusted than is the sea, for the external pleasure and consolation of the world can be soon twisted in bad weather and the joys of the world can soon make an evil conscience.

How good a conscience does that person maintain who does not seek any passing joy and never concerns himself with this world! How restful and peaceful a conscience does that person have who looks only to divine things and sets all his hope on God! How great and sweet a consolation will he have from God if he does not give himself up to the consolation of this world! How many a man often finds in himself his conversion, improvement, and holy meditation that he loses among other people! In your heart, you will find that which you will lose outside of it. A tree does not grow better than in its own ground and earth. Thus, the inner man does not grow better than in the inner ground of the heart, which is Christ.

The human conscience has joy and sorrow. If you use it for divine, inner things, your conscience will give you inner joy. If you use it for external, worldly things, it will give you internal sorrow and heartbreak.

As often as a meditative soul is concerned about sin, so often does it weep inwardly. Then it finds the well of tears and the source of tears with which it purifies and washes itself all night in faith so that it becomes worthy and holy to enter into the hidden holy of holies, where God can secretly speak with it.

Since God is a hidden God (Is. 45:15), the soul with which God is to speak must live in its secret depths (Ps. 85:9 . . . Ps. 34:5–7 . . . Ps. 5:4 . . .). The soul lives the more in its secret depths, the more it cuts itself off from the world. The Patriarch Jacob drew away from his children and friends and spoke with God and the angels spoke with him (Gen. 32:24ff.). God and the angels love the holy soul above all things and will not leave it alone.

24

ON THE LOVE OF GOD AND NEIGHBOR

The aim of our charge is love that issues from a pure heart and a good conscience and sincere faith (1 Tim. 1:5).

In this verse, the apostle teaches us of the highest and noblest virtue, love, and he tells us many things about it. First, he says it is the sum of all the commandments, for love is the fulfillment of the law (Rom. 13:10), in which all the commandments are contained and without which all gifts and virtues are fruitless and impure.

In addition, he says that true love is to proceed from a pure heart. By this he means that love for God arises from a heart pure from all worldly love (1 John 2:15–17 . . .). He, who has [such] a heart [is] purified of all creaturely love, so that he does not commit himself to any temporal thing, regardless of its name, or set the peace of his heart on it, but only on God (Ps. 73:25–26 . . .). His love proceeds from a pure heart. Again, it is a pure love if it proceeds in pleasure and joy (Ps. 18:2–3 . . .).

Third, the apostle teaches us that love is to proceed from a good conscience. The false love of an evil conscience loves neighbor for the use or benefit that can be gained from that love. True love will not knowingly attack a neighbor with words or deeds, or oppose him secretly or openly. It will not bear hatred, envy, wrath, or anger in its heart, so that the man's conscience will not speak against him in his prayers before God.

In the fourth place, love is to come from undefiled faith that one does not use against his belief and Christianity, that does not deny God in secret or openly, that continues in tribulation or in good days, or in misfortune or good fortune. This is the whole of the verse in 1 Timothy 1:5. We wish now to look at each section of the verse.

I

First, the Apostle Paul says that love is the summation of the Law, that is, the love that comes from true faith is the most noble, best, and highest work and fruit of faith that a man can do and that pleases God best. God does not demand a great, high, and heavy work from us to serve him, but he changed the difficult worship of the Old Testament with its many commandments into faith and love and he gave us the Holy Spirit to help us as Romans 5:5 says: *"By the Holy Spirit, God poured out his love into our hearts."* In this, we hear of the true source of virtue.

Therefore, love is not now a heavy work but is easy for a pious, faithful man. Its commandments are not difficult, says John in 1 John 5:3. John understands that it is not difficult for an enlightened Christian, for the Holy Spirit produces a willing, good heart. God does not demand great art and brilliance from us, but only love. If this is warm and deep without falsity, it is pleasing to God. In it, God finds more pleasure and more joy and happiness than in all the art and wisdom of the world. And, indeed, where there is no love, with all the wisdom, art, works, and gifts everything is impure and counts for nothing; indeed, it is dead as the body is without life (1 Cor. 13:1ff.).

Great intelligence is common to pagans and Christians and great works are common to believers and unbelievers. Love alone is the proper test of a Christian and distinguishes false Christians from true Christians, for where there is no love, there is no good thing, even if it is costly and seems to be great. The reason for this is that God is not there. *For God is love and he who remains in love remains in God and God in him* (1 John 4:16).

Love is dear, both to God and to the man who practices it. All other arts, intelligence, and wisdom, if they are not grounded in love, destroy the body, bring about sorrow, weariness, and laboriousness, which is the torment and pain of the body. Only love makes things better, brings about new life, and preserves both body and soul. It is not hurtful to anyone but brings rich fruits. The person who loves receives love as a payment. Virtue is its own payment. Sin and wrongdoing bring forth evil payments.

All other powers of the body and the soul fall away and become weary, but true love is never weary, and never ceases as do knowledge, the gift of languages, and faith (1 Cor. 13:8; Rom. 12).

Everything that is to please God in our acts must proceed from God. Nothing pleases God that he does not bring about in us by himself. God himself, however, is love and therefore everything must proceed from faith that is pleasing to God. So, too, prayer must proceed from deep love. Consider what kind of prayer proceeds from a heart full of wrath and enmity. If such a person prayed his Psalter the whole day it would still be an abomination before God. True meditation arises in the spirit in faith, in love and not in words (Jn. 4:23 –24). Consider the Lord Christ who with a merciful heart said, *Father forgive them* (Lk. 23:34). The person who does not love God does not pray. However, prayer is a joy for the person who loves God deeply. He who loves God serves him with his heart. The person who does not love him does not serve him, even if he carries a mountain for him.

Therefore, nothing useful or better can happen to a man than that God's love be awakened in him.

Everything that a Christian does in external works and acts love must do as the soul does everything through the body. The soul sees, hears, tastes, and speaks through the body. Thus, in external works and acts love is to do everything in you. If you eat, drink, listen, speak, punish, praise, let it be done in you completely through love, just as Christ did everything in love. If you look upon your neighbor, look upon him with merciful love. If you listen to him, listen to him with love. If you speak to him, speak to him with mercy.

Maintain the root of love at all times in yourself through faith and then nothing can proceed from you except good and you will begin to fulfill commandments of God, which are all contained in love (1 Cor. 16:4). Because of this, a holy teacher once said: "O love of God in the Holy Spirit, a sweetness of the soul and a godly life of man! He who does not have you is dead although he is alive and he who has you will never die before God. Where you are not, man's life is a continual death; where you are, man's life is a taste of eternal life." Thus note how love is the summation of all the commandments.

II

Man is to love God with a pure heart. The heart is to be pure from all worldly love. God is to be man's highest and greatest Good (Ps. 16:5 . . . Ps. 17:4, 18 . . .). Man is to have all his pleasure and joy of his heart in God.

Therefore, God is to be the most beloved thing for our soul, because he is the highest and greatest Good, and because he himself is all goodness and all virtue. God is nothing other than pure grace, love, kindness, patience, faithfulness, truth, consolation, peace, joy, life, and blessedness. He has presented all this [to us] in Christ. The person who has Christ has all of this, and he who loves God loves God's truth, mercy, goodness, and all virtues.

A true lover of God loves everything that God loves and is saddened by everything that saddens God. Therefore, man is to love righteousness because God himself is righteousness. Man is to love truth because God himself is truth. Man is to love mercy because God himself is mercy. Man is to love meekness and humility for the sake of the meek and humble heart of Christ. Again, a true lover of God is to hate all vice, for it is against God and the enemy of God and [is] a work of the Devil. Therefore, a true lover of God hates lies because the Devil is a liar and so also with all the other vices. Every man who loves sin, such as lying and unrighteousness, is a child of the Devil as John 8:44 says, and every man who loves Christ as a Savior and Sanctifier loves the example of the holy life of Christ, his humility, meekness, patience, and he is a child of God.

Such love you must request from God with a pure heart so that he ignite it in you through the love of Christ. God will willingly ignite the flames of his love in your heart if you ask him to do so and if every day, indeed, at all hours and at every moment, you direct your heart toward this. If love is weak and cold, indeed, if it goes out for a while in you, and you stumble, stand up again, ignite it once again. It is eternal life. The love of God will not go out. It will enlighten you once again. You are to pray daily to God that he will nevermore allow the divine flames of love to go out in your heart.

This is the love of a pure heart that is pure of all the love of the world and creatures.

III

The love of a good conscience is the love of neighbor. The love of God and the love of neighbor are one thing and must not be divided. The true divine love cannot be better noted or proven than in the love of neighbor. *Anyone who says he loves God and hates his brother is a liar; for he who does not love his brother whom he has seen cannot love God whom he has not seen. And we have this commandment from God, that he who loves God should also love his brother* (1 John 4:20–21), that is, the love of God cannot dwell with the hatred of man, or in a hateful heart. Again, if you do not practice mercy with your brother whom you see and who needs your mercy, how are you to love God who does not need it?

1. Faith unites with God, love with men (1 John 4:16). *He who abides in love abides in God and God in him.* Body and soul make one man. Faith demonstrates that the love of God and man make a true Christian. God intends good for all men. He who acts in such a way is one heart and mind with God, but he who does not is against God and is the enemy of God because he is the enemy of his neighbor.

2. It is a quality of love that it is chiefly concerned for the trespasses of its neighbor (Gal. 6:1), and therefore the trespasses of your neighbor are your mirror, in which you are to learn to know your weaknesses, and that you, too, are a man. Therefore, you are to help to bear his weaknesses and burden with patience, humility, and meekness.

3. Such people, who do not willingly stumble into evil but who quickly stand up straight again, punish themselves and admit their guilt. With such people one can soon be compassionate, and can have mercy for them. Those who do not do this do not have the meek spirit of Christ. If one quickly judges the trespasses of one's neighbor without compassion, it is a certain sign that such a person lacks the merciful love of God and of the Holy Spirit and does not have God in himself. A true Christian who is sanctified by the spirit of Christ carries all men in compassionate mercy and in a merciful love as Christ did and as he demonstrated to us by his example. Thereby, each Christian proves himself. The love of God, indeed, God himself, has fallen away from that man who does not find the love of neighbor in himself. He ought therefore to be in dread and in his heart to be repentant, to seek forgiveness from his neighbor so that God with his love might come to him once again. Everything that a man does in faith and love will then once again be good, holy, and godly. Then a man will practice God's love and mercy with joy for the sake of the indwelling love of God and it will be a joy for him to do good as God said (Jer. 32:41).

4. Outside of love everything that is in man is devilish, and everything is evil in its very foundation. This is the reason why

Satan can do nothing good, for there is no love either for God or man. Therefore, everything that Satan does is evil in its very foundation. He seeks and intends to do nothing other by his acts than to do dishonor to God and to bring corruption to man, so as to perfect his enmity against God and man. Therefore, he seeks such hateful hearts through which he can practice his envy and wrath. In this, man can see who are the children of God and who of Satan (1 John 3:10).

IV

Love must arise from sincere faith, that is, it must love God in fortune and misfortune. He who truly loves God is pleased by everything that pleases God. He who loves God must also love his cross that God gives to him. This is shown to us in the example of Christ our Lord, who took up his cross since it was the will of God. *I have a baptism to be baptized with; and how am I constrained until it is accomplished* (Lk. 12:50). Therefore, all the holy martyrs bore their cross with joy.

Those who have deep love for God do not find it difficult to bear their cross, for their cross is the yoke of Christ (Mt. 11:29). A magnet draws a heavy piece of iron toward itself, and likewise a heavenly magnet, the love of God, ought to draw the burden of our cross toward itself, so that it becomes light and easy. Why then should man's heart be troubled? Sugar makes bitter food sweet. How much then, ought the sweetness of divine love to make the bitter cross sweet? Because of this, the great patience and joy of the holy martyrs arose, for God made them drunk by his love.

25

ON THE LOVE OF NEIGHBOR IN PARTICULAR

Whatever overcomes a man, to that he is enslaved (2 Pet. 2:19).

There is no more difficult and burdensome a service than for a man to serve the sinful affectations and particularly enmity. These bind and burden all the bodily and spiritual powers and never allow man's thoughts to be free. The man who practices love is truly free in his heart and is no servant of wrath, envy, covetousness, usury and mammon, pride, lying or slander, nor does he owe his body to these. Love makes him free from all of these things and does not allow him to be conquered by hurtful vices. He is truly free in Christ through the spirit of freedom, for where the spirit is, there is freedom (2 Cor. 3:17). Such a person, who walks in the love of Christ, is no longer a servant of sin, nor does he owe his body to sin for the love of God has freed him through the Holy Spirit.

Now we see how the love of God stretches itself over all men. This is testified to not only in his word, but also in the whole of nature. The heavens are given to all men. They cover all men; they are mine and my neighbors'. The sun is mine and my brother's. The greatest as well as the lowest man lives under the same sun, in the same air, on the same earth and by the same water.

We are to treat our fellowman as God treats us. God himself gave nature as an example, that we are to be of the same mind to all men and not to love anyone more or less than another. As he is minded toward us, so we are to be minded toward our neighbors, and as we act toward our neighbors, he will act toward us. He testifies in our hearts to convince us how he is minded toward us. We are to be so minded toward our neighbor.

The test lies in our heart and conscience. We are to enter there and to ask ourselves how we stand with our neighbor, good or evil. As we find ourselves there, so we will also find ourselves with God. The way in which we act with our neighbor, God will act with us. *With the pure thou dost show thyself pure; and with the crooked thou dost show thyself perverse* (Ps. 18:26–27). That is, if you have a perverse heart against your brother, God will be so toward you.

Therefore, our brother is a test for us, established by the love of God, that is, God wishes to test us in our neighbor [to see] whether our love is righteous before him. God does not need our service in the slightest way, but our neighbor does.

God has directed us to our neighbor and has laid out the commandment in our consciences that we are to order ourselves in all things toward our neighbor as well. At all times, indeed, at every hour, we are to be minded toward our neighbor as God is minded toward us. None of us can remain with God in grace without forgiving his neighbor. There is no need of this for God's sake. The sins of the whole world were done away with at once, and perfect forgiveness was achieved through the death of Jesus Christ. Yet each of us is like the servant whose debt the king forgave in his grace so that he did not have to pay it. Yet, when the servant treated his brother so unmercifully, the king took away his forgiveness again and he became an evil servant and was damned because of his treatment of the brother. The conclusion to the story goes as follows: "*So also, my heavenly father will do to everyone of you, if you do not forgive your brother from your heart*" (Mt. 18:35). Again: *With the measure by which you measure, you will be measured* (Lk. 6:38).

Thus, a man is not here for himself but also for his neighbor's sake. So strong, indeed, is the commandment of love for neighbor that if it is broken, God's love turns away from us and man is judged and damned immediately by the strongest righteousness.

If we thought about this, we would never become angry with our fellowman and we would not allow the sun to go down on our wrath (Eph. 4:26). Although Christ by his death on the cross, once and for all and perfectly, paid and atoned for the sins of the world, and although the eternal King has forgiven us all for our great sins and granted us this forgiveness out of grace, nevertheless, if we hate our brother, do not love him, and do not forgive him, the great merit of Christ will be lost for us and it will be as it earlier was for us before the eternal blessedness was achieved through Christ.

Thus, God has bound us to the love of our neighbors. He does not wish to be loved by us, aside from the love of our neighbors. Insofar as we look to the love of our neighbors, so far also we look to the love of God. Therefore, God did not create one man better than another so that we might not have reason to despise another and to lift ourselves over another, but to live with each other as children of one Father in peace and unity and to have a peaceful conscience.

If you hate your brother, you hate God who has forbidden you to hate your brother and so God will hate you. This is your judgment and damnation. You will lose at one time the forgiveness of sins and the precious merit of Christ and his redemption.

It is not possible for the blood of Christ, which was poured out from love, to be shared fruitfully with a heart full of enmity. Indeed, in the Parable in Matthew 18:35 we see that God was not as angry over the great debt of ten thousand talents as he was over unmercifulness. He can forgive the debt but he can not forgive unmercifulness. Therefore, we are to consider the divine counsel: *So also my heavenly father will do to everyone of you* (Mt. 18:35).

26
WHY OUR NEIGHBOR IS TO BE LOVED

Owe no one anything, except to love one another, for he who loves his neighbor has fulfilled the law (Rom. 13:8).

In the Prophet Micah 6:6–8, we read the following: *"With what shall I come before the Lord, and bow myself down before God on high? Shall I come before him with burnt offerings, with calves a year old? Will the Lord be pleased with thousands of rams, with ten thousands of rivers of oil? Shall I give my firstborn for my transgression, the fruit of my body for the sin of my soul?"* He has showed you, oh, man, what is good; and what does the Lord require of you—namely to keep God's word, to practice love, and to walk humbly with your God?

In this question and answer the prophet teaches us what proper, true worship consists of, namely, not in external ceremonies or sacrifices, for what can a man give to God? God is, of course, before everything, and he does not need this. Nor is he appeased *victimis humanis* [with human victims] if one sacrifices men. He has not commanded this and it is an abomination to him and it is an insult to the sacrifice that occurred alone through Christ, whom God ordained to bear the sins of the world. The true, proper worship, which is pleasing to God, consists internally in pure faith, which the prophet here describes as keeping God's word, as the practice of faith, love, and mercy, and not in sacrifice but in true humility as David points out in Psalm 51:17: *The sacrifice acceptable to God is a broken spirit; a broken and contrite heart, O God, thou wilt not despise.*

True worship must proceed from the ground of the heart out of faith, love, and humility. The Apostle Paul counsels us to this in Romans 13:8–10. This passage is an *enconium caritatis, et debitum proximi perpetuum* [a praise of love and the continual duty toward neighbor]. By this, we can properly serve God. The reason is that man cannot serve God with anything except with that which God brings about in our hearts, for God is to be served with nothing other than that which he brings about in our hearts. God is to be served with nothing else except service given to neighbor with love and pleasure.

The apostle admonishes us to such love and uses a good and dear argument that is pleasing to those who love Christian virtue, and he says: "Love is a glorious virtue in which all virtues are summed up and it is the fulfillment of the Law." This argument was not used by the Apostle Paul so that we might be able to bring to perfection the law by our love and thereby to earn blessedness and eternal life, which would indeed occur if our love were perfect, but he wished to portray for us the greatness and worth of this virtue to inspire us to strive toward it. Our righteousness and blessedness are grounded on Jesus Christ and on his merits, which are ascribed to us through faith.

Out of his righteousness flows love for neighbor and other virtues, and these are called the fruits of righteousness to the praise and honor of God (Phil. 1:11). Since it is the most glorious and greatest virtue for you, we wish to treat a bit further and to discuss yet other bases on which we might build in love.

1. The chief basis is found in 1 John 4:16: *"God is love and he who abides in love abides in God and God in him."* Who would not eagerly be and abide in God? Who would not eagerly wish that God would be and abide in him? On the other hand, who would wish that Satan would be in him and he in Satan? This occurs, however, if love is not there but enmity. The Devil is an enemy of man, but God loves man. Listen to what John says in the same place, for he speaks further in verse 7: *"He who loves is born of God and knows God."* Is it not comforting to be a child of God and to be born of God and to know God truly? He who does not have love in his heart and has not experienced its power, its life, its blessings, its goodness, its kindness, its long-suffering, and its patience cannot freely know God, who is love alone. The knowledge of God and Christ must proceed from the experience and reception of Christ. Who can truly know Christ who does not know anything about love? Christ is pure love and meekness. He who has this virtue and practices it, he truly knows Christ. Two Peter 1:8 speaks of this. . .

2. The Lord says in John 15:8–9: *"By this shall all men know that you are my disciples if you love one another as I have loved you."* What is it to be a disciple of Christ? It is not only to be a Christian in

name and to confess Christ with the mouth alone *externa quadam professione*, but to belong truly to Christ, to be loved by him deeply, to have a part in him and to enjoy all his blessings. That man does not belong to Christ who does not have the love of Christ, nor does he have any part in Christ. Such a man has no faith and therefore Christ will not acknowledge him as his own. Just as a man knows an apple by its taste and a flower by its smell, so one knows a Christian by love.

3. Saint Paul says in 1 Corinthians 13:2 that all the great gifts are nothing without love. To know many languages, to do miracles, to understand many mysteries, does not make a Christian but faith, which is active through love, does. God has not demanded great things of us (to do miracles or the like) other than love and humility. On the last day, God will not ask how learned you were in the arts, in languages, and in great knowledge, but how you practiced love by faith. *I was hungry and you fed me, and so forth* (Mt. 25:35). Therefore, Paul says in Galatians 5:6 *"that neither circumcision nor uncircumcision counts for anything in Christ,"* that is, no preeminence, no gift, no appearance before the people, but only faith that is active through love.

4. John says the same thing in 1 John 4:20–21: *"If anyone says I love God and hates his brother he is a liar, for how can one love God whom he does not see, if he does not love his brother whom he can see?" For this commandment we have from him that he who loves God must also love his brother*, that is, God's love can not be without the love of neighbor. He who does not love his neighbor is an enemy of God for the enemy of man is the enemy of God because God loves man.

5. Love is a law of nature out of which all good for the human race arises and without which the human race must perish. Everything that happens that is good for man arises and has its source in love. Therefore Paul called love the bond of perfection (Col. 3:14). The glorious fruits that arise out of love he described in Romans 12:9. And, therefore, the Lord in Matthew 7:12 said, *"Whatever you wish that man would do to you, do so to them; for this is the Law and the prophets."* And the pagans have also learned from nature that what you do not wish to happen to you are not to do to another. This statement, the Emperor Severus, who was adorned with many virtues, continually spoke and made into a law.

6. Love is a beautiful image and foretaste of eternal life. What

a blessed situation it will be when the elect love each other together, rejoice in each other, dwell with each other in eternal graciousness and kindness, have pleasure in each other that is not to be fathomed. All this will happen in love. Therefore, he who contemplates the image of eternal life, indeed, he who wishes to have a foretaste of it, he will find great joy and pleasure in it, and will have much rest and peace in his heart.

7. The purer, warmer, and deeper love is, the nearer it is to godly quality and nature, for in God, in Christ, and the Holy Spirit the purest, sweetest, warmest, noblest, and deepest love exists. Love is pure if one does not love for the sake of one's own gain and enjoyment, but for the love of God alone, because God loves so purely and cleanly without any self-purpose. Therefore, he who loves his neighbor for the sake of his own purpose does not have a pure love or a godly love. This is the difference between the pagan love and that love held by Christians. A Christian loves his neighbor in God, in Christ, purely, and he loves all men in God and in Christ. The pagans knew nothing about this but they soiled their virtue with self-honor and self-purpose. We must love our neighbor deeply if we are to love him without hypocrisy, without falsity, and if the love is to proceed from the heart and not from the mouth by which many are led astray. Love is to be warm if there is a deep mercy and compassion there, for man is to take the neighbor's need upon himself as his own, he is to *share his life with his neighbor, indeed*, give up his life for his brother (1 John 3:16), as Moses and Paul who wished to be burned for their brothers (Ex. 32:32; Rom. 9:3).

8. Out of this it follows that we must and ought to love our enemies (Mt. 5:44 . . .). In this, the priority, preeminence, and glory of Christians consist: to conquer nature, to rule over flesh and blood, the world, and all the evil in the world with good and with virtue (Rom. 12:21). This is the Christian nobility (Ex. 23:5 . . . 1 Cor. 9:9 . . . Rom. 12:20 . . .). It is not enough that you do not harm man, indeed, not even your enemy; you must do good to him or you are not a child of God. Otherwise you do not love your neighbor.

9. He who does not endeavor to practice Christian love separates himself from the spiritual body of Christ, the Church, and loses all the blessings of Christ (Eph. 4:5). There is one faith, one

baptism, one God, one Lord. Just as members that are separated from the head are not able to have the life and power of the head but are dead, so all those who do not live in love separate themselves from the one head, Christ, and are not able to participate in the movement and fullness of his body. Therefore John [in 1 John 3:14] says: *He who does not love his brother remains in death, he is dead although he is alive.*

10. All good gifts and success must be requested of God through prayer and without prayer there is no help, consolation, salvation, and no blessing or fortune can come to us. However, no prayer will be heard or come to God if it is not prayed in faith and out of love. Therefore, the Lord said, *"Where two or three are gathered together in my name, what they request I will give them and they will receive from my Father"* (Mt. 18:19).

Thus we are to live in love for there is peace and unity. However, wherever there is peace, there is the God of peace (Rom. 15:33), and wherever the God of peace is, there the Lord gives his promised blessing and life forever and into eternity (Ps. 133:3).

27

WHY ONE MUST LOVE ONE'S ENEMIES

I say to you love your enemies and pray for those who persecute you, so that you may be the sons of your Father who is in Heaven (Mt. 5:44–45).

1. The first reason [for loving one's enemies] is that it is God's commandment, and the Lord gives no other reason than this: that you might be the children of your Father in heaven. When we were his enemies he loved us (Rom. 5:10). The Lord wishes to say: If you do not love your enemies, you cannot be the children of your Father. If one is not the child of God, whose child is he? Ah, have we yet so much to learn? How far are we yet from the fruits of the childhood of God, since in the true children of God there is to be so much love that they love enemies?

2. One John 3:14 states: *"He who does not love his brother remains in death."* Why? Because he does not have the true life in Christ. The spiritual, heavenly life consists in faith toward God and in love toward neighbor as Saint John himself said: We know that we have come from death into life since we love the brethren. This is the fruit and the witness of the new life given in Christ. Therefore, enmity against the neighbor is eternal death. He who dies in enmity dies in eternal death, and of this the Lord Christ faithfully warned us.

3. If a man hates his neighbor, all his good works, worship, and prayer are lost, as Saint Paul says: *"If I gave all my goods to the poor, deliver my body to be burned, and have not love it would profit me nothing"* (1 Cor. 13:3).

4. It is a mark of high, noble, and godly mind to forgive injuries. Look at God and note how patient he is, how quickly he forgives (Ps. 103:8). Look at the Lord Jesus and how patient a lamb he was, how he did not open up his mouth (Is. 53:7). Look at God, the Holy Spirit. Why did he reveal himself in the form of a dove (Mt. 3:16)? Without doubt, because of the gentleness and meekness. Look at Moses, with what great patience he bore the sin and

JOHANN ARNDT

insult of the people (Num. 12:3). . . . Look at David, how he endured Shimei (2 Sam. 16:10).

> *Que quisque est major, magis est placabilis irae,*
> *Et faciles motus mens generosa capit.*
> That is,
> The greater the hero, the sooner is his anger placated.
> The nobler the mind, the sooner is it forgiving.
> Mantua
> *Ardua res vicissa alios, victoria major*
> *Est, animi fluctus composuisse suos.*
> That is,
> To conquer an enemy is a great task;
> To conquer oneself is yet greater.
> *Parcere subjectis et debellare superbos,*
> *Hac est in magnis gloria magna viris.*
> That is
> To spare the small and battle the proud
> Is the greatest victory for the greatest men. (*Aeneid* VI, 853)

"Vera charitas nulli nouit indignari quamsibi" [True love is stirred up against no one easier than against oneself]. True peace consists not in great fortune but in the humble suffering of opposition. Publ[ius]: "In genuitas non recipit contumeliam" [A brave mind is not capable of any vice]. Seneca: "Si magnanimus fueris, numquam judicabis tibi contumeliam fueri" [If you have a brave mind you can accept insults brought against you]. If someone should cut off the sunlight [to a room] and say there was nothing but darkness, it would not make it so. Consider this. *Genus magnum vindictae est ignoscere* [Great revenge is quickly forgiven]. Excellent people have practiced such a glorious, wise rule of life. Pericles, for example, a Greek orator, allowed a man who had slandered him the whole day to accompany him to his house in the evening so that he could not take offence and he said: It is no great art to attack virtue, but to follow it. Phocion, an Athenian prince, after he had done many glorious deeds, was condemned to death by envy. When he was asked if he wished to say something to his son he answered: "Nothing, except this, that he will not attempt to avenge this act of his fatherland." The Emperor Titus, when he was endangered because

138

two brothers were attempting to gain power and had sworn an oath to get it to kill the emperor, invited them as guests one evening and in the morning took them to a theater where they saw a play and he allowed them to sit beside him and he conquered their evil through great grace. When Cato, the wise counsellor of Rome, killed himself, Julius Caesar said: "I have lost a great victory, for I wished to forgive Cato all the injuries which he did to me."

5. He who cannot be moved to meekness toward his enemies through the great patience and humility of the Son of God will never be moved by a saint's example and much less by the example of a pagan. What greater injustice and evil is there than that the children of men, the crowns of his heart, should have treated the one innocent and righteous Son of God so badly, have slandered him, beaten him, crowned him with thorns, whipped him, laid him on a cross, and brought the greatest evil upon him? Yet God forgave everything out of grace and the Lord prayed: *Father, forgive them* (Lk. 23:34).

6. To this end, your Redeemer and Sanctifier placed his example before your eyes so that he might be a powerful medicine for your whole life, such a medicine indeed that would press low everything that is high in you, give life to everything that is broken down in you, cut off everything that is unchaste in you, and make better everything that is corrupted in you. How can pride be so great in a man that it is not able to be healed with the deepest lowliness and humility of the Son of God (Heb. 5:8)? How can covetousness gain so great a hand in man that it is not able to be healed through holy poverty of Christ? How can the wrath of man become so great that it cannot be healed through the soft meekness of Christ? How can the search for revenge be so bitter in man that it is not able to be healed through the great patience of the Son of God? How can a man be so loveless that he can not be stirred through the great love of Christ and be ignited by his blessings with love? How can anyone be so hard of heart that Christ cannot soften him with his tears?

7. Who would not like to be similar to God the Father and his dear Son, Jesus Christ, and God the Holy Spirit, and carry the image of the Holy Trinity, which chiefly consists in love and forgiveness? This is the highest characteristic of God, to be merciful, to spare, to be gracious, and to forgive. Who would not say that

that is the most beautiful of virtues by which man might become similar to the highest God and the most virtuous, highest people in the world?

8. Finally, the highest step of the virtue is to conquer oneself, to forgive, to forget, and to change wrath into grace.

Fortior est qui se, quam qui fortissimus, vincit Moenia, nec virtus altius ire potest [The Highest victory is to conquer oneself, above which the virtue never steps higher]. It is as Proverbs 16:32 reads: *"He who is slow to anger is better than the mighty and he who rules his spirit than he who takes his city."* Virtue cannot rise any higher. It has no higher position or grade. At such a point it rests in God and finds its end in God and is completed in God.

28

HOW AND WHY THE LOVE OF THE CREATOR IS TO PRECEDE ALL CREATURELY LOVE. HOW THE NEIGHBOR IS TO BE LOVED IN GOD

Do not love the world or the things that are in the world (1 John 2:15).

Man's heart was created by God so that it was not able to live without love. It must love something whether it be God, the world, or itself. Since man must love something he ought to love the very best thing, which is God himself, and he ought to give this affection, which God planted in the heart and ignited through the Holy Spirit, back to God again and to ask that God ignite his love in him more and more. God first loved you and ignited your love with his love. You are to love him in return if you wish to be loved by him. *He who loves me will be loved by my father* (Jn. 14:21).

If God's love is in us we cannot intend evil for any man. God's love intends no evil for any man and can wish evil for no one. He who does not will evil for any man, because of the quality and the power of the love of God, will not be deceived by any man nor led astray by word or deed. Note that the love of God works in us.

There are many—indeed, most—people possessed of worldly love to such a degree that God's love never comes into their heart. As a result, they bear witness to their neighbors with false love, with judgment and deception. The world and everything that is in the world is not to be loved or God's love will be hindered and rooted out by it. How is the nothingness and the vanity of this world to be reckoned against the greatness and supremacy of God? Just as God in infinite ways surpasses all his creatures, so his holy love, in a totally surpassable way, without any comparison, is more noble and more precious than any other love by which a creature is loved. Therefore, all creatures are far too small and paltry, that because of their love and for their sake, God's love should be destroyed.

Saint Paul says in 1 Corinthians 9:7: *Who plants a vineyard without eating any of its fruit?* Thus, who wants you to love more than he who planted the love in your heart, through whose love you live? Through the love of God in Christ all of us live. In this same love, we are to keep ourselves our whole life long whatever comes to us because of it. Just as sailors in great storms upon the sea cast out their anchor by which the ship is held firm, so if this world, which is a stormy sea, moves the ship of our heart through the waves of manifold vice, pride, wrath, impatience, covetousness and fleshly lust, we are to hold firm to the love of God and Christ as to an anchor and not quickly tear away from the love of Christ (Rom. 8:38ff.). So also in spiritual need, if sin, death, the Devil and hell, trouble and misery, strive against us as the waves of a sea, we are to hold firm to the love of God and Christ. This is the mountain that was pointed out to Lot when he left the fire at Sodom. On that mountain his soul was to be saved (Gen. 19:17).

Thus, a Christian must flee the Sodom of this world and hold firm to the love of God if he does not wish to fall on the streets of worldly lusts, which are worse than the fire at Sodom. The love of God protects a man from the world as Joseph [was protected] from Potiphar's wife (Gen. 39:9).

A man loves this world so much only if he has not tasted the love of God. A man hates, envies, deceives, and judges his neighbor only if he does not have the love of God. Where does so much sorrow and trouble come from? It comes only from the fact that man does not love God deeply. The love of God is so dear and sweet that it consoles a man in all troubles and makes him joyous and consoled even in death.

It is the quality of love to consider great that alone which it loves, and it forgets everything else so that it might gain only the beloved. Why does a man not forget everything that is in the world—honor, pleasure, and wealth—so that he might have God alone, since he says that he loves God? In earlier times the saints of God have done this. They searched after the love of God and its sweetness, so much so that they forgot themselves and the world because of it. For this reason they were considered fools in the world and yet they were among the wisest. Who is the wisest? The man who seeks above everything else the highest good. Therefore, those are the greatest fools in the world who held these holy people to be fools (1 Cor. 3:9, 4:10).

A true lover of God seeks and loves God as if there were nothing else under the heavens except God, and thus he finds God in everything that he was ever able to love in the world. God is everything. He is the true honor and joy, peace and pleasure, wealth and glory. You will find all this in God better than in the world. If you love something beautiful, why do you not love God who is the source of all beauty? If you love something good, why do you not love God who is the eternal good? No one is good except God (Mt. 19:17), who is the highest Good in his being. All creatures are good because they have received from the highest goodness of God a small spark and drop and yet they are wrapped around with much imperfection.

Why do you not now love God much more, the source and the fountain and the highest perfection of all good who is essentially good and who is the source of all good in all things? The less earth or earthly weight a thing has in itself, the easier is it lifted into the heights and the sooner does it do so. Thus, the more a man's heart is weighted down with earthly things, the less does it lift itself up and the less can it rejoice in the love of God. The less earthly love the more godly love and the more love of neighbor [there is]. These last two are not to be separated.

From this it follows that he who loves God also loves his neighbor and he who cuts off God also cuts his neighbor off.

29

ON THE FORGIVENESS OF THE NEIGHBOR,
WITHOUT WHICH GOD DRAWS BACK HIS GRACE

When anyone sins against a man he sins against the Lord (Num. 5:6).

[He who outrages man outrages God. He who wishes to be reconciled with God must be reconciled with his neighbor, for the love of God and the love of neighbor are not able to be distinguished. The love of the neighbor is a test of the love of God in man. These are the two goals of our whole life. Therefore, God made his love visible in Christ. As in Christ God and man were bound together, so are the love of God and the love of neighbor bound together, just as all the lines of a circle come together in their middle point. An image, an example of the love of neighbor is found in Job. For the love of neighbor, God created man in the beginning. Loving is much easier than hating. Love and reconciliation bring peace. Every virtue is its own payment. Reconciliation comes about when the one who is guilty acknowledges his sin. He must be repentant or nothing will occur. In the way in which one treats his neighbor, God will treat him. This is upheld by many passages of Scripture.]

30
ON THE FRUITS OF LOVE

Love is patient and kind; love is not jealous or boastful; it is not arrogant or rude. Love does not insist on its own way; it is not irritable or resentful; it does not rejoice at wrong, but rejoices in the right. Love bears all things, believes all things, hopes all things, endures all things (1 Cor. 13:4–7).

The tree of life stood in the middle of Paradise and bore fruit. If a man ate of this fruit, he would live forever as the Lord said in Genesis 3:22–23. . . . Thus, God established in the middle of Paradise the Christian Church, Christ Jesus, so that all the faithful might receive life and power from him. The whole of Christianity consists in faith and in love. God is pleased with the whole life of a Christian for the sake of faith in Christ. If a neighbor is to be served, however, this service must arise in love, for all the virtues without love, indeed, even faith itself, are dead and count for nothing (Jas. 2:17). Faith alone makes one righteous, yet where love does not follow, faith is certainly not proper but is hypocrisy even if it does miracles. Just as the body is dead without the soul, so the inner spiritual man, whose members are all the virtues, is also dead without love and all the members of the virtues are dead without love. Therefore, Saint Paul demands such faith, which is active through love (Gal. 5:6). The noble fruit that this tree bears is pointed out to us by Saint Paul in 1 Corinthians 13:4ff. in fourteen different ways.

1. Love is long-suffering. Long-suffering is the first fruit of love, which we can in no way better know than in Christ Jesus our Lord. In Christ we must not only seek this fruit as on the tree of life, but we must also eat his noble fruit, indeed, practice it *in sanguinis et succum* [in blood and sap]. Look to the Lord Christ with how great long-suffering he bore the evil of the world and by this action attracted sinners to repentance (Rom. 2:4). Do so also and the meek Christ will live in you and you with him. As a member with his head you will remain united.

2. Love is kind. Look to the kindness of your Redeemer. Where does one hear more gracious lips (Ps. 45:2)? Each man is surprised at the graciousness that went forth from his mouth (Lk. 4:22). You too ought to act so, for Christ speaks through your mouth, and remain united with him so that your speech will proceed only from deep love.

3. Love is not jealous, that is it does not seek vengeance but forgives and forgets as the Lord did (Ps. 103:9–10 . . . Ezek. 18:21–22 . . . Jer. 31:3 . . . Is. 43:25). You ought to act in the same way. Forgive and forget so that God will forget your sin also. Then you will have the mind of the Lord Christ and will remain united with him.

4. Love is not arrogant or rude, that is, true love draws the neighbor to itself not for the ill purpose of scolding, slandering, or insulting him. Such secret intention love does not have in itself but it is open, public, and upright of mind. Look to the Lord Jesus Christ. He revealed his heart to friend and foe and from the depths of his heart he intended good for all men and sought from his heart the salvation of all. You too ought to act so, for the goodness and faithfulness of Christ is in you. As Christ intended in his heart, so ought we to act to one another, or we are not united with Christ as members with the head.

5. Love does not insist on its own way, that is, it is not eager for praise, pompous and blown up. Look to the Lord Jesus when a woman lifted up her voice among the people and said in Luke 11:27–28: *"Blessed is the womb which bore you, the breasts which gave thee nurse." The Lord said: "Indeed, blessed is he who hears the Word of God and keeps it."* Thus, he turned the praise that was intended for him humbly away from himself and gave it to the one he loved, to God. You ought to do also. Thus, the humble Christ will live in you and you in him. This is the proper love, which turns itself away from praise and gives praise to the other person.

6. Love is not irritable as an obstinate, inconsiderate person, but it allows kindness to shine from its eyes. Look to the Lord Jesus, the gracious image. *"He will not be stubborn nor discourage* says the prophet (Is. 42:4). He looked upon every man with merciful eyes. You ought to do this also. Thus, you will have Christ's appearance as an image in yourself and you will be united with him.

7. Love does not seek its own, that is, joy for true love is if it

can serve another purely without any self-gain so that many can be pleased. God so acts. He gives us everything and has no use from it. If you serve God, God has no use of it, but you do. Therefore, God has commanded you to be pious, to fear God so that you might enjoy his love and can have the blessing from it. Look to the Lord Jesus. In the smallest ways he did not seek his own but all that which served for our salvation (Mt. 20:28). He had no gain from it. A tree gives its fruit to each man without discrimination of persons and has no gain from its act but it gives in as good a way as God gave to it. If it were in a better situation it would also give without any envy. Thus, Christ gave himself to us as a possession. Indeed, God gave himself to us as a possession in Christ, so that everything would be ours in Christ, even God himself. He is the best and the highest good and shares himself with us. You ought to act in a similar way. Then you will be a tree of righteousness for God's praise (Is. 61:3). Then, Christ will grow and flourish in you. He will be the living bind and the ever-growing palm tree (Ps. 92:13).

8. Love is not bitter, that is, if wrath takes the upper hand, in the highest degree, so that it curses in its mouth against the neighbor and spews out all sorts of poison and blasphemes and curses a neighbor. Look to the Lord Jesus. No bitterness proceeded from his mouth but only blessing and life (Is. 11:3, 42:2). When he was cursed . . . (Lk. 10:3, 11:42) no evil bitterness was sought but a sermon of repentance by which deep improvement might come about. *Therefore see to it that no root of bitterness spring up and cause trouble and by it the many become defiled* (Heb. 12:15).

9. Love does not seek to harm nor does it think on evil. Look to the dear God and his Father's heart as he spoke in Jeremiah 29:11–14. . . . *"He who has thoughts of peace toward his neighbor has God's heart and Christ's mind and is united with him as a member with its head."*

10. Love does not rejoice in unrighteousness and does not laugh in enmity if injustice or unrighteousness comes to the pious as Shimei did when David fled from Absalom (2 Sam. 16:6). Look to the Lord Jesus. He had a deep compassion with Peter. Note how he looked upon him so sorrowfully (Lk. 22:61). With this attitude he raised him up again (Ps. 146:8 . . .). The Lord Christ wept over the corruption of men and the fall of Jerusalem (Lk. 19:41). Thus, if you see a man fall, pity him and be merciful to him, help him bear

his burden and you will fulfill the law of Christ (Gal. 6:10), for he bore all our burdens. Thus you will be a true member and his life will be in you and the life of the head must make the members alive.

11. Love rejoices in truth and in justice. Look to your Redeemer, how he rejoiced in his spirit when the seventy came again and how he praised his Father (Lk. 10:21). Look to the holy angels concerning whom the Lord said that they rejoice over our repentance (Lk. 15:10). Act in a similar manner and you will have an angelic, indeed, a godly mind.

12. Love bears everything so that the bond of peace will not be broken. Therefore, it bears the mistakes of its neighbor with patience, as Saint Paul says: *"To the weak I became weak that I might win the weak. I have become all things to all men that I might by all means save some"* (1 Cor. 9:22). Love believes all, that is, it does not consider evil of its neighbor. Love hopes for all things, that is, it wishes that all goodness be fulfilled for its neighbor. It endures all so that the neighbor may be well served and made pious. Look to the Lord Jesus. He suffered and bore everything for our sins, the highest insult, pain, and the highest poverty, so that we might have in him and through him honor and joy.

13. Love is not weary and never ceases. Look to the dear God. His mercy endures forever by those who fear him (Lk. 1:50; Ps. 103:17 . . . Is. 30:18 . . . Rom. 8:39 . . . Ps. 8:6–7 . . . Is. 54:8). Although the Lord says in Jeremiah 15:6: *"I am weary of mercy,"* this is only to be said of those who openly stand against God's mercy, despise God's grace, and act wantonly (Jude 4). In other cases, his love is not weary but remains eternal for all those who fear him as he stated in Isaiah 54:10. . . . Thus, our love is not to be weary, not even for our enemies, but we are to say out of a merciful, ever-enduring love, *"Father forgive them."* Thus, Christ lives and prays in you (Lk. 23:34).

14. Love is the greatest of all virtues for *God is* love (1 John 4:16). Love is also a fulfillment of the Law and all the commandments are included within it (Rom. 13:10). It is also eternal although faith, hope, and the gift of languages cease, and in the end of faith, holiness is achieved. All virtues and blessings that come to our neighbors and all good and living gifts are false and unclean without love. It gives us an eternal witness that we have inherited

blessedness through faith in Christ. Therefore, a Christian is not to strive so eagerly for gifts or arts as he is for love (Eph. 3:19), *to know the love of Christ which surpasses knowledge, that you may be filled with all the fullness of God and with all the fruits of love.*

31
SELF-LOVE AND SELF-HONOR CORRUPT
AND BRING TO NOTHING THE HIGHEST AND MOST
BEAUTIFUL GIFTS OF MAN

*If I speak with the tongue of men and of angels and have not love I am
as a sounding brass or a tinkling cymbal* (1 Cor. 13:1).

[Love is the greatest virtue for God is love. There is a true love
and a false love. Without true love all gifts are worthless, indeed,
harmful. True love takes and gives everything in simplicity without
self-honor. Without such pure love all gifts are worthless. All self-
love and self-honor are from the Devil. This is the fall of Lucifer
and Adam and the evil life of all men. This evil life must be
changed through Christ for the end of his incarnation is our rebirth.
Out of this new birth all our works and gifts must come. Only thus,
in faith and love, are they pleasing to God.]

32

GREAT GIFTS DO NOT INDICATE A CHRISTIAN AND A MAN PLEASING TO GOD, BUT FAITH THAT IS ACTIVE THROUGH LOVE DOES

The kingdom of God does not consist in talk but in power (1 Cor. 4:20).

[God does not demand great art from us but faith, love, and the mortification of the flesh. Not great gifts but a new creature counts before God. God has given gifts for the edification of the Church. Without faith and love, Christ does not acknowledge a person to be his own. Love is the true, new life. God, Christ, and his Spirit, the Church and the eternal life, are all pure love. He who is without love is a dead member of the Church.]

33

GOD DOES NOT LOOK UPON WORKS OR UPON A PERSON BUT JUDGES WORKS ACCORDING TO THE HEART

Every way of a man is right in his own eyes, but the Lord weighs the heart (Prov. 21:2).

[God does not look upon the person but he judges the person and all works according to the heart. Self-honor corrupts all good gifts. Everything that is to be pleasing to God must arise out of faith and love. Out of evil hearts come unfitting sacrifices, unfitting repentance, unfitting adornment, unfitting demands for signs, unfitting prayer, unfitting fasting, unfitting alms-giving, unfitting joy, and unfitting martyrdom. Examples of all these are found in the Scriptures. Everything lies in the heart.]

34

A MAN CAN DO NOTHING FOR HIS HOLINESS. GOD ALONE BRINGS IT ABOUT IF MAN ONLY GIVES HIMSELF TO GOD, TO HIS GRACE, AND ALLOWS GOD TO ACT WITH HIM AS A PHYSICIAN ACTS WITH A SICK MAN. THE MERIT OF CHRIST IS NOT IMPUTED TO ANYONE WITHOUT REPENTANCE

God made Christ Jesus our wisdom, our righteousness and sanctification and redemption (1 Cor. 1:30).

[Everything that belongs to holiness, Christ merited for us, for a fallen man cannot help himself. We cannot create ourselves and much less can we redeem and sanctify ourselves. Therefore, Christ had to come and he alone is our physician. As soon as a man is repentant, Christ works in him. Yet, a man cannot even do that by nature, but grace must train him. If he follows grace, then faith and love come. Without faith, Christ's merit does not help us and, therefore, Christ first taught repentance and promised the forgiveness of sins thereafter. Faith cannot accept any sparkling sins. This is indicated by the example of Zacchaeus. Christ himself creates a good will in us.]

35

WITHOUT A HOLY CHRISTIAN LIFE, ALL WISDOM, ART AND OTHER KNOWLEDGE, INDEED, ALL LEARNING OF ALL OF THE HOLY SCRIPTURE, IS USELESS

Not everyone who says to me Lord, Lord, shall enter the kingdom of heaven but he who does the will of my Father who is in heaven (Mt. 7:21).

[The Christian life is rooted in love. True love loves God and neighbor and nothing else. He who does not have this love is a hypocrite and God's word is useless to him. Self-honor makes everything an abomination before God. This will be discovered by the false prophets on the judgment day. The giving of alms for self-honor without love is useless as is the hypocritical practice of fasting and the chastisement of the body. Examples of this abound among the heathen and the Papists. All wisdom, knowledge, and work is nothing without the love of God and neighbor.]

36

THE PERSON WHO DOES NOT LIVE IN CHRIST BUT CLINGS WITH HIS HEART TO THE WORLD HAS ONLY THE EXTERNAL LETTERS OF THE SCRIPTURE AND DOES NOT TASTE THE POWER AND THE INNER MANNA

To him who conquers I will give some of the hidden manna, and I will give him a white stone, with a new name written on the stone, which no one knows except him who receives it (Rev. 2:17).

With these words we are taught that only those taste the sweetness of heavenly consolation and joy in the word of God who conquer, that is, who conquer their flesh, the world, and all honor and glory of the world and the Devil. Those who mortify their flesh together with all its lusts and desires through daily sorrow and penance, who die daily to the world and to themselves, so that their whole life is a bitter cross, these will be fed inwardly from above by God with a sweetness of the heavenly manna and will be given the joyous wine of Paradise to drink. The others, however, who have their consolation in the world, cannot taste the hidden manna. The reason for this is that each thing unites itself with that to which it is like. Opposites do not cling to one another. God's word is spiritual and therefore it does not unite itself with a worldly heart. The food that does not enter the stomach does not give strength to the body and it is thus with the soul that does not taste the power of the divine word or the bread of heaven, that does not change it completely and totally into itself, that is, into life.

Everything tastes bitter to a man who is suffering from a fever. Those who lie sick with the fever of this world in the search for worldly possessions, in covetousness, pride, and pleasure, taste the Word of God as bitter, indeed, it disgusts them as ones sick with fever. Those who have the Spirit of God, however, find in it the hidden bread of heaven. Those who have the spirit of this world have no taste for they receive nothing from it.

155

As a result, many men gain little pleasure, joy, and spiritual desire from the Holy Gospel, although they hear it daily, for they do not have the Spirit of God. They do not have heavenly minds but rather earthly hearts. He who wishes to understand the Word of God properly and gain power from it and eat of the bread of heaven must endeavor to conform his life to the Word of God and to the life of Christ. Thus, God feeds the humble with his grace (1 Pet. 5:5), the meek with his love, the patient with his consolation, and he makes his yoke easy and his burden light (Mt. 11:30). The sweetness of the bread of heaven is tasted under the yoke of Christ and therefore it reads: *He has filled the hungry with good things and the rich he has sent empty away* (Lk. 1:53).

Thy words are spirit and life says the Lord (Jn. 6:63). If they are spirit and life they cannot be experienced by any unspiritual, carnal, arrogant heart and mind, but one must appropriate them in the spirit in silence, in quietness, with deep humility and holy, great desire, and one must practice them in life. Otherwise, man has nothing from the Word of God other than the external husk and letter. Just as a person who hears the sound of a harp but does not understand what it is has no joy in it, so it is with one who does not discover the power of the divine Word if it is not practiced in his life.

Therefore, John says in Revelations 2:17, *"I will give him a good witness and with the witness a new name which no one knows except him who receives it."*

This is the witness of the hidden spirit, which gives witness to the Word of God. Moreover, the spirit of the Word of God gives witness to our spirit (Rom. 8:16) and the two agree, unite with one another, and are one spirit (1 Cor. 6:17) and this is the new name that no one knows except him who receives it. No one knows the sweetness of honey except the man who tastes it, and no one understands the new name of the witness of God in the heart except he who discovers it. That man alone understands the consolation of God who experiences it. This is the new witness and the new name that no one understands except he who receives it, and it is new because it proceeds out of the new birth from above.

Blessed is the man to whom God gives a taste of himself in his heart. Thus, in earlier times, God fed the prophets with his sweet bread of heaven by the voice of his eternal Word, which came to them. From it they were able to speak since they experienced it and in this way the Holy Scriptures came into being.

At the present time he does not cease to speak with all men and to feed them internally with his Word in their souls. Most men, however, are far too hard of hearing and too deaf to his Word and they would rather hear the world than God. They would rather follow their own lusts than the Spirit of God. Therefore, they cannot eat the hidden manna. They would rather eat the hidden tree of death and their fleshly lusts than the tree of life.

It is, therefore, a great blindness and foolishness that men will not understand that in God there is greater pleasure and sweetness than there is in the world. For the person who has once tasted God's goodness, the world and all its lusts are great bitterness. Our first parents let themselves be fooled by the world and ate of the forbidden fruit and, thereby, ate bitter death. We are still so blind and foolish and we still eat from the forbidden lusts of the flesh by which we die (Rom. 8:13).

The person who eats of me, said the Lord Christ, the tree and the bread of life, will live into eternity (Jn. 6:51). To eat of Christ means to believe in him and to have the pleasure, joy, love, consolation, and happiness of heart in him (Eccles. 24:29). The world gives only small, paltry, temporal things and you will be served for this with yet greater desires. God gives great, high, and eternal goods and yet before this men are so lazy and bear about their mortal, human hearts. Where does one find anyone who serves God with as great obedience and sorrow as he does Mammon and the world? For the sake of a little money, a man will often walk a long way, but for the sake of eternal life he will hardly lift a foot from the earth.

The prophets charged the great trading cities, Tyre and Sidon, with buying and selling their merchandise over the sea and yet not lifting a foot for the eternal good (Is. 23:1; Jer. 47:4; Ezek. 27:12–13).

In all places, the world is sought and loved more than God. Many learned doctors study day and night so that they might receive honor from the world, but for the sake of eternal honor and glory, they do not take the time to say even one "Our Father." Many endeavor to achieve nobility and chivalry in battle, but they will not fight against one vice of their flesh. By such a battle they could gain eternal, heavenly nobility. Many a man is a conqueror of many lands

157

and people and does not know how to conquer himself. How many of you are there who seek temporal things and because of this lose yourself and your soul and blessedness? All those who do this have not tasted the hidden manna of the divine Word. They do not conquer but allow themselves to be conquered by the world. He who wishes to taste manna must for the sake of God's love despise the world and conquer it. He who can do this will discover the sweetest consolation of the Holy Spirit, which no one understands except the person who receives it.

The tree of life must first be planted in us if we are to eat of its fruits. The heart must be turned first from the world to God if you are to discover heavenly consolation. You allow the consolation of the world to be a great joy to you and you do not think that God's consolation can bring more joy than the whole world. What God does is at all times nobler than what the creature does. The teaching that comes from above through the inspiration of the Holy Spirit is much nobler than that which is learned by man's understanding through great work. An apple and a lily made by nature are much nobler and better than that which an artist makes from pure gold. In a like manner, the very smallest spark and glance of the consolation of God is nobler and better than a great sea full of the joys of this world.

If you wish to have the noble consolation of God, you must despise the consolation and joy of this world. If you wish to hear properly you must turn your ear to me. If you wish to understand me, you must turn your heart to me. If you wish to see me, you must turn your eyes to me. If you turn your whole heart to God with all your thoughts you will see, hear, understand, taste, and discover him.

Men now praise others by saying, "With the help of God, how rich, powerful, wise and learned a man is," but they say nothing concerning a man's meekness, humility, patience, and meditativeness. Thus, one man now only looks upon another man with external eyes. He does not see the internal, which is the best and noblest [part]. One says: "This man has seen many lands and cities." Ah, had he seen only God, that would have been the best thing. One says: "This man has heard and served emperors, kings, princes, and lords." If he had truly heard God in his heart and served him properly, he would have served better and have heard something [worthwhile]. Many say out of a pure love for the world: "We live in a learned time; this is a period *doctum et eruditum saeculum* of great intelligence and culture." They do not know that the true art of loving Christ is better than all knowledge, that faith is almost completely extinguished (Eph. 3:19; Lk. 18:8), that few are truly learned by God (Is. 54:13), and that there are few who wish to learn from Christ the true, humble, and meek life (Mt. 11:29). The most intelligent are often strangers to the life that is from God and have not learned that in Christ a righteous life exists (Eph. 4:18–21). They believe that everything depends on the art of words although true erudition and intelligence does not consist of words but in *rebus* (things) and in the righteous, eternal wisdom. On this, one can see more in *Tractat de antique Philosophia* [The treatise of ancient philosophy]. If any one says that it is now an *impium seculum* [godless world], the ancient times were nearer to the truth and Word of God.

People say that a man has a good table and kitchen. He who has truly tasted God's Word has tasted the hidden manna, the eternal, enduring, living bread of life (Jn. 6:35). Such a man has truly a glorious table that God has prepared (Ps. 23:5).

What man who has truly tasted God and his Word may taste any evil, and what may one have as joy who has not tasted God and his Word? God himself is that joy which stands above all created joy. He is the eternal light that is above all created light. He wishes to pierce our hearts with his hidden beam of joy, to purify our spirit and all powers, to enlighten them, bring us joy, glorify them, and make us living. When will the time come when God with his presence, with everything that he is, will satisfy us?

As long as this does not occur there will be no perfect joy for us. Because of this we must take pleasure in the little crumbs of consolation that fall from the table of our Lord until the true joy of eternal life beings (Is. 55:1–2).

"Behold I stand at the door," says the Lord in Revelations 3:20, *"and knock. If anyone hears my voice and opens the door I will come into him and eat with him and he with me."* Listen dear man, if a nobler guest comes to you, will you leave him stand outside? It is a great shame to let a friend stand outside for long and to wait at the door. It is a greater shame to let your God stand outside who wishes to be your guest. You do not need to feed him; he will feed you. You are

to eat his bread of heaven and hidden manna with him. Does not a great Lord bring his kitchen with him when he comes to his poor friend's dwelling place?

The Lord says, "Hear my voice and open unto me." In a house in which there is the noise of this world, no sweet music can be heard. In a like manner, God cannot be heard in a worldly heart for it is not opened toward God and does not let him in. Therefore, such an earthly heart cannot taste the heavenly manna. When the tumult of this world is still in the heart, God comes and knocks and allows himself to be heard. Then you can say with the prophet Samuel: "Speak, Lord, for your servant hears" (1 Sam. 3:10).

The Epistle to the Hebrews in chapter 6:4 speaks concerning this internal, spiritual, and heavenly meal and says that those who are enlightened and have become partakers of the Holy Spirit have tasted the heavenly gift, the good Word of God and the power of the coming world. In this we hear where the Holy Spirit is in man and that if he is not hindered, he feeds the soul daily with the hidden manna of the good living Word of God that comes forth from God's mouth from which we live.

The royal Prophet David experienced this through the Holy Spirit in his heart and in his soul (Ps. 16:11 . . . Ps. 34:9 . . . Ps. 23:5 . . . Ps. 63:4 . . . Ps. 36:8ff. . . . Ps. 70:4–5 . . .). In these verses he describes what kind of people they are who are fed inwardly by the good Word of God, namely, those who are poor and wretched in spirit and soul and who cling to the consolation of God alone, who are worthy to taste the heavenly gifts concerning which Psalm 84:1 speaks: *"How lovely is thy dwelling place, Oh, Lord of Hosts! My soul longs, yea, faints for the courts of the Lord."* In this, David teaches us that the smallest pleasure of eternal life is more than the greatest joy of this world, and that one day there is better than a thousand years here. He who has once tasted this will find everything that is in the world bitter. The world will become for him wearying and boring, for he has discovered something better and more lovely.

Concerning this, the eternal wisdom in Ecclesiasticus 24:27–28 said: *"I am sweeter than honey and he who eats of me will hunger after me."*

This is a holier hunger and thirst, which no creature can satisfy except God himself with his love. Thus, the saints of God are made drunken as Solomon says in Song of Songs 5:1: *"Eat my beloved and drink my friend and be drunken."*

God allows his beloved to go away so that he can draw her to him so that she forgets earthly things. If it can happen in this life that we eat a crumb of the hidden manna and taste a small drop of the heavenly wine, how much more will happen in the new life where we will have the well itself?

On the cross, the Lord said, *"I thirst"* (Jn. 19:28). He thirsted to awake in us a holy, spiritual, heavenly thirst. Just as he extinguished and satisfied our spiritual hunger and thirst, so we ought to satisfy his hunger and thirst. He hungered and thirsted more for us than we do for him as John 4:34 says: *"My food is to do the will of God."* God's will, however, is the blessedness of men. If we thirst as much for him as he for us, he will with his spirit, mildly and sweetly, give us something to drink, so that streams of living water will flow into our bodies, that is, everything will be spiritual, gracious, loving, and consolatory for us. Indeed, he will give us to drink a great stream of his goodness, so that our body and soul and all our powers will rejoice in God as if a great stream of heavenly joy flowed into our souls. There is nothing so great as the human soul in its joy and freedom that contain God, Heaven, and earth. There is nothing so small as the human soul in its nothingness and humility if it humbles itself under all creatures before God.

37

HE WHO DOES NOT FOLLOW CHRIST WITH FAITH, A HOLY LIFE, AND CONTINUAL REPENTANCE CANNOT BE REDEEMED BECAUSE OF THE BLINDNESS OF HIS HEART BUT MUST REMAIN IN ETERNAL DARKNESS. HE CANNOT KNOW CHRIST PROPERLY NOR CAN HE HAVE A PART IN HIM OR IN HIS COMMUNITY

God is light and in Him is no darkness at all. If we say we have fellowship with Him or we walk in darkness, we lie and do not live according to the truth. But if we walk in the light as he is in the light, we have fellowship with one another (1 John 1:5–7).

To understand light and darkness properly, we must notice the description and definition of light.

God is light says Saint John (1 John 1:5). However, what is God? God is a spiritual, eternal, infinite being, all powerful, merciful, gracious, righteous, holy and true, only wise, of unspeakable love and faithfulness. God, the Father, Son, and Holy Spirit, one in being but three in persons, is the highest Good and is the essential Good in everything and is the true eternal light. Therefore, he who turns from God, from his love, mercy, righteousness, and truth, turns away from his light and falls into darkness. On the other hand, if God is a light, the Devil must be darkness, and if God is love, the Devil must be pure wrath, scorn, enmity, hate and envy, sin and vice. He who now turns himself to sin turns himself to darkness and to the Devil and cannot be redeemed from this until he turns away from darkness to the light, from sin to righteousness, from vice to virtue, from the Devil to God (Acts 26:18).

This is called repentance and faith alone brings it about. He who believes on Christ repents and turns from his sins, that is, from the Devil to Christ. Just as Adam turned by his sins from God to the Devil, so man, by true repentance and cessation from sin, turns himself from the Devil to his beloved God.

From this it follows that a man cannot be enlightened without converting from his sins to God, for *what does light have to do with darkness* (2 Cor. 6:14)? Refusal to be repentant is darkness and with it the light of the true knowledge of Christ has no fellowship. It is impossible for those who are able to be enlightened by the spirit and light of eternal truth to live in darkness and impenitence. Therefore, Saint Paul speaks to the Jews in 2 Corinthians 3:16: *"When a man turns to the Lord, the veil is removed,"* that is, darkness, blindness, and ignorance, and he is enlightened in Christ.

The greatest blindness and darkness of the human heart is unbelief with all its fruits, pride, covetousness, fleshly lust, wrath, and so forth. He who is possessed with these cannot know Christ, the true light, and much less can he properly believe on him, trust on him, and be blessed through him. How can a man who is full of stinking pride know the humble heart of Christ? How can he who is full of fierce wrath and envy know the merciful heart of Christ? How can he who is full of inconsistency and the search for vengeance know the great patience of Christ? He who does not understand the meekness, humility, and patience of Christ does not properly understand Christ or faith either. If you wish to know Christ properly, you must have, by faith, a heart like he had; you must taste his meekness, humility, and patience in your heart and then you will know who Christ is. If you wish to know a good fruit and plant, you must touch and taste it and then you know it. So too it is with Christ, the tree of life. Taste and touch in faith his humility, meekness, and patience; eat of his fruit and you will find rest for your soul and will receive divine consolation, the divine grace. Otherwise, your soul will find no rest. God's grace and consolation cannot bring light into a faithless heart in which Christ's meekness and humility does not exist, for to the humble he gives grace (1 Pet. 5:5).

What good is Christ for a man who does not want to have any fellowship with him? Now those who live in the darkness of sin have no fellowship with the light that is Christ. Therefore he is of no use to them. Thus John says in the passage noted [I John 1:6–7 . . . and in the following chapter 2:8].

As long as a man remains in such sins as in the most frightful darkness, he cannot be enlightened by Christ, the true light, nor come to a true knowledge of God, for if a man is to properly understand God and Christ he must know that God is pure grace

163

and love. No one can know what love is, however, except the person who does it and has it himself. Thus, the knowledge of each thing arises out of experience, out of the act and discovery, out of the work of truth. He who does not practice love does not know what love is, even if he speaks much about it. Christ is pure love, humility, meekness, patience, and simple virtue. He who does not practice this does not know who Christ is, and he does not know him even if he bears his name and speaks much about him. God's Word is pure spirit and he who does not walk and live in the spirit does not know what God's Word is, even if he speaks much about it. Who can know what love is who has not practiced any love? Knowledge and understanding proceed out of experience. How can one know what light is who has sat in a dark tower all the days of his life and has not seen light? Now faith and Christian life are light in man as the Lord said in Matthew 5:16: *"Let your light so shine before men that they may see your good works and give glory to your Father who is in heaven."*

If we contemplate the holy life of Christ, we see it as pure love. Let us learn from him in true faith his love, humility, meekness, and patience just as he commanded us. Thus, we will be glorified and enlightened with this light in his image as with Christ himself, who is the true, eternal light, as Saint Paul said in Ephesians 5:14: *"Awake you who sleep, in sins and the pleasures of the flesh, and you will be enlightened in Christ."*

Therefore, those who do not awake from the sinful sleep of this world, the lust of the eyes, the lust of the flesh, and the private life, cannot be enlightened by Christ.

That person is enlightened who appropriates the noble life of Christ to himself and follows Christ in faith. He who does not follow Christ in his life loves darkness more than light and, there-fore, he is not enlightened, as Christ said in John 8:12: *"I am the light of the world and he who follows after me, in faith, love, hope, patience, meekness, humility, the fear of God, and prayer, he will not walk in darkness but will have the light of life."* The true followers of Christ only have the light of life, that is, the true enlightenment and light of the knowledge of Jesus Christ. Because of Christian faith and life, Saint Paul called the believer a light as he said in Ephesians 5:8: *"Once you were in darkness but now you are light in the Lord."* Saint Paul understood this of faith and other Christian virtues (1 Thess. 5:5 – 8).

The Holy Spirit flees from the deceitful and *in every generation passes into holy souls and makes them friends of God and prophets* (Wis. [1:5;] 7:27). Since the spirit flees the godless, how can they be enlightened? Indeed, the Lord says in John 14:17, *The world cannot receive the Holy Spirit*, that is, carnal, unrepentant people.

So that man might have a perfect example of all the virtues, the Son of God became man and with his holy, virtuous life he became a light to the world so that all men should follow him, believe on him, and be enlightened by him. The pagans, who did not love virtue so much, mocked the Christians, since they knew that Christ was pure virtue and yet they did not follow him in their lives. Plato, Aristotle, Cicero, Seneca, and the wisest pagans said: "If a man sees virtue it will shine as brightly as the morning star." Those who have seen Christ in faith have seen this beautiful morning star, indeed, the Word of life itself, and touched it with their hands (1 John 2:1). If the pagans loved virtue, and desired to see it, how much more ought Christians to love it, for Christ is virtue alone, love alone, and meekness alone, indeed, God himself.

"*To love Christ*," says Paul in Ephesians 3:19, "*is better than to know everything.*" He who loves him loves his humility and meekness and eagerly takes this to himself out of love for Christ. Then he is enlightened and daily glorified in the image of Christ (2 Cor. 3:18). "*To the humble, God gives grace,*" says Peter in 1 Peter 5:5. Therefore, Bernard says, "Flumina gratiae deorsum non sursum fluunt" (The streams of grace flow under us and over us). How is the grace of light and knowledge of God to come to man who does not walk in the holy life of Christ, but in the path of Lucifer? *Faith and the fear which comes with faith does not let us be unfruitful in the knowledge of Christ* (2 Pet. 1:8). Christ lives in the humble man, and knowledge of power and might and of the fear of God rests upon him as it did upon Christ himself. Christ is in the man in whom his light and life is, since all of this is he himself. Therefore, the gifts of the Holy Spirit rest in such men as they did in Christ himself as Isaiah 11:2 has pointed out.

Therefore, Peter said in Acts 2:38, *Repent and you will receive the gifts of the Holy Spirit* —the Spirit of God that enlightens the heart rests only in the repentant and faithful.

He who is redeemed from the blindness of his heart and from eternal darkness, indeed, from the Devil himself, let him follow

Christ according to faith in true conversion and improvement. The nearer he is to Christ, the nearer he is to the eternal light; the nearer he is to unbelief, the nearer to the Devil and darkness. All this hangs together: faith, Christ, and all virtues; and disbelief, the Devil, and all sins.

The holy apostles followed Christ in faith, denied the world, denied themselves, denied everything they had, and lived in unity. As a result, they were enlightened from above and received the Holy Spirit (Acts 2:1ff.). A rich young man (Lk. 18:23) did not want to do this but he remained in the darkness of this world and was not enlightened to eternal life. *For he who loves the world does not have the love of the Father in him* (1 John 2:15).

Therefore, John said in 1 John 2:11, "*He who does not love is in darkness and walks in darkness and does not know where he is going, because the darkness has blinded his eyes.* In all his sermons, Tauler says that without righteous practice of faith, without dying, denial, and rejection of oneself, without turning into one's heart, without the inner, still Sabbath of the soul, no man can discover in himself the divine light.

In a word, insofar as the works of darkness are extinguished in man, the man will be enlightened. Again, the more evil nature, flesh, and the world rule in man, such as the lust of the eyes, the lust of the flesh, and the pride of life, the more will darkness be in man and the less grace, light, spirit, God, and Christ. Therefore, he cannot be enlightened without true repentance.

The person who does not wish to pay for one sin gives cause for many sins to arise. One sin grows out of another and spreads like a weed. Just as darkness always grows and becomes greater, the further away the sun goes, so the further away the noble life of Christ is from us, the more sin and darkness grows in us until one finds oneself in eternal darkness. On the other hand, the person who begins with one virtue, through the power of God's grace, discovers that it grows in him and matures into others, for all hang together, as Saint Peter in 2 Peter 1:5–8 points out, making a beautiful golden chain: "*Make every effort to supplement your faith with virtue, and virtue with knowledge, and knowledge with self-control, and self-control with steadfastness, and steadfastness with godliness, and godliness with brotherly affection, and brotherly affection with love, for if these things are yours and abound, they keep you from being ineffective or unfruit-*

ful in the knowledge of our Lord Jesus Christ," that is, he who does not practice these virtues does not know who Christ is. The person who grows in these virtues through faith grows in Christ. The man who is wrathful, covetous, proud, and impatient has not matured much in Christ but in Satan.

We are to grow into a perfect man, that is, as a child matures in largeness of body, so a Christian is to mature in faith and in virtuous life until he becomes a perfect man in Christ. *Whoever lacks these things is blind and short-sighted and has forgotten that he is cleansed from his old sins* (2 Pet. 1:9), that is, Christ has not rooted out and taken away all our sins with his blood and death. Therefore, we are not to continue in sins, but the death of Christ is to be fruitful in us so that we die to our sins and live in Christ. Otherwise, the purification of and payment for our earlier sins is of no use. If we die to our sins, do penance, and believe in Christ, our earlier sins are passed away and forgotten. However, if we do not wish to die to our sins, we keep all the ones we have committed earlier, we must repent for them in eternal damnation and we cannot pay for them [fully] throughout eternity. Thus, a man can be damned for the sake of wrath alone and if he gives it up all his sins are forgiven for Jesus Christ's sake. If he does not do this, Peter says he is blind . . . (2 Pet. 1:9).

This is the chief reason why we should be repentant and leave our sins. Although Christ died for our sins and paid for them all perfectly, we will not participate in his merit and it will be of no use to us if we do not do penance. Although a man has forgiveness for all his sins through the merit of Christ, yet the forgiveness of sins is not promised to the unrepentant person, but to those who leave their sins. The sins that a man does not wish to leave and does not intend to leave are not forgiven but only those over which a man brings true regret and sorrow. Thus it says in Matthew 11:5: *The Gospel is preached to the poor*, that is, forgiveness of sins. An example: There is a man who lived many years here in covetousness and usury as Zacchaeus, in unchastity as Mary Magdalen, in wrath and vengeance as Esau. He heard that he must leave these sins or the blood and death of Christ would be of no value to him. He came then and said: "O God, I am sorry," and he left his sins, prayed to God for grace, and believed on Christ. Thus, all his former sins were taken away and forgiven out of pure grace and this happened without merit because of the holy blood and death of Christ. The person who does not intend to leave his covetousness, wrath, usury, unchastity, and pride, and yet wishes at the same time to have forgiveness of sins, will not get this and must atone for all his sins in hell for he does not have true faith that purifies and makes the heart better. Therefore, Saint Paul clearly and precisely said: *"Those who do this will not inherit the kingdom of God"* (Gal. 5:21). Sin must be left or one will be eternally damned and lost.

If true conversion to God is present, forgiveness of sins and God's grace is also present. If regret and sorrow are present, God's grace is present. If God's grace is present, Christ is present, for outside of him there is no grace. If Christ is present, his precious merit is also present. If his merit is present, the payment of our sins is present. If the payment of our sins is present, righteousness is present. If righteousness is present, peace and a joyous conscience are present, for righteousness and peace kiss one another (Ps. 85:11). If a joyous conscience is present, the Holy Spirit is present. If the Holy Spirit is present, joy is also present, for the spirit is a joyous spirit. If joy is present, eternal life is also present, for eternal life is eternal joy.

Note that the light of eternal life is present in those who live in Christ and in true daily repentance. This is the beginning, and the death of Christ is the foundation. On the other hand, if repentance is not present, forgiveness of sins is not present. If true healing, regret, and sorrow are not present, grace is not present. If grace is not present, Christ is not present. If Christ is not present, his precious merit is not present. If his precious merit is not present, payment for sins is not present. If payment for sins is not present, righteousness is not present. If righteousness is not present, peace and joyous conscience are not present. If joyous conscience is not present, consolation is not present. If consolation is not present, the Holy Spirit is not present. If the Holy Spirit is not present, joy of the heart and of conscience is not present. If joy is not present, eternal life is not present, but only death, hell, damnation, and eternal darkness.

Note that the person who does not follow Christ in his life through true repentance cannot be redeemed from the blindness of his heart, indeed, from the eternal darkness.

38

THE UNCHRISTIAN LIFE IS THE CAUSE OF FALSE, MISLEADING DOCTRINE, HARDNESS OF HEART, AND BLINDNESS. ON THE ETERNAL ELECTION

The light is with you for a little longer. Walk while you have the light, lest the darkness overtake you (Jn. 12:35).

Because Christ and faith are denied by an ungodly life and almost done away with, what will happen to his doctrine? His doctrine, word, and sacrament were given to us that they might be practiced in a holy life and that, out of word and sacrament, a newborn, holy, spiritual man ought to come forth as a good fruit out of a noble seed. That person is a Christian who is born anew out of spirit, word, and sacrament, as out of Christ. He believes on Christ and lives in Christ. As a child is brought up by his father, so a Christian is brought up by God and Christ through faith.

Since we do not wish to practice Christ's teaching and life, but act against it with our lives, how are we able to be born out of God and what good is his teaching to do us? What good is his light, then, since we walk in darkness? If the light fades, darkness must come, with false teaching, error, and deception. Therefore, the Lord warned us when he said: *Beloved children walk in the light while you have the light, lest the darkness overtake you*, that is, error, deception, hardness of heart, darkness, and blindness, just as hardness of heart came upon the Pharoah, the Jews, and Julian—who was by his punishment finally convinced in his conscience that the crucified Christ still lived and was a true God since he said "Vicisti tandem Galileae" [You have conquered finally, Galilean]. It would have been better had he said "Miserere" [Have mercy on me] but he could not say this because of his hardness of heart. He had despised and rejected the grace of Christ. Therefore, it did not come to him.

Such hardness of heart is the true darkness, which finally falls upon those who will not wish to walk in the light. It is a proper punishment for those who sin against the truth as Pharoah did: *"Who is the Lord that I should heed his voice, I do not know the Lord"* (Ex.

5:2). Therefore, he had to feel the Lord's power and God demonstrated his might and strength to him and established him as an example, made him a drama and spectacle for the whole world so that man might experience how God could act against man.

Since the Jews would not listen, God struck them with blindness and hardness of heart as Moses had long before prophesied would happen to them (Deut. 28, 32:21): *"If you will not hear my voice, I will strike you with blindness and hardness of heart."* Thereafter they were set to work (Is. 6:9). Out of this we can see that such a hardening of the heart is a proper punishment for unbelief and the rejection of God and his truth, as Saint Paul clearly stated in 2 Thessalonians 2:10–12. . . . Here we see out of what causes such blinding and hardening of the heart arises.

The person from whom God takes away his promised grace is harshly struck down and cannot arise again. This happened to Pharoah and Julian. The person from whom God has withdrawn his light must truly remain in darkness. He withdraws his light from no one, however, except from those who do not wish to walk in the light. He withdraws his grace from no one except those who force it away from themselves.

Therefore, Paul in Romans 9:18 openly says: *"He has mercy on whom he will have mercy and he hardens the heart of whomever he wills."* He wishes to have mercy on all those who will take his mercy and he will harden all those who sin against the offered grace and push it away from themselves, as Paul clearly says concerning the Jews in Acts 13:46: *"Since you thrust the word from you, and judge yourselves unworthy of eternal life, behold, we turn to the Gentiles."* The Gentiles were happy however, praised the word, and were faithful. As a result, many of them were brought to eternal life, that is, as many of them who did not thrust away from themselves the word of grace as the means of faith. Since the Jews did this, they were not able to be faithful, for God ordained no one to life who thrust his word away from himself.

The decree of election and ordination to life occurred in Christ with this addition: God offered his grace alone through the Gospel and whoever would take it was ordained to eternal life, but those who thrust it away from themselves considered themselves not worthy of eternal life, as Saint Paul said, that is, they brought it about themselves that they were not worthy of eternal life and they closed themselves off from the grace intended for all and they blotted out their names from the Book of Life, that is, out of Christ, through their hardness of heart, by which they thrust the Word of God away from themselves. Therefore they were not able to be faithful.

Now, however, they not only thrust God's word away from themselves, do not take for themselves teaching from Christ as the Jews and Turks, but also do not walk in Christ's footsteps or take on his holy life, and do not wish to walk in the light but in darkness. Therefore, God draws away the light of his Word and of pure teaching. For he says in John 8:12: "*I am the light of the world, he who follows me walks not in darkness, but has the light of light.*"

From this it follows that the person who does not follow Christ in his life must walk in darkness, that is, be counselled in error, deceived, hardened, and blinded. Look on the proud, the pompous, the glorious, the wise, the learned, and the mighty of this world, how they are counselled in error, deceived, and blinded. What is the cause? They do not live in Christ, they do not follow him in their life, and therefore they cannot have the light of life.

What is the cause of so much deception and error, which Saint Paul in 2 Thessalonians 2:9 called the working of Satan and the lying power? These arise more and more because the whole world does not follow Christ in its life. *What fellowship has light with darkness? What accord has Christ with Belial?* (2 Cor. 6:15), that is, the pure teaching and light of the knowledge of God does not remain with those who live in the Devil, in darkness, in pride, covetousness, and pleasure, for how shall the pure, divine teaching remain where an impure, ungodly life is practiced? Pure teaching and an impure life do not go together and have no fellowship.

If we wish to keep his teaching, we must follow another path and cease to follow an unchristian life. We must follow the Lord Christ, awake from our sins, and thus be enlightened by Christ with the light of true faith (Eph. 5:14). Therefore, he who does not walk in the footsteps of Christ in his love, humility, meekness, patience, and fear of God must be deceived, for he does not go on the way that leads to truth.

If we live in Christ alone and walk in love and humility and direct our total energy and theology to this, we are to mortify the flesh and live in Christ, Adam is to die in us and Christ to live in us, we are to conquer ourselves and are able to overcome the flesh, the Devil, and the world. [If this were the case] there would not be so much disputation in doctrine and all heretics would fall by themselves.

Why is it that four hundred false prophets led Ahab astray and counselled him to go to war (1 Kings 22:6)? The answer is his godless, tyrannical life. Out of such a life follows such a false light that he had to believe lies that led him to his own destruction. The true Prophet Micah told him the truth, that he would be overcome in the war, but he would not believe him. The false prophets said that he would gain peace. This new lie, he believed. As a result, the dogs licked his blood, as he deserved.

One may say as Saint Paul did in 2 Corinthians 4:4, *"The god of this world has blinded the minds of the unbelievers to keep them from seeing the light of the Gospel."* Indeed, what is this other than what God in Isaiah 29:13–14, 1 Corinthians 1:19, warned against all hypocrites who speak of Christ and his teaching with their mouths and deny it with their deeds? Will they not be given false prophets by God just as were given to Ahab? He said clearly enough, *"People draw near to me with their mouth and honor me with their lips, while their hearts are far from me, but the wisdom of their wise men shall perish and the understanding of their discerning men shall be hid, their prophets and seers shall be blinded so that the Word of the Lord shall become as a sealed book or as one which they can not read"* (Is. 29:13–14).

To the Jews, Saint Paul in 2 Corinthians 3:16 said that a covering would hang over their eyes so that they would not be able to see their Messiah in their own prophets; but when a man turns to the Lord the veil is removed.

39

THE PURITY OF TEACHING AND OF THE DIVINE WORD IS NOT MAINTAINED ALONE WITH DISPUTATIONS AND MANY BOOKS BUT ALSO WITH TRUE REPENTANCE AND HOLY LIFE

Follow the pattern of the sound words which you have heard from me, in the faith and love which are in Christ Jesus. Guard the truth which has been entrusted to you by the Holy Spirit who dwells within us (2 Tim. 1:13–14).

The pure teaching and truth of the Holy Christian faith must necessarily answer sects and heretics and defend itself according to the example of the holy prophets who preached firmly against the false and idolatrous prophets in the Old Testament. It must also follow the example of the Son of God who earnestly disputed against the Pharisees and scribes in Jerusalem. Again, it must follow the example of John the Evangelist who wrote his gospel against the heretics Ebion and Cerinthus and who wrote his Revelation against the false church of the Nicolites and others. We also see how Saint Paul defended the doctrine of the justification by faith (Rom. 3:21ff., 4:1ff.), of good works (2 Cor. 9:8ff.), of the resurrection of the dead (1 Cor. 15:1ff.), and of Christian freedom (Gal. 5:1ff.) and other doctrines. These examples were followed and continued also by the holy bishops and fathers of the early Church against the pagan idolatrous religion and other heretics who arose out of it. These men wrote many well-argued defenses. To this end the chief councils were set up by the great Christian emperors against the arch-heretics Arius, Marcedonius, Nestorius, and Eutyches and in our own time the false practices of the Papists and other sects have been made known throughout the whole world by that precious man Dr. Martin Luther and his writings.

It is not enough only to write against sects and heretics, to preach and dispute, to maintain pure doctrine and true religion as the Apostle Paul indicated (Tit. 1:9) so that one may dispute with and conquer those who contradict sound doctrine. These activities have fallen into great misuse in our time so that beside the many, heavy disputations, polemical sermons, writings and tracts, Christian life, true repentance, godliness, and Christian love are almost forgotten. It is as if Christianity consisted only in disputations and the production of polemical books, and not far more in seeing to it that the Holy Gospel and the teaching of Christ is practiced in a holy life.

1. Look at the examples of the holy prophets and apostles, indeed, the Son of God himself. They not only strove firmly against false prophets and idolaters but they also firmly undertook repentance and a Christian life and spoke out in opposition so that religion and worship would not be destroyed by impenitence and godless life, so that the Church would not be laid waste and the lands and peoples punished with hunger, war, and pestilence as experience has indicated can happen. Isaiah 5:6 states that if there are not grapes to be found in the vineyard of the Lord but only wild grapes, the Lord God will lay the vineyard waste. This is indeed an earnest warning that godlessness is the cause of God's withdrawing his word from us. What did the Lord Christ preach other in John 12:35: *"Walk in the light while you have it so that you do not fall into darkness?"* What is it to walk in the light other than to follow Christ in life? What is it to fall into darkness other than to lose the pure doctrine of the Gospel? From this it is thus clear that no one without true repentance and a holy life can be enlightened with the light of truth. For the Holy Spirit, which enlightens the heart, flees from the godless and continually gives itself to holy souls and makes prophets and friends of God (Wis. 7:27). *The fear of the Lord is the beginning of wisdom* says Psalm 111:10 and therefore godlessness is the beginning of foolishness and blindness.

2. Thus, true Christian knowledge and understanding of Christ and pure teaching does not consist alone in words but in deed and in a holy life as Saint Paul says in Titus 1:16. . . . In this passage we hear that Christ and his word are denied by a godless life, indeed, more clearly denied than it is with words (2 Tim. 3:5 . . .). What kind of true knowledge of Christ can there be that one does not demonstrate in deed? He who has not tasted and discovered Christian love in his heart cannot know Christ properly. How is one to confess in his need? A person who confesses Christ's teaching and not his life confesses only half of Christ, and he who

preaches Christ's teaching and not his life preaches only half of Christ. There is much written and disputed concerning teaching but little concerning life. We may be well served with polemical books on doctrine, but true repentance and Christian life are served little with them. For what is teaching without life? [It is] a tree without fruit. Truly, he who does not follow Christ in his life does not follow him in his teaching, for the chief article of the teaching of Christ is: *Love with a pure heart, a good conscience and a sincere faith* (1 Tim. 1:5). As a result, many a man learns much concerning discussion and disputation over polemical articles so that he might look good, but in his heart he is an evil man full of pride, envy, and covetousness, and there is no basilisk worse. Saint Paul, not without reason, ties faith and love together (2 Tim. 1:13) and this is to indicate that teaching and life are to agree together.

3. We do not of course say that through our power and piety blessedness is achieved, for we are brought to blessedness through the power of God (1 Pet. 1:5). Thus, it is clear that a godless life stands against the Holy Spirit with all his gifts among which the gifts of faith, knowledge, understanding, and wisdom are not the smallest. How can the truth of pure doctrine be upheld without a holy life? Clearly, the godless who do not follow Christ cannot be enlightened with the true light. On the other hand, those who walk in the light, that is, who follow Christ in their life, are enlightened by the true light (Jn. 1:9), which is Christ and which protects them from all error. The holy and spiritual Tauler said: "If a man gives himself and resigns himself to God and denies his will and flesh, the Holy Spirit begins to enlighten him and to teach him properly since God keeps the true Sabbath and rest-day in his heart and frees it from all evil lusts, willings and work."

4. Not without cause does the Lord say in John 14:6, "*I am the way, the truth, and the life.*" He calls himself first "the way" because he has pointed the way out to us. How [has he done so] however? [He has done so] not only through his holy teaching but also through his innocent life. His life is nothing other for us than true repentance and conversion to God, which leads us to truth and to life in which the whole of Christianity consists, in which all the books and the commandments are contained. In this Book of Life, namely, Christ, we are to study throughout our life, namely, in true repentance, in living, active faith, in love, hope, meekness,

patience, humility, prayer, and the fear of God. This is the proper path to truth and to life that is in all, Christ himself. He is the narrow way and the small gate (Mt. 7:14), which few find, and the only Book of Life, which few of you study, yet everything is contained in it that is necessary for a Christian. Thus, we do not need any other book for our holiness. The Holy Scriptures do not contain many books so that we might know that Christianity does not consist in numberless books but in the following of the Lord Christ. Thus, Solomon writes in Ecclesiastes 12:12–13: *Of the writing of books, there is no end. The sum of all doctrine is: Fear God and keep his commandments.*

5. What does it mean that the enemy sowed weeds among the wheat while the people slept (Mt. 13:25). [It means] nothing other than that, since they slept in the unrepentance and security of their sins and were drunken in the love of this world and concerned themselves more about temporal things than about eternal things, the enemy spread the seeds of false doctrine everywhere. Indeed, he sowed, in the ground of pride, sects and divisions and rabbles. Through pride both angels and men lost the true light. All error has its source in pride. If Satan and Adam had remained in the humble life of Christ, there would never have come into the world any deception. Therefore, Saint Paul said properly in Ephesians 5:14: *Awake you who sleep and you will be enlightened by Christ.* [He said this] to point out that the enlightenment cannot come unless a man give up the sleep of a sin, that is, unrepentance, security, and godlessness (Acts 2:7 . . . Jn. 14:17 . . .). What is the world, other than pure godless life?

6. What is it that the Lord means [in Matthew 7:20]: "By their fruits you shall know them?" [It means] nothing other than that true and false Christians must be known by the fruits of their lives, not by how much they shout "Lord, Lord." With the appearance of true doctrine, false Christians cover themselves over as with the fleece of a sheep. In their hearts they are yet less than true Christians. From an evil life no one can make any other judgment concerning doctrine but that the doctrine must also be false and evil since the life is evil. Thus, the Anabaptists and Papists make judgments concerning our doctrine. Are they wrong? Yes, for it does not follow in any way that a doctrine must be false because the people practice it with a godless life. If this were so, Christ and the

apostles must have taught falsity, for there were so many evil people at their time. Therefore, an evil life is no test of doctrine but of person, whether one is a false or a true Christian if he lives and teaches in a fashion different from correct faith and acts against faith. The Lord Christ says no to this. There are false Christians, evil, unfruitful trees that belong in the fire (Mt. 7:19).

7. And finally there is true faith that is active through love (Gal. 5:6), by which man becomes a new creature, by which he is newborn, by which he is united with God, by which Christ dwells in us (Eph. 3:17), lives in us, and works in us, by which the kingdom of God is established in us, by which the Holy Spirit enlightens and purifies our hearts (Eph. 4:23). On this, there are many beautiful passages. One Corinthians 6:17 reads: *He who is united to the Lord becomes one spirit with him*. What does it mean "to be one spirit" with Christ other than to be of a like mind, heart, and thought with Christ? This is indeed the new, holy, noble life of Christ in us. Again, 2 Corinthians 5:17 reads: *If anyone is in Christ, he is a new creature*. What does it mean "to be in Christ?" It does not only mean to believe on him but also to live in him. Again, Hosea 2:19 reads: *I will be betrothed to you in eternity, indeed, I will promise myself to you in faith*. What is this other than that a man will become completely, spiritually united with Christ so that where faith is, there is Christ. Where Christ is, a holy life exists in man. Where Christ's life is there is his love and where his love is, there is God himself, for God is love. There also is the Holy Spirit. Everything that is necessary must be together there and cling together as a head with its members and as a source out of which activity and fruits are to follow. This relationship and unity of Christian faith and life is described in 2 Peter 1:5ff. *"Make every effort to supplement your faith with virtue and virtue with knowledge, and knowledge with self-control, and self-control with steadfastness, and steadfastness with godliness, and godliness with brotherly affections, and brotherly affection with love. If these things richly exist in you, you do not let them become bad or unfruitful in the knowledge of our Lord Jesus Christ. The person who does not have these is blind and taps with his hand and forgets his purification from former sins.* Peter says expressly: The person who does not have such unity and Christian faith does not know Christ; he has lost faith and walks in darkness. That is true faith which renews and makes the whole man alive in Christ so that Christ lives and remains in him and he in Christ.

40
SOME BEAUTIFUL RULES FOR A CHRISTIAN LIFE

Train yourself in godliness, for while bodily training is of some value, godliness is a value in every way, as it holds promise for the present life and also for the life to come (1 Tim. 4:7–8).

This verse is a description of the Christian life and teaches us how a Christian is to carry out his life in the best possible way, namely, with godliness that contains all Christian virtues in itself. The apostle gives two significant motives. First, it is of use in every way. If man's godliness is in all his walks, works, and deeds, it makes everything good and chaste and blesses everything. Second, it has its reward in this life, as is to be seen in the cases of Joseph, Daniel, and others. In the eternal life we will reap without ceasing (Gal. 6:9).

I
If you are not able to practice a perfect life as is commanded in God's word and as you very much would like to, you are nevertheless to wish [to practice this life]. Such holy desires are truly pleasing to God and God accepts them as acts, for he looks on the heart and not on works. Nevertheless, at all times you are to mortify your flesh and not allow it to rule.

II
In all things that you think or do, see to it that you protect purity of heart and that you do not become impure with proud thoughts, words, and deeds, with wrath and similar carnal and devilish works, for through these your heart will be opened up to Satan and closed to God.

III
Endeavor to maintain the freedom of your soul so that you do not make it into a servant and thing possessed by earthly things by your inordinate desire for temporal goods, for your soul is nobler than the whole world. How then are you to sell it and make it

subservient to ignoble, temporal things of nothingness, which are nothing in themselves, and allow your heart to cling to these nothingnesses?

IV

Shun the sorrow of this world, for it brings about death that arises out of covetousness, envy, out of sorrow for food, and out of unbelief and impatience. Divine sorrow, which comes out of the knowledge of sins and out of a consideration of the eternal pains of hell, is sanctifying and brings about regret for blessedness that no one regrets, and it begets joy and peace in God (2 Cor. 7:10). No man ought to be sorrowful for temporal things but for his sins.

V

If you cannot take up your cross with joy as is intended for you to do, take it up at least with patience and humility and let the divine providence and the divine will of God be your consolation at all times. God's will is good at all times and seeks our best and our blessedness in all things. If God wishes that you be sad or happy, rich or poor in spirit, low or high, honored or unhonored, know that it is for your good and that it is thus his pleasure. God's pleasure is to be your pleasure, indeed [it is to be] your consolation that God deals with you as it pleases him and that he thereby seeks your blessedness (Ecclus. 39:21 . . . Ps. 145:17 . . .). It is always better to allow God to work and perfect his will in you and by you, for it is always directed to good, than for you to perfect your will in yourself, a will that is always directed to evil.

VI

If God gives you heavenly consolation and joy, accept it with humble thanks. If God, however, takes away his consolation, know that this is a mortification of the flesh and is better than the joy of the spirit. Pain and suffering make a sinful man much healthier than do joy and happiness. Many of you come by too great spiritual joy into spiritual pride. God knows well whom he will lead into eternal life through the path of full, heavenly consolation and light and whom he will lead through an unlovely, sad, stony, and harsh path. It is much better for you that you thus go into eternal life in the manner in which divine wisdom ordains it for you, than in the manner your own will and pleasure demands (Eccles. 7:4 . . .).

179

VII

If you cannot bring to your beloved God many and great offerings such as meditation, prayer, and thanksgiving, bring to him what you have and can, and with these, a good will and holy desires, and hope that you might please him in your worship. To have such a holy desire, indeed, to wish to have one, is not a small gift or sacrifice. It, too, pleases God. Our meditation, holy desires, prayer, and thanksgiving are as great before God as we desire them to be. God does not demand more from you than his grace works in you and you cannot give him more than he has given you. Pray to your Lord Jesus Christ that he make your sacrifice and gifts perfect with his perfect sacrifice for our perfection is in him; in us, it is in part. Speak as follows: Dear God and Father, take my meditation, faith, prayer, and thanksgiving in your dear Son, and do not look on it as it is in itself but [as it is] in Christ; thus, it will give you pleasure as a perfect work; my Lord Jesus will make that perfect which is lacking in me. Thus, our meditation, prayer, and thanksgiving succeeds and even if it is in itself weak and dark, and has its shortcomings, it is a great perfection, a great light and glory from the merit of Christ. It is unlovely in the same way as a naked, miserable child is when he is naked and unclean. If a man adorns it, however, and cleanses it, it brings pleasure. Your old acts are in themselves nothing, but if they are adorned with Christ's perfection, all your works truly please God. Apples that are brought in in golden trays are seen as particularly valuable. Apples in themselves are not considered so great, but they are more lovely if they are brought in in golden trays. So it is with our prayer, meditation, and thanksgiving in Christ (Eph. 1:6 . . .).

VIII

Your sins and manifold trespasses ought indeed to make you very sorrowful, but not dejected. Even if they are many, know that much more grace is present with God and much more mercy (Ps. 130:7). If they are great, remember that Christ's merit is greater (Ps. 51:2 . . .). If you are sorry for your sins God also regrets his punishment (Ezek. 33:11, 18:23). The forgiveness of sins follows regret. It occurs as often as the sinner is sorrowful. As soon as the leper said to the Lord in Matthew 8:2–3, *"Lord you can truly cleanse me,"* in that very moment the Lord said to him *"I will do so; be cleansed."* God also purifies you as quickly internally and says *"Take heart, my son; your sins are forgiven*" (Mt. 9:2). This is an image and mirror of internal purification and the forgiveness of sins. This great mercy of God toward men ought not to cause man to sin more, but to love God more and more deeply (Ps. 103:1 . . .).

IX

External insult, rejection, and injury you are to not only accept without anger, wrath, and the desire for vengeance, but you are to think also that it is a test of your heart by which God wishes to reveal what is hidden in you, whether there is meekness and humility in you or whether there is pride and wrath. *Qualis quisque apud se latet, illata contumelia probat* [When someone suffers insult his actions thereafter indicate what is hidden in him]. If there is meekness and humility in you, you will conquer all insult with meekness. (1) Indeed, you will consider it to be a chastisement of the almighty, as David said when Shimei attacked him . . . (2 Sam. 16:10). (2) The suffering of insult is a great part of the injury that Christ suffered and that the true members of Christ must bear as Hebrews 13:13 indicates: *"Let us go forth to him outside the camp bearing abuse for him."* Note with how meek a heart Christ bore his abuse. For the sake of his patient heart we, too, are to bear our abuse with meekness. Do not say: "Ah, ought I to suffer this from such a knave?" Ah, for the meekness and the patient heart of Christ you are to suffer it. (3) God is so good and faithful that he will give much more honor and grace for undeserved injury. King David held it for a certain sign that God would honor him again when he suffered injury from Shimei and this indeed came about, for he said: *"It may be that the Lord will look upon my affliction and that the Lord will repay me with good for this cursing of me today"* (2 Sam. 16:12). Therefore, you have not to be concerned what man says against you but you should be happy that the spirit of glory stands above those who despise and curse, as Saint Peter says in 1 Peter 4:14.

X

You are to learn to conquer and forgive all your enemies and wrongdoers with good deeds and goodness. The search for vengeance, wrath, and striking back does not make one victorious over an enemy because *in virtue est victoria, non in vitio* (the victory is in virtue not in vice). Wrath, the desire for vengeance, and striking back are sins and vices and therefore man cannot conquer with them, but only with virtue. No Devil drives out another Devil and no vice will drive out another vice and no search for vengeance or blow will conquer one who is antagonistic to you but it will only make him worse. If someone saw a person who was full of curses and evil sayings and wished to strike him with his fists, would he heal him? Of course not. An evil, poisonous man is full of curses and, therefore, one must heal him with softness. Look what the Lord God himself did to conquer us. Did he not conquer our evil with goodness, our wrath with love? Did not his goodness attract us to repentance? This path Saint Paul described in Romans 12:21. . . . This is the victory.

XI

If you see that someone else has received a gift from God that you do not have, do not envy that, or begrudge it, but rejoice in the fact and thank God for it. The elect and the faithful are one body, and a gift, an adornment of one faithful member, is directed to the whole body and its honor. On the other hand, if you see someone in misery you are to hold it for your own misery and sorrow over it, for it is a common human sorrow under which all flesh is cast. The man who has no compassion and no mercy is not a member of the body of Christ. Did not Christ consider our misery to be his own and thereby redeem us from our misery? Therefore, Saint Paul said: *"Bear one another's burdens and so fulfill the law of Christ"* (Gal. 6:2).

XII

A distinction is to be made between loving and hating one's neighbor. You are indeed to hate sins and vices in man as the work of the Devil, but you are not to hate the man himself but to have mercy on him, since such vices dwell in him, and you are to pray to God for him as the Lord Jesus Christ on the cross prayed for the persons who did evil to him (Lk. 23:34). You are also to know that no man can please God who hates his neighbor within himself. God's pleasure is to help all men (1 Tim. 2:3). If you seek the destruction of a man, that action is against God and against God's pleasure. Therefore, no man can well please God who seeks the destruction of another. The Son of Man has come not to destroy men's lives but to save them (Lk. 9:56).

XIII

Since you know very well that all men are sinners and filled with error you are to consider yourself as the weakest and most erring man and as the greatest sinner, *Omnes homines fragiles, puta te autem fagiliorem neminem.* (1) Under God all men stand in the same damnation and by God there is no distinction. *We have all sinned and fall short of the glory of God* that we are to have before God (Rom. 3:23). (2) If your neighbor is a greater and more frightful sinner, do not think that because of this you are better before God. *He who thinks that he stands, take heed, lest he fall* (1 Cor. 10:12). If you humble yourself and lower yourself before all men, God will raise you up with his grace. (3) You, indeed, need his grace and mercy as the greatest sinner. And where there is much humility there is much grace. Therefore, Saint Paul considered himself to be the greatest and chief of sinners . . . ([Tim. 1:15–16] . . . 2 Cor. 12:9).

XIV

True enlightenment brings with it the insult of the world. As the children of this world have their inheritance upon this world in temporal honor, passing wealth, earthly glory (which they hold as the greatest treasure), the children of God have their treasure in poverty upon earth, insult, persecution, injury, suffering, death, martyrdom, and pain. Like Moses, they consider the injury suffered for Christ's sake to be higher than the treasures of Egypt (Heb. 11:26). This is true enlightenment.

XV

The true name of a Christian that is written in heaven (Lk. 10:20) is the true knowledge of Jesus Christ in faith, through which we are planted in Christ, indeed, have our names written in Christ as in the Book of Life. From this, living virtues spring forth that God will praise on the final day (Mt. 25:34ff.). On that day, all the treasures gathered together in heaven will be brought forth (1 Tim. 6:19) and all the works that were done in God will be brought to light (Jn. 3:21). One can find no saint who is not honored through such virtue and such virtue will nevermore be forgotten (Ps. 112:6). It is the name written in the Book of Life (Rev. 2:17, 3:12), faith, love, mercy, patience, and similar things. These virtues when practiced indicate true saints and eternal names in heaven. In the Second Book more mention is made of this.

41

PROPER SUMMATION OF THE FIRST BOOK.
THE WHOLE OF CHRISTIANITY CONSISTS IN THE
REESTABLISHMENT OF THE IMAGE OF GOD IN MAN
AND THE ROOTING OUT OF THE IMAGE OF SATAN
IN HIM

And we all, with unveiled face, beholding the glory of the Lord, are being changed into his likeness from one degree of glory to another; for this comes from the Lord who is the spirit (2 Cor. 3:18).

In the true knowledge of Christ, his person, his vocation, his blessings, his heavenly, eternal goods, consists eternal life (Jn. 17:3). All this is ignited by the Holy Spirit in our hearts as a new light that becomes ever brighter and clearer as a polished brass or mirror, or as a small child grows and matures daily in body. A man is newborn in his conversion if the righteousness of Christ is given to him through faith. Then the image of God will be daily renewed. He is not yet, however, a perfect man (Eph. 4:13) but a child who must yet be trained by the Holy Spirit and become conformed from day to day with Christ Jesus.

The whole of the Christian life upon earth is nothing other and can be nothing other than a raising up of the image of God in a faithful man. Thereby, he continually lives in the new birth and the old birth is daily extinguished and mortified in him (Rom. 6:4). This must be begun in this life but will be perfected in the next. If he has not so begun before the final judgment day and before his death, it can nevermore throughout eternity be established in him. In conclusion, I wish to reiterate once again what the image of God and the image of Satan is, for in these two things true Christianity consists. I wish also to clarify many articles of the Scripture: original sin, free will, repentance, faith, justification, prayer, the new birth, renewal, sanctification, the new life, and obedience. On these, note the following:

The soul of man is immortal soul given glorious powers by God, namely, understanding, will, memory, and the powers of movement and desire.

This soul held itself to God and set forth the image of God as a portrait within itself so that God and his eternal, unchangeable will, Christ Jesus our Lord, and the Holy Spirit might be seen and known in the soul of man as in a mirror. This is what Saint Paul refers to when he says that the glory of the Lord shone forth in the renewed image of God (2 Cor. 3:18).

God's substance and being is good and holy and thus the substance and being of the soul in the beginning and in its original was good and holy. As in God's being there is no evil, so also there was no evil in the human soul. Everything that was in the soul was good just as it was in God who is the only Good (Deut. 32:4; Ps. 92:15). As God was rational and wise, so the human soul was also rational and wise, full of the knowledge of God, full of spiritual, heavenly, eternal wisdom. The divine wisdom had arranged all things by measure and number and weight (Wis. 11:21) and knew all heavenly and earthly powers in all creatures and this light shone also in the mind of man.

Just as the understanding of the human soul was holy, so also was man's will and in all things the will was conformed to the will of God. The human soul was like God, righteous, good, and merciful, long-suffering, patient, kind, meek, true, and chaste (Ex. 34:6; Ps. 103:8; Joel 2:13; Jon. 4:2). As the will of man was conformed to the will of God, so also all its affections, desires, lusts, and the movements of its heart were holy and were conformed to the divine, eternal mind and movements in a perfect way. As God is love, so also the affections and movements of man were nothing but pure love. As God the Father, Son, and Holy Spirit are bound together and united with an unspeakable, eternal love (Jn. 10:30, 17:11), so all the affections, movements, and desires of man's soul were ignited with a pure, perfect, clean, total, burning love from the whole soul and from all its powers (Deut. 6:5; 1 Cor. 13:4). Man, therefore, loved God and his honor more than himself.

God's image shone forth in the soul. In a like manner, the body was the image of the soul with all its living, bodily powers and was holy, pure, without any inordinate movements and lusts, beautiful, lovely, and glorious, at all times healthy and filled with energy, immortal with all its internal and external powers and thoughts, without any sadness, suffering, pain, weariness, sickness, age, and death. In a word, the whole man was perfect in body and soul; he was holy, righteous, completely pleasing to God. The body must also be holy and conformed to God if man is to be the image of God as Saint Paul says [in 1 Thessalonians 5:23], *Your body, spirit and soul are to be holy*. The body and soul together are a man. He performs his works in a spiritual and physical fashion at the same time and if the holy, righteous soul is to work through the body and in the body, it must have a holy instrument that does not strive against it. As the soul was ignited in the pure love of God, so also the life and power of the body was ignited in love for God and neighbor. As the soul was merciful in all its powers, so also in all its powers the body was moved to mercifulness with it. As godly purity was in the soul, so also the whole body, together with all internal and external powers and thoughts, was ignited in perfect purity and chastity. Thus, the body was conformed to all the virtues of the soul as a holy, coworking instrument. Thus, the first man in his innocence was able to love God with his whole heart and soul and with all his strength and his neighbor as himself (Deut. 6:5; Mt. 22:37). If God commanded the heart, he commanded the whole man with body and soul and all his powers. You must understand the use of the word "heart" in the Scriptures as meaning all the powers of the soul: understanding, will, affections, and desires. When God commanded the soul, he commanded the whole man with all his being, life, and all his powers. These must be conformed to God and renewed in Christ. Thus, we must walk in a new spiritual life and in the spirit (Gal. 5:16; Eph. 4:23).

Just as man had perfect holiness, righteousness, and love, so did he also have the perfect joy of God in his soul and the powers of his life. Wherever there is divine holiness there also is divine joy. These two are together eternal and they are the image of God. If we do not have the perfect holiness and righteousness of God in this life, we must lack also his perfect joy. The righteousness of Christ must be begun in all faithful here on earth so that this spiritual joy may also truly be begun here and be discovered in the kingdom of God by those who have meditated on it and practiced it. God's spiritual joy will be as great in each Christian as is God's love in him (Phil. 4:4; Ps. 63:11; Ps. 84:2–3). Since love will be made perfect on the final day, so also will joy be made perfect as the Lord Christ said in John 16:22: *For love is life and joy alone*. Where his love is not there is no joy, nor life, but only death in which all Devils and unrepentant hardened men will remain eternally. Where does a father find joy? In the love of his children. Where does a bridegroom find joy? In the love of his bride (Is. 62:5). How much more will unspeakable joy out of love be experienced by the Creator who made us with the kiss of his mouth, that is, in Christ whose kisses are most dear (Song 1:1), and in him and through the love of the Holy Spirit who comes to us and makes his dwelling place with us (Jn. 14:23). The image of God, which consists in conformity with God, you are not to understand as if a man were like God in all things, in so great a holiness as God himself is, for God is inconceivable, immeasureable, and infinite in all his being, virtues, and characteristics. Therefore, man can only carry the image of God, as was clearly pointed out in this First Book, chapter 1.

This discussion of the image of God is clear, certain, and true. God made man to his clear, bright mirror so that if man wished to know what God was, he could look into himself and see in himself God as in a mirror. Indeed, he discovered God's image in his heart.

The image of God was man's life and blessedness. The injurious Satan had begrudged him this, however, and brought the greatest deception and haste to destroy the image of God in man, through disobedience and enmity against God. No greater haste is used and has ever been used than the Devil uses today. The whole human race has given Satan its highest good although it ought to be and remain eternally under another Lord. According to his great deception and haste Satan was not able to find anything higher by which he could have deceived man and tear him away from God than that by which he himself fell and which deceived him. Such desires he impressed upon our first mother through the most beautiful and most lovely animal in Paradise in the friendliest and best way. What can be a better counsel, a higher and wiser one for man, than that he be God himself? Through this suggestion the image of God in man was destroyed and Satan's image was impressed upon him, [an image] that was nothing other than to wish to be God himself.

When this desire and great pride were impressed upon man, the fall followed with disobedience and the refusal to follow the Law of God concerning the forbidden tree. Then the image of God was extinguished, the Holy Spirit turned away from man, and the image of Satan was impressed upon him. By this, man became

Satan's physical possession and obedient to Satan and Satan was man's lord and raged over man's soul as a wrathful giant rages over a poor child, darkens and blinds its understanding, turns its will from God by the highest disobedience, makes all the powers of the heart antagonistic to God, and poisons it with the greatest evil. In a word, the whole image of God was killed in man and Satan's image was planted in him, which he sowed with his evil practices, and thus man was born as his child according to his image with all sins and enmity of God. Thus, man died an eternal death, for just as the image of God and the eternal life and blessedness of man once existed, now the theft of the image of God, eternal death, and eternal damnation existed (Eph. 2:1; Col. 2:13).

All troubled hearts understand this death best when they have to suffer great spiritual temptations and experience the Devil's tyranny, raging, and wrath against the poor soul beyond the normal power of sin. If the Holy Spirit remains still in this suffering and does not comfort them and enliven them with living comfort, Satan comes to them, kills them with his death, and frightens their soul with the dread of hell. Then the whole body suffers, the heart is made pale. This is the mark as Psalm 6 and Psalm 38 indicate. Then all the words of God are dead for man and he finds no life in them and experiences no meditation and spiritual life in them. This is truly spiritual death. Then all man's holiness, righteousness, worthiness, strength, power, honor, esteem, art, and wisdom lie in filth. Here, nothing can help except God's grace.

Learn now, O dear man, how great an abomination above all abominations original sin is, namely, the lack of the original righteousness of God and the original unrighteousness planted in man by the Devil, because of whom the sinner is cast away from God and damned to eternal death in which he must eternally remain unless he receives forgiveness of sins through faith for Christ's sake. So that you might better understand this, I will better review for you this abomination that holds your body and soul captive. Pray and admonish each man for God's sake and for the sake of his blessedness that he learn and daily consider these articles so that he might learn to understand his sorrow and his misery properly and learn to understand by this original sin in him as his face in a mirror, and sorrow and weep daily because of it.

The whole Christian is and must not be anything else than a

spiritual battle against original sin and the rooting out of this by the Holy Spirit and by true repentance. The more you extinguish original sin the more day by day you will be renewed to the image of God. Those who do not mortify this in themselves daily through the Holy Spirit are hypocrites, no matter how holy they appear externally before the world. All that which has not died to itself and once again been renewed through the Holy Spirit according to the image of God is unchaste.

From this you see how very necessary the new birth and renewal are. You will understand all of this better if you contemplate the image of Satan according to the law of God. First, just as the Devil does not love God but is his enemy from the heart, so he poisoned the soul and poured his whole enmity toward God into the soul so that it would not love, honor, and call upon God or trust God but would be his enemy and flee from him. Just as the Devil lives in his blindness without God and thinks not on God's will, so he blinded the human soul so that it too would live without God and not think on his will. This darkness in the mind of man is a grievous, frightful disruption of the light and image of God and a grievous sin, so that man says: *"There is no God"* (Ps. 14:1). Because of this blindness the whole human race is an abomination before God in his being.

A small spark of natural light remained in the human understanding. If out of this light of nature a man concludes that there is a God (Rom. 1:20), he also knows that God is righteous as all the pagan philosophers say. However, the spiritual life for God and his righteousness is completely dead in man. The conscience that is the Law of God and that all men carry in their hearts in the creation tells each one what is right. An unchaste man thinks at times there is a God and God is chaste and, for this reason, you ought also to be, since unchastity is an abomination before God. But this thought, which is proper and good and is a small light, is half darkened just as a small spark is extinguished and put out by water. The evil desire and seething of the flesh keeps the upper hand. A blasphemer and murderer thinks at times that there is a God who is true and who does not wish man to die, but preserves him, but this spark does not last long and is conquered by devilish wrath and search for vengeance and thus the spiritual life in love and truth is completely dead and extinguished in the carnal man.

JOHANN ARNDT

The wise pagans reached good conclusions by the light of nature. They believed that there is a God who rules the human race, but how quickly because of the blindness of their hearts were they overcome so that they doubted in God's providence, as their books testify. Out of this original blindness and inherited darkness, disbelief and doubt arose in which all men are rooted by nature and, for this reason, they are an abomination before God. They do not live in faith and deep trust on God. The natural man knows nothing at all about this spiritual life and its works. He does not call upon God but gives himself over to himself and to his own wisdom, power, and strength, which is the greatest blindness.

Out of this blindness arises the despising of God and the sense of security. The Devil did not humble himself before God, but remained proud. Thus, he poisoned the soul with this vice of rejection of God, self-certainty, and pride, so that the soul does not humble itself before God but remains in its pride and does everything internally according to its own will, without any view to God. Just as the Devil gave himself over to his own wisdom and might and ruled by himself, so he also poisoned the human soul so that it gave itself over to its wisdom and might and wished to rule by itself. Just as the Devil sought his own honor, so also does man, and he does not ask concerning God's honor. Just as the Devil raged against God, so the soul raged against God with impatience. Just as the Devil cursed God's name and was unthankful to his Creator and became unmerciful, wrathful, and a searcher after vengeance, so the soul of man was also corrupted with this poison. As the Devil eagerly wishes to rule over man and honor himself, so he corrupted the human soul, so that a proud man looks upon his neighbor as a fool in his heart, as a lost man worthy of nothingness, as one soiled with the greatest sins, and he desires to have him for his footstool. As the Devil is a murderer, so he also made the soul a murderer. At this point I wish to tell you a thousand times that God calls upon and speaks to the soul at all times and not to the external members. The heart, the soul, is the murderer, liar, and not the hands or the mouth. If God says, *Call unto me in your need* (Ps. 50:15), he offers this to the soul, not to the mouth. The person who does not know this remains a fool in the Holy Scripture and does not understand anything about original sin, repentance, the new birth, or any other article.

Daily we observe this devilish evil, frightful pride, hate, and envy against the neighbor, which would rather die than offer or leave its life to its neighbor. We wish a neighbor to be with us or not with us, according to our evil, wrathful soul. The Devil has strewn the human soul with such abominable envy and man is Satan's image because of the great wrath, anger, hate, envy, and enmity. Thus, he portrays himself and sets his image in the human soul.

God has planted in man a pure, chaste, clean, marital love that is to rear up children according to the image of God. There is no holier pleasure and love than to continue the image of God and to increase the human race to God's honor and to man's eternal blessedness. Indeed, if a man had reared a thousand children in his innocence and had been able to continue the image of God and his honor, there would have been a most holy, high pleasure and joy, for everything would have proceeded out of love to God and for the human race as the image of God. God created man in a holy and deep pleasure and joy, and 'had joy and pleasure in him as by his image. In a similar way, man would have raised up his likeness in holy pleasure, and would have had joy and happiness in it as the image of God. No long sermon is needed to describe how Satan made impure with his impurity this pure, chaste, marital flame of love. Man reared his own likeness as an irrational animal in his blindness and fervor. How is holy marriage wasted with such inordinate vice by the unclean spirit?

Satan is not righteous and is a thief and a robber and thus he sowed the human soul with his thieving quality. The Devil is a slanderer, a sophist, a blasphemer, and is opposed to both God and man. He twists the words and works of God and man as he did when he deceived our first parents. Thus, he sowed in the human heart poisonous, twisted, lying acts and continued the devilish quality, namely, lying, blaspheming, slandering (Jn. 8:44). This poison is so unspeakably rooted in the human soul in so many thousand ways that one can not find enough words to describe it, as Psalm 5:10 and Romans 3:13 and James 3:5–6 . . . point out. The evil, poisonous quality of lying and false tongues you are to understand as nothing else than the devilish, diabolic poison in the soul. In his law, God complains not only about the mouth, tongue, hands, and feet but about the whole man, his heart and soul, the source of all evil, concerning which he has given enough for us to understand in the two final commandments (Ex. 20:16–17). This, learn well.

This is the image of Satan that the Devil, in place of the image of God, impressed and planted in the human soul so that such an evil manner of life would sin, would blaspheme, would bring his neighbor to nothingness, and would be the greatest pleasure and joy of man. Many a man who wishes to be a good Christian often seeks an opportunity to spin out some poison against his neighbor and when this occurs he says: "Now I am satisfied, I wanted to do that to him for a long time. A great millstone has fallen from my heart; I am as if newborn." O wretched man, do you not know who has brought such a slanderer and Devil to birth in you? Do you not see whose image you carry? Thus, all other qualities of the Devil and Devil's seeds and roots press into our soul such as pride, covetousness, unchastity, as daily experience indicates clearly.

You wretched man, look at this image of Satan, which is original sin. You must learn to know in your heart how the soul is sown with the Devil's image and quality and is completely wasted in a most abominable way, is so evil that no one can see to the depths of the human heart. You yourself cannot consider and speak enough about how great an abomination exists in your heart. I ask that you allow this to be said to you a thousand times and two thousand times a day; no poison is so great, so deep, so ill that any creature is able, either angel or man, to root this sin out of human nature, to drive it off and to cut it out. This is impossible for all men with all their powers, for how can a person help himself with his own powers that are completely corrupted and are spiritually dead? Man must remain eternally in this corruption unless there comes to root out sins a mighty person who is Lord over sin and death who also can change human nature, renew it and make it pure. Thus, you see that justification is no human work and you see also how necessary the new birth is, for no soul can live internally out of its own powers in any other way than in its own weakness, its own inherited quality and evil, in sins against all the commandments of God and especially those on the first tablet. This is truly enmity against God. In this, understanding and will are captured, completely dead, and by their nature are not able to fear, love, trust, call upon, honor, praise, and give homage to God, nor to turn themselves to him. Insofar as concerns the second tablet, there is yet a spark of free will remaining in the soul, but this only rules external works on the second tablet. It is very weak and powerless and can in its own way only tame the desires and the evil lusts and rule over them, but external works cannot be perfected, as one notes in the virtuous pagans. To change the heart, to turn to God, to purify evil lusts, is impossible; for this it is necessary to have divine power. The internal, poisonous root remains. It is as if someone has put out a fire so that the flame cannot be brought to life again and yet it remains eternally, internally always glimmering and yet not ignited.

If this free will in the natural, external life and being did not exist, men would not be able to live together. Therefore, the Lord God did not allow Satan to tear out all natural powers and affectations from the human soul. There remains then the law of nature, the marital, natural love between married people, parents and children, or the human race would not be able to exist. The person who wishes to perfect externally all his evil lusts and desires according to his evil nature will break down human community and cast his body on the secular sword. As a result, God allowed the natural flame of love to remain so that by it we might know and sense what a high good and beautiful image of God the perfect love of God is, and how great a good we have lost. In spiritual matters, however, touching upon holiness and the kingdom of God, what Saint Paul said in 1 Corinthians 2:14 still remains true: *The natural man knows nothing of the spirit of God; for him it is foolishness, he cannot conceive it,* that is, he has no spark of spiritual light, but he is completely blind in the full, divine, spiritual life, for which alone man was created, so that he might see with the internal eyes of his soul, in the spiritual light of God's presence and his deep love for him, that he might walk with him and before him eternally and that he might allow him to rule him in this life.

Natural man has not the smallest spark from this spiritual light in the kingdom of God. By nature all men must remain in this blindness if God does not enlighten them. This is true, spiritual, original blindness in things that concern the kingdom of God. In addition to this, there often also comes natural blindness, which arises when the evil of man takes the upper hand, puts out and darkens even the small, natural light of virtue and honest work belonging to the external life. Thus, the whole soul is beaten down and darkened with blindness and it would have remained so eternally if Christ had not enlightened it.

Behold now, dear man, what would you be if Christ had not begotten you anew through his spirit, made you to a new creature, and renewed you again to God's image? However, all this is only begun in this world in great weakness. Look upon yourself, you who are a new creature of the Holy Spirit. How weak and small is the image of God in you? How paltry is humility? On the other hand, how great are mistrust, pride, and impatience? How cold and weak is your prayer? How weak is your love for your neighbor? How small a spark of pure spiritual chastity is there in your heart? How great a flame of fleshly unchastity? How great is your self-love, self-gain, self-honor and the fervor of evil desire? By the spirit of God, you must fight and strive with the old Adam, with the image of Satan in you, until your grace. Therefore, pray, weep, wail, seek, knock, and the Holy Spirit will be given to you, who will daily renew the image of God in you and extinguish the image of Satan.

Thus, you will learn to trust and build not on yourself, but on God's grace and you will learn that God's grace must do everything in you. Thus, you will learn through faith and will seek, pray for, and receive from and out of Christ divine knowledge and understanding against your blindness, Christ's righteousness against all your sins, Christ's healing against all your impurity. Christ's redemption, power, victory, and strength against death, hell, and the Devil, and the forgiveness of all your sins against the whole kingdom of sin and of the Devil, eternal blessedness against your spiritual and bodily sorrow and misery and in Christ alone you will find eternal life. On this more is discussed in the Second Book.

42

CONCLUSION AND THE CHIEF REASONS FOR THE ORDER OF THE FIRST BOOK. HOW A MAN IS TO PROTECT HIMSELF AGAINST SPIRITUAL PRIDE AND HOW NO TRUE, SPIRITUAL GIFT CAN BE RECEIVED WITHOUT PRAYER

What have you that you did not receive? If then you received it, why do you boast as if it were not a gift (1 Cor. 4:7)?

At the conclusion of the First Book, I must remind you once again of certain, necessary points:

1. In this book, repentance is described and set forth extensively and in many ways in its fruits, and this is done for many reasons. The majority of chapters in this book describe nothing other than the fruits of repentance, namely, renewal in Christ, daily mortification and crucifixion of the flesh, denial of oneself, rejection of the world, practice of love and so forth. I have described these in different manners but in clear ways for many reasons. First, repentance is the beginning and foundation of true Christianity, of a holy life and walk, indeed, the beginning of our blessedness through true faith. True, continual consolation can nevermore be bound and rooted in the human heart if it does not first, properly and fully enough, know original sin, the abominable, frightful, deadly, hellish, devilish poison and evil (Ah, man cannot complain about it sorrowfully enough!) with all its fruits. And truly without this all books of consolation are useless if this fundamental is not first laid down and if you do not first properly know your sorrow and misery, and especially how great an abomination original sin is. It is the quality of our pretentious self-seeking nature that it always wishes to be consoled before it acknowledges its sin, false quality, and evil.

The way of our weak nature is a twisted quality and manner of life and completely against the Holy Scriptures. The strong have no need of physicians but the sick do (Mt. 9:12). Christ, the true physician, and his medicine and all consolation are of no use to you without the knowledge of your sickness, for a true Christian life is nothing other and is not to be anything other than a continual mortification of the flesh. Let this be said to you once and a thousand times. Only those belong to Christ whom he will nevermore leave without consolation. Such knowledge of your own weakness through the Holy Spirit and contemplation of the Gospel carries with it consolation and leads you to Christ. You do not wish to turn to the inopportune judges and destroyers of the present world but to know that such judges and destroyers are miserable, blind people who do not know their own sorrow and misery and do not understand what Adam and Christ are, how Adam must die in us and Christ live in us. He who will not learn this remains in his blindness and darkness and does not understand what true repentance, faith, and the new birth are. In this, the whole of Christianity consists.

2. You are to be warned of spiritual pride if our dear God, through his grace, begins to work spiritual gifts in you, new virtues and knowledge, (1) that you do not ascribe these to yourself and your gifts but to the grace of God, (2) much less that you hold these virtues, which have been begun in you, as your righteousness before God than as a piece of that righteousness, (3) that you do not use these for your own homage and acclaim but that in the humble fear of God you give God alone the honor and not yourself and that you do not think in your heart: "I now have a powerful faith, I have much knowledge and other things of the same kind." Guard yourself, for this is the seed of the Devil, which he sows among the good wheat. (4) All gifts are not yours but God's and without God's enlightenment you remain a dead, stinking piece of earth. If God does not place his gifts in you, you remain an empty vessel. The treasures a man places in a chest are not those of the wretched, naked chest but of him who placed them in it. Similarly the gifts are not yours; you are only an empty vessel for them. Ought the wretched vessel to be proud because of foreign good? In the Second Book you will see more about this. (5) The Lord has power at every hour to take his possession and goods from the small chest to place them in another chest or to keep them by himself. Behold, God can take his gifts away from you again at every hour and, therefore, do not be proud but be afraid (Rom. 11:20). (6) You must give a detailed reckoning for such goods to your Lord. (7) If you have such

beautiful gifts, do not think you will have them all the time. O dear Christian, it is only the beginning; you will need much more. (8) You are to know that no perfect, good gift will come to you from God without prayer (Jas. 1:17), but that which you have in you is as a shadow and a seed that can bring forth no fruit and fades away before it ripens. This you can see in my prayer book [the *Garden of Paradise*]. Such heavenly gifts must be prayed for before God and without prayer do not come into the heart. To have a small taste of this, read the tractate concerning prayer in the following book. You must look to two things in prayer: first, that the image of Satan be destroyed in you—unbelief, pride, covetousness, pleasure, wrath, and so forth; second, that the image of God might be raised up in you—faith, love, hope, humility, patience, the fear of God. Look to the holy prayer of the Lord, the "Our Father." This goes against you and for you. If God's name alone is to be hallowed, your name and pride must cease. If God's kingdom is to come, Satan's kingdom must be destroyed in you. If God's will is to be done, your will must become nothing. Note that there are two parts for every useful prayer book by which according to the order of the "Our Father" heavenly, eternal goods and gifts are to be sought and prayed for. They are included in the prayer of the Lord as taught by God. In the "Our Father," all the treasures of body and soul and goods are contained as in a summation, which we temporally and eternally need. Therefore, the Lord God, our dear Father, is willing to give to us what his dear Son has commanded us to request of him. Of this, we will speak at another place and time.

Book Two

LIBER VITAE CHRISTUS

Foreword

Dear Christian reader, as in nature the end of each thing is the beginning of another, so also is it in the Christian life. The old carnal man must first die before the new spiritual man can arise. And since our carnal life is completely against the holy life of Christ, as has been clearly pointed out in the First Book, it is necessary that we deny our carnal life before we can begin the spiritual life of Christ or follow Christ. For example, you must first cease to be proud before you can begin to be humble. Therefore the spiritual Christian life must necessarily begin with repentance. For this reason the First Book was composed as is clearly indicated by the order of the chapters and by the conclusion.

Since the doctrine of repentance is treated once again in the chapters of this Second Book, it is necessary that I briefly indicate the order of the chapters of this book. Since the chief section of the First Book treated the knowledge of the dreadful, deadly, and damnable poison of original sin, which cannot be fully enough treated, it is necessary that the Second Book begin with our eternal wellspring Jesus Christ, in whom we find a remedy and help by faith against the aforementioned grievous poison of original sin and against all of the sorrow and misery arising out of it. This matter is treated in the first three chapters of the Second Book. However, since faith, which brings forth good out of the gracious well Christ Jesus, must bring forth living fruit, this is treated in the three following chapters [in 4, 5, 6]. If the fruits of righteousness and of the spirit are to grow in us, the fruits of the flesh must die. This is the daily, true, active, and righteous repentance in which a Christian must continually live and act. By it he is to mortify the flesh and the Spirit is to rule in us. As a result a clear discussion of the distinction between flesh and spirit and of the characteristics of daily repentance is necessary. These are treated in the four following chapters [that is, in 7, 8, 9, 10]. Since a new man is daily to arise out of such daily repentance and mortification of the old man (for a true Christian life is not anything other than a continual crucifixion of the flesh), one can find no better order of life than that which Christ our Lord presented to us by his example. Christ's life is to be our mirror. We begin, therefore, with his poverty, shame, contempt, sadness, tribulation, suffering, and death. His holy life is the crucifixion of our flesh. To this belong prayer, love, and humility. These matters are treated in the following fifteen chapters [chapters 11 to 25].

By this lowliness and humility of our Lord Jesus Christ, we climb up as on a true ladder to heaven into the heart of God, our dear Father, and we rest in his love. In Christ's humanity we must begin and arise into his divinity. There, in Christ, we see into the heart of our dear Father in heaven, we contemplate God as the highest, eternal, essential, infinite good, as the immeasurable power, as the unfathomable mercy, as the unsearchable wisdom, as the purest holiness, as the unassailable and infinite righteousness, as the sweetest goodness, as the noblest beauty, as the loveliest graciousness, and as the most gracious loveliness, as the kindest blessedness. These are the chief aspects of the contemplative life. These are treated in the eight following chapters [chapters 26–33]. Since such contemplations cannot occur without prayer, the ten following chapters treat prayer and the beautiful praise of God [chapters 34–42]. And finally, since such godliness must lead to the persecution that Christ Jesus experienced, the following fifteen chapters [chapters 44–58] treat patience under tribulation, the chief spiritual trials and how to overcome these. May God help us that we all may be true followers of Christ and not be ashamed of his holy life but follow the Lamb of God where he goes, so that he might lead us to the living water of life and wash away all tears from our eyes. Amen.

[**Chapter One.** Our great illness demands a great divine remedy. We cannot bring this about through our own powers. Christ's great mercy must bring it to us. He has given himself to us completely so that we can make use of him at all times. He is the greatest gift, the All in all.

Chapter Two. Each Christian can find consolation in the merits of Christ. The following give witness to these merits: the general promises of God, God's precious oath, God's promise not to think on our sins any longer, the sacrifice of Christ, God's reiteration of his oath, the eternal covenant of grace that he made with all the faithful and reiterated in baptism, the death of Christ by which the covenant was established, the general call of God to all men, the inner testimony of the Holy Spirit, the example of the repentant sinner whom God received, the abundant payment of Christ for our sins, the infinite and eternal payment, the perfect and effective obedience of Christ, Christ's royal victory over all our enemies, Christ's royal high priesthood.

Chapter Three. The foundation of our righteousness is God's mercy in Christ. This righteousness must be received by grace alone so that man might be made righteous from within, so that our heart will turn from itself to Christ, so that Christ's righteousness will become ours through faith, because faith is God's work and not man's. Thus, our righteousness has an eternal ground. It is based on no creature. Rather, it is built on God's truth and bound to it. Thus, Christ alone receives honor and he is the highest consolation, honor, wisdom, and victory.

Chapter Four. A Christian is not only justified by faith but is also sanctified. The fruits of the spirit must be truly found in him, even if they are weak. Test yourself according to the Ten Commandments; judge your works according to your heart. Christ taught us that we should be forgiving, because our life is a path to death. God's judgment will be frightful. The unforgiving will be damned. Therefore, judge your Christianity according to the heart. Be certain that it is internal and not a mere external appearance.

Chapter Five. By true repentance and a holy life man achieves true wisdom. In the Psalms David suggested that there were two ways to achieve it: continual prayer and continual desire to practice God's word despite trials and tribulations. True Christians are those who do not merely know and hear God's word, but practice it. This is shown at many points in the Scripture. Since man is so dreadfully corrupted, he must become a new creature. Therefore, we must continually pray and always be alert so that we hear the voice of the inner teacher, Christ.

Chapter Six. The perfection and holiness of man consist in the union with God in Christ; this is eternal. It occurs through faith and by grace and man can do nothing to bring it about, but must resign himself to God and deny his own will. Self-will and self-love are our greatest corruption. Therefore, Christ must convert him; man cannot do it himself, Christ's grace and power must work all goodness in him.

Chapter Seven. In each Christian are two opposing men: Adam and Christ. Adam must die and Christ will then live. For this to occur, watchfulness, prayer, and struggle are necessary so that Adam may be overcome. If Adam lives in you, you are not God's child, but a child of the Devil. This teaches us that by nature we are all evil in Adam and all together good in Christ. He is the remedy against spiritual pride.

Chapter Eight. God has described conversion in many ways. Two of these are the parables of the lost sheep and of the prodigal son. In these are indicated the unconverted heart of the sinner, the penitent heart of the repentant sinner, the merciful heart of the Father God. Seven things move us to repentance: God's mercy, Christ's warmth, the warning of temporal punishment, temporal death, final judgment, eternal pain in hell, the joy of eternal life.

Chapter Nine. Through firm warnings and gracious promises God calls us in many ways to repentance. The converted heart must turn itself to God. Word and sacrament call and attract us to him. We must not strive against grace and the spirit, but allow ourselves to be healed and as the lost sheep to be brought back to the correct path. We must continually sigh for this grace that will bring us to the right path. Each man must look after himself, must become pure, and changed inwardly. He must be converted to God with fasting, and with a humble heart ask God not to punish him. God looks after such people. One must be truly in earnest, however, and there must be no hypocrisy in him. To be capable of receiving grace, the heart must be contrite. We are moved to repentance, because God is gracious, merciful, patient, full of great goodness, and will not punish us from the moment we are sorry for our sins.

Chapter Ten. A repentant heart believes itself unworthy of all of God's goodness. It is necessary that a repentant man deny himself, hate himself, take up his cross and follow Christ. For this reason, the repentant man in the Old Testament put on sackcloth and sat in ashes. An image of the repentant and humble man is Mephibosheth (2 Sam. 9). Other examples are the prodigal son, the Canaanite woman, and others. The greatest pain of the repentant heart is that it has offended to God. The consideration of unthankfulness brings with it great fear. A repentant heart does not trust in its own powers and considers them only shadows. This is daily spiritual death. A repentant heart will be eternally united with God.

Chapter Eleven. All those who are in Christ are new creatures. The name "Christian" is the highest name and yet the lowest name in the world. Christ was most humble, and yet raised above all.

Chapter Twelve. Christ is the only way. We remain in him through faith, love, and hope. All the other virtues are tied to these three in which the imitation of Christ is rooted. The light of light shines in us through them. They are the fruit of the Lord.

Chapter Thirteen. Christ is the Book of Life according to his merits and by his example. His whole life was a continual struggle; it stood in great poverty, he was despised, he suffered much. His holy poverty was the first aspect of his sorrowful life and it had three grades. He was poor in temporal goods, he had few friends, he gave up his divine power and glory and gave himself over to all creatures for our good. He humbled himself in the deepest way. He gave up his divine wisdom, his divine glory, and holiness. In a word, he gave up everything, which is the world. How foolish that we do not suffer so. How far we are from the way of Christ.

Chapter Fourteen. A second aspect of Christ's suffering was the way in which he was despised; in this Christ was a gift and an example to us. He who still loves the world does not have Christ in him.

Chapter Fifteen. Christ sorrowed over the way he was despised. In Psalm 109:22, he expressed his sorrow over the great dread of heart, over physical weakness, and over his rejection. The following consolations are to be remembered against the rejection of the world: You carry the image of Christ, you learn humility by this, you are among the number of the saints, in heaven you will be praised, you will not arise to eternal shame and punishment, you stand with God in grace, God has given you tribulation so as to test you, God changes trouble into blessing and does so that you will thank him, God stands at the right hand of the poor.

Chapter Sixteen. In all his sufferings, Christ's glory was that of God, his Father. We have the greatest glory in heaven if we are persecuted in innocence. Let us, therefore, follow Christ as an example, whose only glory was that God was his Father, that he was God's only begotten Son, that to unthankful man he did only good, that he died out of love for us, that he was glorified at the right hand of God, that he was the only head of his Church, and that God revealed his name throughout all the world. The person who praises him, praises the Lord.

Chapter Seventeen. Christ suffered much from slander and therefore no Christian can be safe from it. Against slanderers, each man must console himself out of God's word with the examples of Christ and the saints. From these he must learn patience and meekness, and pray for those who speak falsely against him. We must revive ourselves from the cool springs of the divine Word. Slandering is a hellish storm, but it soon passes. God allows men to speak falsely for a number of reasons and he makes a medicine out of their poison. God has the hearts of all men in his hands. Those who speak evil fall into hell. There are many words of consolation in the Psalms against those who speak ill of one.

Chapter Eighteen. The third aspect of Christ's tribulation was his unspeakable sorrow and pain. He experienced this because sin is an unspeakable evil, because he suffered for the sins of all men, because he loved God his Father perfectly, because he loved the human race, because he was forsaken by God, because he was true God, because he had an innocent, holy, tender body. Since Christ suffered such tribulation, we ought also to suffer willingly out of love for him.

Chapter Nineteen. The crucified Christ is the Book of Life, written internally and externally. He points out to us the greatness of our sins, God's righteousness, the great love and mercy of the Father, the gracious will of God to make us holy, the highest wisdom of God, the great patience and meekness of God, the deep humility, and the many glorious fruits of the redemption. Thus, Christ the crucified is and remains the true Book of Faith and Life.

Chapter Twenty. Without prayer, no man can know God and Christ. Prayer has three steps. There is oral prayer, inner prayer, and supernatural prayer. By it, man learns to know and taste God properly. It often occurs in an instant, in which the soul seeks to gain it. By oral prayer one comes to inner prayer and through this to supernatural prayer. By prayer we are drawn to God. One must, however, pray with a whole and not with a half heart, according to the example of Christ. One must not doubt that prayer brings results. Take for example Jesus when he prayed and learn to persevere in prayer. Thus, like him, you will be certain that you will be heard. Especially consider Christ's suffering and death, for by such consideration, prayer will be awakened and made strong. If you are also suffering trials, pray the more firmly and remain humble, for the prayer of the lowly and poor in spirit is as pleasing to God as is the prayer of those firm in faith.

Chapter Twenty One. The whole life of Christ was simple humility. Christ taught us humility with his words and with his deeds. He taught it particularly in his act of washing feet. Humility acknowledges its nothingness and God's greatness. By it man prays properly and loves all things that God loves. Such love is directed toward neighbor and judges no one, but judges only itself. Humility strengthens the knowledge of God and hope. It makes man loving and friendly and like Christ. It creates inner peace, and brings about silence. In short, it is a little room, full of heavenly treasures. Man gains it, however, through meditative prayer and contemplation of the crucified Christ.

Chapter Twenty Two. All works that are pleasing to God must come out of a humble faith. The man who accepts a humble faith protects himself from idolatry. Although there are many who do not know it, the Devil controls their hearts, for idolatry is internal and spiritual. It exists when your heart clings to something and rests in something other than God. Man's heart makes idols; therefore, the Devil is called the God of this world. Protect yourself from living idols by true humility. Give all honor to God.

Chapter Twenty Three. Man is nothing. He is as a shadow or a dream. If he forgets this, he falls away from God into his own nothingness. Such pride is the greatest sin and the greatest punishment. In this, the fall of Satan consisted; he wishes to be God. It is the greatest foolishness to seek help and consolation among creatures with the Devil.

Chapter Twenty Four. Love is the greatest of all virtues, but man can easily err in love, particularly in the love of God and neighbor. He who loves God for temporal things loves himself more than God, for he loves God and divine things for his own sake. Such impure love brings impure fruits. Others love God so that they will not be punished; this is a weak love. Still others love him so that he will give them wisdom. Some love virtue so that they can have the name of virtue. This is not true love. There is also a disordered love, given to neighbors. Our love must be ruled by the Holy Spirit and ordered according to Christ's example. Such pure love does not find any difficulty too great. It follows the Beloved in his virtues even though it is weak. This love works all good things in man, without compulsion and with joy, just as God, the essential

Love, always does good. The lovers of God receive everything by prayer from God. Test your love according to four characteristics that one finds in Christ's love. In love the will of man must be cast down, all enmity must be put away, one must serve as Christ served, one must be like him in all ways, except for the fact that one is not sinless. There is no prayer possible without love.

Chapter Twenty Five. The marks of true love are in us: the shunning of worldly love, patient acceptance of the rejection of this world, joyous endurance of all martyrdom and pain, resignation, prizing the cross of Christ above all the treasures of this world, continual meditation on Jesus and his works of love in his incarnation, his holy teaching, the mystery of his life and death, his resurrection, and his ascension. In all these mysteries we are daily to study.

Chapter Twenty Six. There are five special indicators of the love of God: the incarnation of Christ, Christ's suffering and death, God's indwelling under and in us that comforts us in trial, God's love illuminating creatures, the beautiful and the ugly, and God's love that we know from his loving essence. Worldly love is pure deception.

Chapter Twenty Seven. In the crucified Christ one sees the purest and most perfect love. He who tastes this wishes nothing else, for Christ is loved by the believing soul. In this love of Christ all our works are to occur. This highest good God is prepared and willing to give to us. The taste of this love brings more joy than the whole world. If this leaves one, there is more suffering than if the person lost the whole world. Without this love all of life is bitter for the faithful man.

Chapter Twenty Eight. God, the perfect Good, must be known and tasted in spirit and in truth. This happens in the soul of man. That fallen man must first be converted to God and by faith cling to the Lord. Then he will taste internally in his heart God's graciousness. After this, he begins to reject the world and loves God above all things, the perfect above the imperfect. Thus, the loving knowledge of God does away with the love of the world.

Chapter Twenty Nine. God does everything to turn fallen man again to himself. A foolish man does not understand this, however. We are to contemplate the physical and spiritual goodness of God: the physical, such as the protection of angels, the planets, the air, the fish and the animals, the earth at large, which is God's arena. We are also to contemplate the spiritual blessings of the Holy Trinity. These are to be found in the messengers of God, which God sends to us. Do not these ignite you to love? You cannot escape the love of God, so give yourself to it completely. Cling with your heart to it until your heart is ignited.

Chapter Thirty. The loving soul knows God as the highest beauty. When man contemplates it he understands the beauty of all creatures. We participate in the beauty of God in Christ. God's beauty shines out of his creation. How much more will his beauty in Christ enlighten us when Christ is revealed in glory with his elect.

Chapter Thirty One. God gives us power so that we can return good acts to him. Because of this we must ascribe everything we do to the power of God, which controls the whole world. God is over everything and in everything and everything is in him. Consideration of this fact teaches us to know our nothingness and to fear God. As great as God is in his power, so lowly did he make himself in Christ that his humility and lowliness is impossible to fully consider.

Chapter Thirty Two. The soul knows God as most holy righteousness. All sins do away with God's righteousness and stir up creatures to wrath. Damnation results and eternal misery. The judgment of God also gives witness to God's righteousness. No creature can protect himself from it.

Chapter Thirty Three. God orders and rules everything according to his unsearchable wisdom. He called us by name before we were born. He created light and darkness. He ordered everything in his wisdom. He sees and hears everything. Our unthankfulness troubles God, since he created everything for us. The powers of his creatures are hands of the goodness of God; the wisdom of

God also foresaw our suffering. Even if things appear foolish to us, we must praise God's wisdom, which shines forth most brightly in the redemption and renewal of man. Christ illuminates our blindness, heals our twisted will, creates a new heart and mind in us, and by the essential image of God he thus renews again the lost, divine image in us.

Chapter Thirty Four. A guide to prayer containing twelve sections.

Section 1: Before the fall, man needed nothing but after the fall he needed everything. For this reason, Christ became man to show us the way to holiness. Through him, we become the children of God, and in him, we find everything we have lost, if we seek it with continual prayer.

Section 2: The person who does not pray disobeys God's commandment. He rejects the precious promises of God, becomes weak in faith and loses it. He robs Christ, he undertakes a bold existence, he casts himself into the power of the Devil and evil men, and he is the most unfortunate man in life and death.

Section 3: A man of true prayer honors God and his commandments, values the word of God highly; as a tree he grows daily in faith, remains as a dwelling place of the Holy Spirit, battles against sin, opposes the Devil, evil men, and all trials, and rejoices in the Holy Spirit.

Section 4: Life and death is placed before us as before Adam. There are two ways, one of the world and the other of God. On both these ways man must suffer. He who prays, strives, is victorious, and comes to rest. He who does not pray, does not strive, and yet he must suffer much and is damned. The first is better than the second.

Section 5: So as to be awakened to inner prayer, one must consider that God is always wise, that God has promised to hear us, that God loves everyone, that it is as great a sin to pray out of one's own piety as it is not to pray because of one's unworthiness, that God hears us at all places and at all times, that without prayer man can achieve nothing. These facts stir us up to prayer and teach us that God commands us to pray for our sakes, that he comes to us with his knowledge, that prayer awakens us, that God would rather give than we would receive, that God is immeasurably good although man is immeasurably bad, that man is the cause of his misery, that man is able to pray at all times, that he who does not pray brings trouble upon himself, that he who prays continually helps himself. Let us believe and practice this.

Section 6: God has foreseen everything.

Section 7: God has promised to hear us and make souls that are silent, participants in his divine grace.

Section 8: God wishes to hear all persons.

Section 9: Man is not to pray because of his righteousness, nor is he to give up praying because of his sinfulness.

Section 10: Man can trust God in all places, for the kingdom of God is in no one place.

Section 11: A believer is holy and will be heard whenever he prays.

Section 12: We learn that God knows everything before we pray, that we must pray daily, that God is more eager to give than we are to take, that God does not have to be awakened but that we do, that God is immeasurably good, that we are the cause of our misery and not God, and that God must be prayed to at all times and in all places.

Chapter Thirty Five. Prayer is the characteristic of a Christian since he is sanctified by the Holy Spirit, is the dwelling place and temple of the Holy Spirit. The Holy Spirit is the teacher and comforter of the contrite heart. For this reason, suffering is useful since the soul is poor and miserable in it and the Holy Spirit is able to pray through it.

Chapter Thirty Six. The basis of our prayer is God's grace in Christ. This grace makes us alive. Without prayer there is no consolation, no grace, no blessing in our occupation. Prayer protects us against the persecutors who are far from God. Prayer makes us heavenly, ignites us in the love of God, and protects us against sins and misfortune. The second basis for prayer is God's gracious presence. This ought to stir us up at all times and places to speak to God. A third basis of prayer is God's truth. Moses and David were heard in prayer. God has promised to heal all those who suffer. A fourth basis of prayer is God's eternal Word. It is a great consolation to know that faith and prayer have an eternal foundation over which the gates of hell cannot conquer. The power and fruits of prayer are uncountable.

Chapter Thirty Seven. The faithfulness and goodness of God are our consolation in suffering. God himself is the essential life and the life of all living things. Man's life is nobler than that of any creature; the angel's life is nobler, Christ's is the noblest. God's goodness shines forth from all creatures as from the book of nature. His grace, however, is revealed in the Holy Scriptures so that we might know how good and gracious God is, and by it that we might believe, love him, and call upon him. In Christ, all the goodness and graciousness of God is given to us. It awakens us to faith and prayer. The chief reasons that God will certainly hear our prayer are the following: God's highest goodness and graciousness by which he is prepared to give us everything, even himself, God's truth and precious promise, his merciful heart, the intercession of Jesus Christ on earth and now in heaven, the witness of the Holy Spirit in us, the indwelling of God in Christ through faith, the working of the Holy Spirit in prayer, and the fact that God does not forget as a man forgets. Against this, it might be said that I have often prayed and that God has not heard me. Prayer is always heard. Where prayer is not answered according to our will, it is answered according to our needs; where it is not answered in a physical way, it is answered in a spiritual way. Therefore, let us accept God's grace. If it is not heard in this life, it will be heard in the next.

Chapter Thirty Eight. God's word points to seven helps for our weak prayer: our only intecessor Jesus Christ, God the Holy Spirit, God's precious promise, the example of the saints whom God heard, the great warmth and graciousness of God, the great mercy of God, the covenant of grace that God made with us.

Chapter Thirty Nine: The believing soul is consoled when it speaks to God. When it calls upon him, God answers. This is indicated in the whole of the Holy Scripture, which is nothing but a conversation of the faithful soul with God.

Chapter Forty: The goodness of God comes to us in the inner conversation of our faith.

Chapter Forty One. God's word is the rule of our faith, life, and suffering. In suffering, you must pray and sing, for the praise of God will be a great help and power. There are seven reasons for this: God's praise as the end of all creatures, the power of prayer, the example of the Old Testament, the example of the New Testament, the praise of God that filled the saints with the Holy Spirit, the Psalms, the praises to be used at special times and in special cases. Therefore, a Christian ought to praise God daily.

Chapter Forty Two. A Christian can praise God at all times in the stillness of his heart, in the spirit. The following awaken him to praise: God's commandment, our own benefit, God's graciousness, love and goodness, God as our Father and Mother in his redemption of us, the example of the saints, the example of all creatures, and the greatness of God beyond praise possible for him.

Chapter Forty Three. The praise of God is the glory of man because he is thus able to joyously come before God, because thereby he is like the angels, because by it he becomes the instrument of God, because this is his highest joy, because God's knowledge grows in him, and because by it he gains victory over all his enemies.

Chapter Forty Four. The chief causes of Christian patience are the gracious will of God, the end of the world, the hope of coming holiness, the second coming of Christ, God's eternal truth and promise, the eternal consolation in heaven, the example of the saints, the sufferings of Christ, the glorious payment of the crucified One, the deep mercy of God. All these are described in the Epistle to the Hebrews.

Chapter Forty Five. The following consolations will relieve our suffering: All suffering comes from God, it is a mark of love and not wrath, suffering is a small, temporal indication of the eternal suffering we deserve, Christ suffered greatly, Christ said we would suffer, the saints suffered, God is with us in suffering.

Chapter Forty Six. The following things should help us to be patient: In suffering God comes to us, we deserve far greater punishment, God does not mistreat us, God has great patience with us, Christ and all the saints were patient, God promises great goodness to us, his promises are given in truth, suffering gives honor to God and it helps us, Christ made suffering a sanctifying thing, and eternal glory follows upon suffering.

Chapter Forty Seven. Regarding patience in suffering one is to note the statements in the Holy Scriptures and the examples of saints who suffered.

Chapter Forty Eight. God's consolation is greater than man's misery; this is clear in seven ways: God is the Father of mercy, he is a God of consolation, Paul and the saints are examples, the holy word of God and his promises are great consolation, the suffering of the believer is Christ suffering, the basis of all consolation is Christ, Christ's glory is the glory of all believers. To receive this consolation it is necessary to have true repentance and knowledge of sins, faith that clings to Christ, prayer as conversation with God, holy praise of God, and contemplation, the Word of God.

Chapter Forty Nine. Where there is no love and faithfulness, corruption and death follow. For pious and troubled people, faith and hope look to God's power and mercy and bring about patience. They know that God hears man's prayer, that God consoles them in wrong, that God gives his light of grace in darkness, that the suffering of evil men is God's wrath, that righteousness and truth finally come to light, that shame will come upon all those who mock God.

Chapter Fifty. Hope is patient faith that perseveres to the end. God himself is its foundation and rest. He who depends upon temporal things must always stand in dread. Hope is tested by trials; by trials, God breaks down false hope. Like faith and love, hope depends upon God alone. It is awakened by considering time and eternity. Souls that live in hope are the most beloved children of God. They learn to trust upon God alone.

Chapter Fifty One. Against the weakness of faith, the following are useful: Faith is God's work; Christ's love for us is perfect even if our faith is imperfect; God looks graciously on weak faith; he is most concerned about those weak in faith; he who eagerly wishes to believe also believes; no desire will be lost; it is better to be weak in faith than to be proud of strong faith; even weak faith grasps Christ and his goodness; faith is not at all times strong; concern about weak faith is true faith; Christ is with us and in us when we think on him; Christ our high priest prays for us; God's mercy is unspeakably great; God began his work and will bring it to fulfillment; God has given many means to strengthen faith; our faith is grounded in the eternal election of God.

Chapter Fifty Two. In spiritual trials, one is to consider that they are brought about by God, that Christ our head underwent them as well, that many saints experienced them, and that impatience in such trials will not be held against those who undergo them. They are to protect us against spiritual pride and help us to learn patience and hope. Bear sorrow until God takes it away. Do not listen to the judgment of the world and the Devil, but to God's word. Think how God has helped the saints. If you suffer with Christ you will also share his glory.

Chapter Fifty Three. Those who are undergoing trials should remember that these come from God, that the Devil has no power over us and that they lead not to corruption but to holiness. Such trials help to teach us to learn the power of sin, to value the redemption of Christ, to become like Christ, to learn to taste the consolation of the divine Word, to learn to practice faith and patience, to be more strongly comforted, to be more joyous in heaven. Be satisfied that temptations are the will of God. They are the marks of the grace of God by which he makes us in body and soul like to his Son. Victory will certainly follow great struggles of soul. The evils that man must suffer against his will are not accounted to him by God. God has never left the soul alone in trial. Great trials are the special graces of God and those who undergo them are spiritual martyrs. Therefore be patient, for a light will shine forth in the darkness.

Chapter Fifty Four. Satan will test all men. He brings many evil thoughts to each man, but we must remember Christ's suffering and the Devil's intention, Christ's intercession for those undergoing trial, Christ's gracious presence and indwelling, the assurance that our faith will not cease, Christ's victory over the Devil, which is our victory, the example of the saints who so suffered, the example of Christ himself.

Chapter Fifty Five. When God's help appears to be withdrawn, we must remember that God is never far from us. Therefore, have faith and be patient. God has foreseen our situation and will bring about our redemption.

Chapter Fifty Six. When you are suffering, think how Christ throughout his whole life had to endure misery in his body. We are to follow him. Consider the glory of the eternal life and the shortness of the suffering. The elect will enjoy glory with the Lamb of God. Struggle on and you will be crowned.

Chapter Fifty Seven. Against temporal death we are to consider that Christ died to conquer death, that he arose so that we might arise, that God is true, that Christ is all-powerful and glorious, that God is righteous, that there exist examples of those who have arisen. Our bodies were purchased by Christ. There are beautiful examples in nature of the resurrection, particularly of the grain of wheat that must die so new wheat can come forward. Eternal life is opposed to temporal existence. Prayer helps us when we fear death. Our bodies will be glorified. Angels will be present to us; there will be eternal glory for the elect. We must not be concerned about the vanity of this world. This life is a miserable life filled with many sins. Death comes to all men; it is a great victory and brings us to peace. We cannot see God with our physical eyes and therefore we must die.

Chapter Fifty Eight. The misuse of astrology is to be opposed but the heavenly bodies do have influence on our life. God works through nature and Christ pointed the signs of the heavens. The great stars often bring great changes. Sicknesses come about for the most part through the stars. It would be foolish to reject the workings of the heavenly bodies on man for the whole firmament is in man. Nevertheless, all the activities of the stars are brought under the rule of faith and prayer.

Conclusion. My purpose in this book is only that pure doctrine and holy life might arise.]

Book Three

LIBER CONSCIENTIAE

Foreword

Just as our natural life has its steps, namely, childhood, man-
hood, and old age, so also does our spiritual and Christian life. It,
too, has its beginnings in repentance, by which man daily betters
himself. Thereafter follows middle age, more illumination, through
the contemplation of divine things, through prayer, and through
suffering. By all of these the gifts of God are increased. Finally, the
perfection of old age comes. It consists in the full union through
love, which Saint Paul called the perfect age of Christ and a perfect
man in Christ (Eph. 4:13).

Insofar as it has been possible, I have treated this order in these
three books. I believe that in them, insofar as is necessary, the
whole of Christianity has been described although it is not perfectly
described and other things could be desired. The prayer book is to
be added. I wished also to add a fourth book in which one can see
how the Scripture, Christ, man and the whole of nature agree and
how everything in one eternal living source, which is God himself,
flows together and leads to God.

So that you might properly understand this Third Book, know
that it is intended to point out how you are to seek and find the
kingdom of God in yourself (Lk. 17:21). To do so, you must give
yourself completely to God with your whole heart and soul, not
only your reason but also your will and deepest love. Many believe
that it is enough and more than enough if they grasp Christ with
their understanding by reading and disputing. This is now the
general study of theology and it consists in mere theory and knowledge. They do not think that the other chief power of the soul,
namely the will, and deep love belong to faith. You must give both
will and love to God and Christ if you wish to give your whole soul

221

to him. There is a great distinction between the understanding by which one knows Christ and the will by which one loves him. We understand Christ insofar as we are able [to understand him]; we love him, however, as he is. It is of no use to know Christ by knowledge and not to love him. It is a thousand times better to love Christ than to be able to speak and dispute much about him (Eph. 3:19). Therefore, we are to seek Christ with our understanding so that we might also love him with our will and pleasure. Out of true knowledge of Christ comes also the love of Christ. If we do not do so, we do indeed find him but to our great shame, for this is what the Lord said in Matthew 7:21: *"Not all who say to me Lord, Lord, will enter the kingdom of Heaven."* There are thus two ways to gain wisdom and understanding. The first [comes] through much reading and disputation. Those who take this way one calls *doctos*, learned ones. The other way is through prayer and love, and those who take this way one calls *sanctos*, saints. Between the two is a great distinction. The first, because they are learned and not lovers, are blown up with pride. The others are lowly and humble. By the first way, you will not find your inner treasure. By the second way, however, you will find it in yourself. The Third Book treats this second way.

How glorious, precious, and lovely is it that our highest and best treasure, the kingdom of God, is not an external but an internal good that we continually carry with us, hidden from all the world and the Devil himself, which neither the world nor the Devil can take from us. For it, we need no great knowledge of languages, learning, or many books, but a resigned heart given to God. Let us, therefore, turn eagerly and inwardly to this our interior hidden, heavenly, eternal good and wealth. What can we seek externally in the world if we have internally in ourselves everything and the whole kingdom of God with all his goods? In our hearts and souls is the true school of the Holy Spirit, the true, working place of the Holy Trinity, the true temple of God (1 Cor. 6:19), the true house of prayer, in spirit and in truth (Jn. 4:24). Although God, by his general presence, is in all things, and not bound up in them, but in an inconceivable way fills heaven and earth, in a special and characteristic way he is in the enlightened soul of man in which he lives and has his seat (Is. 66:1, 2). There, in his own image and likeness, he enacts those works that he himself is. There in the heart he continually answers our sighs. How is it possible for him to deny them in persons in whom he has his dwelling; indeed, how is it possible for him to deny those concerns that he himself moves and bears? Nothing is more lovely and pleasant for him than to give himself to those who seek him.

For this to come about, a refined, silent, and peaceful soul is necessary. The soul will be peaceful and still if it turns from the world. Even the pagans have stated this: *Animam nostram tum demum fieri sapientem, cum quieta et tranquilla sit* [Our soul will be wise and intelligent if it is silent and peaceful]. Cyprian rightly said: "This is continual rest and security if a man is delivered from the continual storms of this world and raises his eyes and heart from the earth to God, draws near to God with his mind, and understands that everything that is considered high and precious among human things lies hidden in his heart and mind. Moreover, man must not desire and wish anything from the earth because his mind is above the earth and is more than the earth. Oh, how great a heavenly treasure it is to be released from the bounds and strictures of this world. How great a good it is that man does not have to endeavor to seek and search favors from people of high rank but has a gracious gift of God. Just as the sun shines by itself and the day gives light by itself, just as the well springs forth from itself and the rain flows forth and gives moisture from itself, so also the Holy Spirit itself flows into the soul of man that has lifted itself up to God away from the world."

In these words is great wisdom, and in them the summation of this Third Book exists. Often the hidden treasure in our souls arises in an instant. This instant is better than heaven and earth and all the loveliness of creatures. Saint Bernard says: "A soul that has once properly learned to turn into itself and to seek God's face and to taste the presence of God in its interiority would I believe find it less painful and tormenting to suffer a period in hell than, after having known and found such sweetness of this holy practice, to return to the pleasures or more to the displeasure and weight of the world and the flesh and to the unsatisfied desire and unrest of the senses." Such a soul does not only find the highest good in itself when it turns to God, but it also finds the highest misery in itself if it loses God. It notes well that it lives in God as in the source of life if it dies to the world. The more it lives in the world, the more it dies to God. Such a soul that has died to the world works rightly in God and is God's pleasure and joy, a sweet and ripe grape in the vineyard of Christ as the Song of Songs says. The other hearts, which seek the world, are bitter, unripe grapes. The marks of such a soul that has died to the world are as follows: A man draws his will in all things to God's will, self-love is put out, fleshly desire is mortified, the pleasure of the world flees, he considers himself as the smallest among men, he does not easily judge and direct his neighbor, he allows God to pass judgment and sentence, he does not lift himself up if he wishes to be praised, he is not disturbed if he is slandered, he bears all things in patience and complains about no one. An example of such a sacrificed will is to be found in King David (2 Sam. 23:15–17). David greatly wished to drink water from the well at Bethlehem. Three heroes travelled through enemy country to bring the king water. He poured it out before the Lord, that is, he gave up his own will because the three heroes had risked their life for his will.

In this is the true perfection of the Christian life. Perfection is not, as some think, a high, great, spiritual, heavenly joy and meditation, but it is a denial of one's own will, love, honor, a knowledge of one's nothingness, a continual completion of the will of God, a burning love for neighbor, a heart-held compassion, and, in a word, a love that desires, thinks, and seeks nothing other than God alone insofar as this is possible in the weakness of this life. In this is true Christian virtue, true freedom and peace in the conquering of the flesh and fleshly affections. You will read more about this in the Third Book and find out more about this by practice. May the grace of the Holy Spirit lead both you and me. It begins everything in us, continues it and perfects it to God's honor, homage, and praise. Amen.

[Chapter One. The Holy Trinity lives in the hearts of believers. This treasure cannot be known and sought without an inner Sabbath of the heart. The medieval mystic Tauler in particular treats of this. I have used his writings throughout this book.

Chapter Two. The way to this internal treasure is true faith, out of which love and all the virtues spring. Through faith a man turns into himself and keeps the Sabbath in his heart in which God can work. When the heart is empty of worldly love God fills it with heavenly goods.

Chapter Three. Christ, the holy kingdom of God, and all holiness is in faith. Faith gives spiritual freedom, peace, and rest; it unites one with Christ; it makes one certain of eternal holiness; it conquers all spiritual enemies; it gives a spiritual and eternal glory in spiritual priesthood; it renews the whole man; it makes each man a servant of his neighbor in love; it makes suffering less difficult.

Chapter Four. God is sought in both an active and a passive manner, the soul is most beautiful when it is united with God.

Chapter Five. Next to faith, true humility is the best way to commune with God.

Chapter Six. God often reveals himself in an instant in the ground of the soul. The saints experience this revelation as a taste of eternal life. Christ awaits joy and pleasure with his love in the ground of the soul.

Chapter Seven. The soul's worth lies in the fact that it is a dwelling place of God.

Chapter Eight. God calls us through all his words and works, partly through suffering and struggle, to peace and patience, partly by igniting his love in our hearts.

Chapter Nine. True faith purifies the heart from the love of the world and of creatures, from inordinate affections; it brings about proper love and leads one to patience, resulting in great joy and peace.

Chapter Ten. The natural light must fade before the spiritual light, the light of grace, can shine. This spiritual light God himself ignites in the ground of the soul through his word. Out of this light, spiritual powers and knowledge of truth come forth. Among the godless, it cannot shine forth because it still needs a quiet Sabbath of the heart.

Chapter Eleven. God, the most beautiful light, enlightens the soul so that the world may be denied. This inner light enlightens in the interior so that Christian virtues result, especially patience, meekness, humility.

Chapter Twelve. God seeks to bring together a distraught soul and to unite it with himself. Therefore, a Christian must at least once a day turn into his heart.

Chapter Thirteen. Worldly love must leave so that God's love may enter.

Chapter Fourteen. A Christian soul must be prepared to experience great suffering with greater patience and must continue in the love of God despite everything.

Chapter Fifteen. Christ, the Word of the father, allows his voice often to be heard internally in the heart. This occurs in those who walk with him in humility and accept suffering with patience. To the humble, God reveals the secret from Christ. Humility is the true place in which God works.

Chapter Sixteen. Those souls are unholy who because of their own actions do not have the Holy Spirit. Yet God gives it to all who empty their hearts of creatures. If God's spirit is to work in you, you must shun the world and bear suffering.

Chapter Seventeen. The marks of the indwelling of the Holy Spirit are interior punishment for sin, interior dread and divine sorrow, denial of one's own merit and justification before God, love for neighbor.

Chapter Eighteen. A Christian must shun all worldly joy and must turn continually to communion with God. Worldly love must be mortified by suffering and trials.

Chapter Nineteen. The Holy Spirit brings about a childlike internal prayer of the heart that rises above all things. The "Our Father" indicates what we are to pray for.

Chapter Twenty. Any work that is to stand firm must be built on the foundation of humility. For humility it is necessary that six things move us: our nothingness and misery, humility that overcomes the Devil, humility that brings about thirst for God, true sorrow for sin, love of suffering, true peace.

Chapter Twenty One. God himself and not his gifts is to be our highest desire and joy. Our nature twists this. Therefore, a denial of one's self is necessary.

Chapter Twenty Two. Except for the grace of God, man can do nothing that is pleasing to God. Therefore, man is not to seek righteousness in any of his works but only in the grace of Christ and God. If God gives you gifts do not be proud; God gives grace to the humble. If your works are to be useful you are to remember four things: serve your neighbor, give nothing without experience, do nothing for appearance's sake, set God as the goal in all things.

Chapter Twenty Three. All true disciples of Christ must bear their cross. Christ's five wounds teach us this. Therefore we must suffer all things with Christ.]

Book Four

LIBER NATURAE

Foreword

The great prophet Moses tells us that there are two powerful witnesses to God. There is first the greater world and second the smaller world, that is, man. From both these worlds the Holy Scriptures take many glorious examples in many places both out of the great world and out of the heart of man. In these, the Creator and Maintainer of all things is revealed and his image is seen in our heart.

In this book, both these examples, first the great world and thereafter the small world, will be introduced, and it will be pointed out how all creatures are like the hands of guides and messengers of God to lead us in Christian knowledge to God and Christ.

It is therefore unnecessary to demonstrate that this book belongs to true Christianity, although there are some who believe otherwise. If they wish this to be demonstrated, however, let them take Colossians 1:16, 17, and the introduction to the Gospel of John, and many other places in the Old and New Testaments, and let them consider also what the royal Prophet David in Psalms 19, 104, and 139 says. Let them also look at Romans 8:22 concerning the dread of creatures and 1 Corinthians 15:42–52 concerning the resurrection of the dead. If they do so they will be more gracious and kind to me. They will also think better then of our Redeemer, Jesus Christ, who often explained things from the great book of the world of nature by many comforting parables in which he set true Christianity and the kingdom of God before the eyes of his children. They might also lift up the holy sacraments with their substantiality, which were ordered as witnesses and signs of the grace of God and were taken and made holy out of the great world book of nature. Thus, they could give answer also to the holy fathers Ambrose, Basil, Theodoret, and others who wrote many books on the six days of creation.

Let this brief comment be enough to answer any opposition. Let me add that a true Christian is to use the creatures of God to the knowledge, homage, and praise of God so that in all things God might be praised through Christ Jesus our Lord.

Creatures are to lead us to God. Note as well that God acts as a loving Father who calls his child to him and accustoms him to himself with sweet words. If the child does not immediately come, he throws an apple or a pear to him, or a beautiful, colored stone as Israel did to his son Joseph (Gen. 37:3), not so that the child will love the apple or the beautiful clothing, not so that it will hang on to the gift and cling to it, but so that the child will cling to the love of the father and the giver. In a similar way our dear Father in heaven acts with us. With many gracious and friendly words by the prophets and apostles he calls us to himself but he also gives and casts before us many good gifts, many fruitful times from heaven, and he fills our hearts with food and joy (Acts 14:17). These are only the hands and messengers of God that are to lead us to God and to the witnesses and images for us of his love so that we will be able to receive the Giver himself in the creatures and gifts.

But look now, how evilly you act, you wretched man. You remain clinging to the gift, to a hand full of gold and silver, houses and acres, worldly honor and joy, which before God's eyes is nothing other than an apple or a pear by which God wishes to attract and draw you to himself. You treat it as if it were a kingdom. Indeed, because of this God allowed man to be born into this world so needy, so thirsty, so miserably created, naked and empty, hungry and thirsty, so that God might draw him to himself with so many blessings, gifts, and graces, so that man might taste God's love in all things, and so that he might find in the mortal creatures the immortal God, so that man might learn that the eternal, immortal God is able to bring more joy, comfort, strength, and sustenance than the fleeting and mortal creatures.

The great messenger and legate of God, however, and the greatest gift and the strongest hand of God that is to lead us to God is Jesus Christ, the Son of God, in whom are all things and all fullness, who stretches forth his hand to all creatures. *All things are made through him* (Jn. 1:3). *All things exist in him* (Col. 1:17). *He carries and holds all things* (Heb. 1:3).

Therefore, we begin in the first part of this book, namely, to describe the six days of creation in general so that we might know, give homage to, and praise the Creator.

In the second part, man himself will be treated. So that no one will make a quick judgment, I direct the reader to the conclusion at the end of the Second Book. My books are all to be understood according to the symbolic books of the Church, the Augsburg Confession, and according to no others.

Part One:

On the Six Days of Creation in General

[**Chapter One.** *The work of the first day, the creation of light.* Light, in particular the sun, is a symbol of God and of Christ. It symbolized God's essence, the most beautiful light, God's eternal wisdom a beam of eternal light, the warm love of God, and the internal, spiritual light of the soul that is Christ himself. Light brings joy, it awakens those asleep in their sins, it guides us in the right path, it gives us the power of life, it allows us to see the truth and casts out darkness. The sun gives more light than the moon and Christ gives more than reason. The sun adorns the heavens and Christ adorns the Church. Light makes a place pleasant to stay in and Christ makes the heavenly Jerusalem pleasant to stay in. Light reveals all things; from the eternal light nothing is hidden. Light shares itself with all things and God shares himself with men. The light of the sun is also an image of the resurrection. We share in it as we share in Christ's resurrection.

Chapter Two. *The work of the second day, the creation of the heavens.* The heaven is a symbol of God. It is pure, high and wide, like the immeasurable power and wisdom of God. The circle of the heavens symbolizes the eternity of God. The inexpressible roundness describes the continual presence of God. The permanence of the heavens signifies the truth of God and his word. This visible heaven is to lead us to the hidden heaven of the blessed. Our hearts and souls are to be God's heaven. Finally, it is to lead us to the new heavens that God will create.

Chapter Three. *The work of the third day, namely, the division of the waters from the earth.* God placed the earth in the center of the great world. There is a discussion among the learned whether the earth stands upon the water or the water upon earth. Two Peter 35 indicates that the earth stands in the water. This great ball of water and earth hangs on nothing and is borne by the air. The elements hang together and no one is able to move from the other. The firmness of the earth in the water is a symbol of the power and wisdom of God. Internally the earth is a noble, living element and has many seeds in it. These grow forth in herbs and medicines and other plants. Together they symbolize God's wisdom and goodness. The earth brings forth food for man and animal. Bread is the common food for the body. A whole tree lies hidden in a small seed. In the mountains are metals and minerals. Mountains are established by a special order of God. They are to remind us of the mountain of God, that is, the protection of God and the Church. There are many springs on the earth that bring forth water. They are to remind us of the spring of grace, Christ. The dawn is an image of the birth of Christ and our rebirth. Dew makes the earth fruitful and is an image of peace. Out of God's word come forth all fruits. The grass of the earth reminds us of the divine foresight, our nothingness, and the consolation that God has for us. The bread that is available for men teaches us to consider the fatherly heart of God, God's miraculous foresight and power, God's great wisdom, and the strength he brings to man's heart, as well as Christ, the bread of life. God created wine to bring joy to the sad, to strengthen the sick, and to give new life to the old. The oil and balsam are images of the Holy Spirit. The trees that are full of sap, which God planted, are images of the love of God and Christ. The birds and animals in the mountains that God created make known his goodness, power, and wisdom.

Chapter Four. *The work of the fourth day, the creation of the sun, moon, and stars.* We must lift up our eyes to see the stars, the lights in the heaven. This makes us consider their greatness, and the height and greatness of the heaven, which is an image of divine mercy.

Secondly, the stars have a constant and certain pattern. They lead us to contemplate the holy angels and the blessings of God. Thirdly, the stars are active and influence poets, artists, and rhetoricians and all other kinds of natural wisdom. Through the supernatural light of the Holy Spirit a higher grade of gifts can be reached than the natural heavens can bring forth. Such gifts were given to prophets and apostles. The orders of the heavens, signs of the Zodiac, the activities of the heavens, are natural images of God's coming judgment. The stars bring forth natural fruits such as clouds, snow, cold, frost, ice, hail, and other things. The movement of the sun and the moon points out to us the blessings of God. By them, we can see the power and wisdom of God, as well as God's truth. Darkness is an image of the wrath of God, the sign of the final day. Sun, moon, and stars remind us of the goodness of God, and attract us to love God. Thus we are to remember Christ, the Son of righteousness.

Chapter Five. *The works of the fifth day, on the creation of the seas and the waters and the fruits of the seas and the waters.* Many things come out of the sea, particularly minerals and metals. In the sea's ebb and flow we are reminded of God's power. Troubles of the sea remind one of the difficulties of this life. The sea of life is deep with sins. God's grace and Christ's merit is deeper yet, however, and yet more bottomless. For God stills the troubles of the sea immediately.

Chapter Six. *The work of the sixth day, on the creation of the animals and of man.* In the characteristics of the animals one comes to know the power and wisdom of God. God looks after the animals and feeds them. Will he then forget man? God's breath and power is the life of all creatures. God's providence is all wisdom and knowledge, and looks after all things. He has a fatherly concern for all things, and serves and reigns over all. Man was the last and most glorious of the creations, the most beautiful that God made. Particularly beautiful was the human soul.]

JOHANN ARNDT

Part Two:

Concerning Man in Particular

[**Chapter One.** God is the source of all the being and life. We know from the creation of all things that he is an internal wisdom and understanding; he knew all things from eternity.

Chapter Two. God is the highest good, the most perfect good of all creatures. Therefore, turn yourself completely to God and you will be always rich, peaceful, and holy.

Chapter Three. All creatures serve man. Man is the noblest creature and is to serve God with all his powers. Just as all creatures work for man, so man in all his works is to rest in God.

Chapter Four. As an artisan loves all his works so God loves his creation. The nearer the likeness, the greater the pleasure. Therefore, God created man after his image that he might have great pleasure in him, so that man might cling to God and have communion with him, and so that God might be able to share all his goods with man, and so that man in the great love for God might be able to receive these goods.

Chapter Five. God gives himself to us completely through his love and in a perfect way in Christ. Out of this love the incarnation, suffering, and death of Christ came as well as eternal life.

Chapter Six. Man is chiefly responsible to God since he received all things from God. God ordered all things to serve man. All these things call man to be thankful.

Chapter Seven. The world was not only created to serve man's bodily needs but also to teach him spiritual truths.

Chapter Eight. Man owes great thanks to God for he understands the goodness of all the creation and the worth of all creatures that were made for him.

Chapter Nine. The service of the creatures teaches us that there is something in man that is immortal and that this is his soul. The soul alone, however, can have communion with the immortal God and because of this man is more responsible before God for his soul than for everything else that is in the world.

Chapter Ten. There are three powers in man: The lowest is the nourishing power bound to the body, the second is the sensitive power nobler than the first, the highest and most noble is made up of memory, understanding, and will, which are completely spiritual.

Chapter Eleven. Man is indebted to God for two gifts: a visible one, the world, and an invisible one, God's love. Love is the first and greatest gift and the root of all gifts. Therefore, man is more in debt for it than for all other gifts.

Chapter Twelve. Man can fulfill his responsibility through love. God loved him in the highest way. God does not despise any man's love. In this chapter, it is not said that fallen man is able to love enough, but what is discussed is how much he should love.

Chapter Thirteen. In punishment too, God shows his love.

Chapter Fourteen. God loved man in the highest way possible. Therefore, man is to give his whole love to God without ceasing.

Chapter Fifteen. God's love attracts us to love him and all creatures admonish us to love God without hypocrisy out of all our powers, willingly and eagerly. This is the greatest worship one can give to God.

Chapter Sixteen. The creatures teach us how we are to bring the sweet fruit of love in a perfect way to God and how we are to do this out of pure simplicity without pretense or possessiveness.

Chapter Seventeen. Nature teaches us that we are to love God because he is the highest good and because we have all things from him. No man is excused from loving God. One cannot love God out of one's own powers but nature teaches us that we are responsible to love him.

Chapter Eighteen. All the duties that man owes to God are useful for him.

Chapter Nineteen. There are two services that exist: that of creatures toward man and that of man toward God.

Chapter Twenty. Since there are many things that man needs to keep him alive that are less than he is, it is necessary that there be a God that keeps man.

Chapter Twenty One. Creatures are bound to man through their service to him and man is bound to God through his service to God. Both services are useful for man and help him to piety.

Chapter Twenty Two. Man's first love is to be given to God alone and to nothing else. Thereafter, man is to love what God loves most, that is, his neighbor, God's image in man.

Chapter Twenty Three. The order among the creatures indicates that man, who was created in the beginning after God's image, is the end of all creatures.

Chapter Twenty Four. All men are created after God's image, and therefore, they are to love one another. There are two bonds of love in the neighbor. By the first man is tied to God and by the second to his fellow man.

Chapter Twenty Five. All creatures serve all men without distinction. Therefore, man is to make no distinction between men, all were created in God's image. There are two brotherhoods among men, a first, which is a general one, and a second, which is that in Christ Jesus.

Chapter Twenty Six. The person who is united to God through love is also united to his neighbor. This unity is a great good and an unconquerable strength for man.

Chapter Twenty Seven. Nothing is truer than love. Love is our whole good. If we give our love to someone, we have given ourselves totally to him. If we turn to evil things we lose ourselves.

Chapter Twenty Eight. Through love man gives himself to the beloved and is freely changed into the beloved. All lesser things are changed into better things. Therefore, we ought to give our love to God, the most noble and the most worthy.

Chapter Twenty Nine. God alone and no physical thing is worthy of our love, for physical things are not as noble as we are and they cannot return our love. As a result, if we love them, our love would be corrupted.

Chapter Thirty. Nature and reason tell us that the highest and first love belongs to God our Lord. If I give my first love to myself, I do God a double wrong.

Chapter Thirty One. By self-love man makes himself into a God and becomes the enemy of God. Out of this springs self-will, self-honor, and self-praise, the most abominable robbery of God.

Chapter Thirty Two. The love of God is the root of all good in us. Self-love is the root of all evil and brings forth sin, pain, unrest, and sorrow; it makes man proud, weak, poor, and hateful.

Chapter Thirty Three. Out of the love of God arises the knowledge of good and out of self-love comes the knowledge of evil in men. From self-love springs pride and arrogance and all other vices.

Chapter Thirty Four. God's love is the cause of unity among men. Self-love brings about disunity.

Chapter Thirty Five. Man's conscience teaches him what he owes to God. If you wish to be loved you are responsible to love God first.

Chapter Thirty Six. Sadness arises out of self-love, but true joy out of the love of God. The love of God is here imperfect, but in heaven it will be perfect. That treasure can be received through grace and we need no external thing to gain it. Every believer can have the love of God and joy.

Chapter Thirty Seven. Self-love brings about a false joy that finally changes to sadness, for self-love is the root of all vice. It always leads away from God and from divine joy.

Chapter Thirty Eight. Out of self-love arise sorrow of heart, eternal hatred, and the despising of oneself.

Chapter Thirty Nine. God, our Creator and Preserver, is over all things to be honored. Man was therefore created rational. Man honors God with love, fear, obedience, and faith. Nothing is better than to love God, and nothing is worse than not to honor him.

Chapter Forty. By self-honor man robs God of what is his; he sets himself in God's place. By so doing he also drives God from the hearts of other men, and wishes to be honored by them. Therefore, drive self-honor out with repentance and faith so that the love of Christ might eternally dwell in you.

Conclusion. What is written in this book is to be the foundation of the faith of a Christian. The second part of the Fourth Book is taught to us in Scripture and in nature. It tells us what we owe to God.]

Book Five

Part One:

On True Faith and Holy Life

[**Chapter One.** It is difficult to plant Christian teaching in man and to develop a holy life. The devil works against this in three types of people. There are those who believe they are perfect and can no longer sin and it is true that we are perfect in Christ, but renewal takes all of one's life. Others say it is not necessary to be pious, but they do not understand the merits of Christ. Still others are out-right sinners and despise the teaching regarding godliness.

Chapter Two. By the new birth, the image of God is renewed in us. The new creature serves God joyously and willingly.

Chapter Three. The activities of the new man have their roots in the knowledge of God.

Chapter Four. The Word of God is a word of truth, a living seed, the wisdom of God, power and life, defense and nourishment, a source for union with God, a light to our soul, a spiritual guide.

Chapter Five. Christ nourishes our soul, which hungers and thirsts for God's grace, promise, and power, aiding us when we are lost or in tribulation.

Chapter Six. Faith is a gift of Christ, a fruit of the spirit, a gift of God.

Chapter Seven. The highest consolation of believers is the forgiveness of sins. It is gained by true repentance and confession, and constant prayer. It is available only in Christ and in faith in his promises.

Chapter Eight. Justification comes only through faith in Christ.

JOHANN ARNDT

Chapter Nine. He who is justified in Christ begins to lead a new godly life. He is a new creature in Christ, bearing fruits of the Spirit, obeying God's law, living in Christ's strength, distinguishing between good and evil, praising God's gifts and enduring tribulation.

Chapter Ten. *On Prayer*

1. Prayer is a conversation with God, a piece of the inner, spiritual, heavenly life, the characteristic and mark of a faithful Christian's heart, a continual movement of the Holy Spirit since he is a Spirit of grace and of prayer (Zech. 12:10), a work of divine healing. As the natural life moves the body, so the Holy Spirit moves through prayer, tears, holy meditation, heartfelt sorrow for human misery, pleas that sins or the punishment for sins be set aside, intercessions for all men and for those in authority, prayers of the Holy Spirit for knowledge and understanding, consolation, relief in tribulation, protection, strengthening of faith, patience, and all needs; and through prayer and thanksgiving for the goodness of God, by which God might be praised, given homage and honored in all his words and blessings. [Prayer] occurs in secret, in a little chamber, in the heart, in all places, in all occupations, or openly in the congregation in the confession of faith to the honor of the holy Name of God and in thanksgiving for all blessings.

2. All must be done in spirit and on truth, in the depth of the heart, without hypocrisy, before God, not before men except where it is required that God be publicly praised and thanked in the congregation. . . .

3. Prayer is an indicator of a true faithful Christian, a powerful living witness of the Holy Spirit. . . .

[Prayer is a precious work and the highest honor, to be offered to God alone. It must be done in the love of God and the joy of faith with total resignation to God's will and certain expectation of divine help. Prayer strengthens, unites man with God and brings him into the community of angels.]

10. Since our flesh and blood is weak, there are three strong aids for our prayer: (1) *The prayers of our own Intercessor and eternal High Priest* (Heb. 5:7) . . . , (2) *The Holy Spirit who helps our weakness and himself intercedes for us with sighs too deep for words* (Rom. 8:26), (3)

The holy Christian Church which prays for all true members of Christ (Eph. 6:18).

11. Satan steps in to hinder our prayers in many ways and by many means, by disturbing meditation, troubling thoughts, [stirring up] the temptation that prayers will not be heard, [noting our] unworthiness, continuation of sins, and many mistakes. We must learn to oppose him (1) with God's command . . . *"Call on Me in the time of need"* (Ps. 50:15), (2) with his promise . . . *"Before you have called, I will answer"* (Is. 65:24; Ps. 145:18, 34:18), (3) with the Intercessor and chief High Priest Jesus Christ, (4) with the seat of grace . . . (Rom. 3:25), (5) [with the knowledge] that God casts out no poor repentant sinner's prayer (Ps. 102:18–20 . . . Ps. 66:20), (6) that God has commanded us to continue in prayer (Lk. 18:1 . . . Mt. 7:7), (7) [that] God has made us a spiritual priesthood . . . (Rev. 1:6 . . .).

Chapter Eleven. The Christian life has many trials but for consolation we should know that the Christian life is the true worship that will destroy Satan, that it is the noble life of Christ and the fear of the cross in us, that a distinction is made between the children of God and the children of the Devil, that those who live according to the flesh do not belong to the kingdom of God, that the Christian life is the narrow way, that this way Christ himself and the saints have gone.]

Part Two:

On the Mystical Union of the Believer with Jesus Christ, His Head

Chapter One. *The first basis and demonstration of the union of God with man is the creation and redemption of man*

All of nature and each creature were created for the homage and honor of the eternal, true, and almighty God alone. Because of this, all the creatures and works of God together praise and acknowledge the glory and goodness of their Creator, for everything was made so perfect, good, glorious, and beautiful by the highest Artisan and Artist that the Creator himself rejoiced in his works when he saw their perfect goodness, manifold beauty, and truth.

Among all his works there was no visible likeness of the invisible God that was similar to its Creator. Therefore, by a special, marvelous, and miraculous decision of the Holy Trinity, God created man to his image, that is, he produced a living image and likeness of his goodness, holiness and righteousness in man, whom he made as the perfect conclusion and end of all his works. Thus, in a single man, as in a masterful and short extract, the worthiness, goodness, beauty, and excellence of the creation were gathered together. Should not God have created in his image that in which the Creator himself might have joy and pleasure? This image of God in man united and bound God and man together in the closest and firmest way by the likeness of righteousness and holiness. Thus, also, the Lord made his seat and dwelling in man himself. He said that his joy was with the children of man (Prov. 8:31).

However, after the fall of man, by which this union was broken and dissolved, the eternal mercy of God the heavenly Father wished to establish it again by the renewal of his covenant in man through the life-giving word, through faith in the promise, through the incarnation of his only begotten, essential Son, through the rebirth of man and through the mysteries of the holy sacraments. By such means he bound man once again to himself and made him the dwelling place and seat of his Holy Spirit, and thus united him with himself and made him once again holy with his gracious dwelling and indwelling. O unspeakable grace and goodness of the highest majesty of God! O miraculous decision to redeem the human race, praiseworthy in all eternity!

The one, only powerful, greatest, best, only holy, wise, and only eternal God established his seat and dwelling in man, whom he created to his image, who was returned to the enjoyment of the highest good and blessedness, who was reborn to immortal glory, and who was enlightened to a taste of eternal wisdom. God wished man to have rest in him.

Why did God rest after he had created man (Gen. 2:2)? [He did so] because man ought to be God's rest. Therefore, he made man as the last creature and at the end of his creation because he wished to rest in each man. The eternal and most holy God himself spoke of this indwelling (Is. 57:15). Thus spoke the Highest and the Sublime who dwells eternally, whose Name is holy: *I dwell in the*

heights and in holiness and with those who are of contrite and humble of
spirit, so that I renew the spirit of the humble and the heart of the contrite.
Here our most gracious Indweller himself unites his divine height,
majesty, glory, and holiness with man's nothingness; he has made
and ordered the humble and contrite spirit as his dwelling place.
Elsewhere it is said that God sits above the Cherubim (Ps. 80:2),
but concerning man the apostle says: *You are a temple of the almighty,*
living God (2 Cor. 6:16). Indeed, he comes closer to this inner union
when he says: *He who wishes to cling to God is one spirit with Him* (1
Cor. 6:17). What could be more glorious and divine than to be one
spirit with God? What could be more blessed than to be and remain
in God? As the Evangelist John says: *You will remain both in the Son*
and in the Father (1 John 2:14). This our Sanctifier himself stated
when he called the union received from the Father his glory, and
said in John 17:22: *The glory which you have given me, I have given*
them, so that they may be one as we also are one, I in them and you in me.
In this regard he compares himself also to a vine and us to the
grapes on the vine (Jn. 15:2ff.). From him, the life-giving sap and
power, we drink and act. By and through ourselves we can no
longer truly and properly live unless we live in Christ, as the apostle testifies in Galatians 2:20 [and] . . . 2 Corinthians 13:5.

It is a great honor and glory for the chief princes and lords of
the Roman Empire that they bear the sword, apple, and scepter of
the Empire. How much greater honor and glory is it that Christians
are and are called bearers of God and Christ, and are thus one with
the Holy Trinity in that they carry in themselves God, the Conqueror of the world. The evangelist says: *He who is in us is greater*
than he who is in the world (1 John 4:4).

Chapter Two. *The union of God with man is demonstrated through*
the image of God in man
The image of God in man is that conformity with God in
which the likeness of the invisible God is characteristically and
vitally published and shines forth, namely, as a likeness of goodness, righteousness, holiness, immortality, wisdom, mercy, might,
power and faith, and so forth. These characteristics, since they are
essentially and infinitely together in God, God himself wishes to
express in man as a living portrait and image. Every likeness begets
love, but love [results in] attraction and union. What ought God to

247

bind and unite to himself better and firmer with love than his image and likeness? Where ought God to dwell more than in his image? With whom ought he to unite himself more lovingly than with him whom he created to his image and likeness? God the Father is in his only begotten Son, the eternal and essential image of God the eternal Father. Here the essential union of the Father and his image shines forth most clearly. As a likeness of this union, however, and to copy it, the dear God according to his infinite goodness wished also to be united with created man by a gracious indwelling. For this reason he ignited the light of true and perfect knowledge of God in man's reason so that God himself with the light and beam of his divine wisdom might shine in man. The affection of purest and most perfect love he planted in the heart of man so that God, who is love itself, might be strong and active through the love of man. The perfect righteousness, holiness, and truth he placed in man's will so that he himself might bring forth and practice righteousness, holiness, and truth through man.

However, without the indwelling and union of God with man this could in no way occur unless God would unite himself with man by his image and likeness. How supremely good, glorious, and lovely is the statement of the Holy Trinity because of this when it decided and said: *Let us make man in our image* (Gen. 1:26). This is as much as to say: Let us make man, who is to be a living mirror of our divine light and wisdom, our love and goodness, our righteousness and holiness, our truth and immortality, our might and glory, so that we might be seen and shine forth in man as in our living image.

What is God's image in man other than a clear and renewed, brightly shining beam of the unspeakable goodness of God? This goodness indeed has its source and essence in God. In man, however, [it is] a beautiful divine adornment and precious grace out of which the great divine goodness and glory gleam forth and shine. The essential image of the Son of God is called the light of glory (Heb. 1:3) so that in the essential image of God the Father, glory might shine forth as the glory of the only-begotten Son of the Father. Why ought the gracious image of God in man not be simply called a bright renewed light of divine goodness? O the unspeakable love and gentleness of God, which no man's intellect can grasp! What more will the elect be when they are like God and see him as he is himself (1 John 3:2)? Finally the perfect union with God will occur; the conformity with God will be perfect. The greater and more perfectly the image of God shines in us in this life, the greater is the union with God. Therefore, by the perfect image and likeness, the perfect union will be brought about and completed, namely, when we see him as he is.

Therefore, the perfection and full pleasure of man is his union with God; union with God is however, the greatest blessedness. Rejection and separation is the greatest unholiness and misery.

Chapter Three. *By the word of God a union of God and man is established*

That the divine revealed word is a bond of the union between God and man the very first commandment testifies. [That commandment] was given to man in Paradise and by it the Lord God bound man fast to himself. By the act of disobedience, the dissolution and division of the most holy union immediately followed and the image of God was lost. Nothing is nor can be called more disturbing, frightening, and abominable, for when man lost the image of God, he lost himself and fell from light into darkness, from truth into lies, from righteousness into unrighteousness, from holiness into all kinds of shame and sin, from the glorious and beautiful adornment into an abominable, hateful nakedness, from freedom into heavy servitude and the power of the Devil, from life into death, from heaven into hell, from Paradise into external misery, from health into many and manifold illnesses, from the greatest wealth into the deepest poverty, from blessed rest into hard and heavy work, from the sweetest pleasure and joy into all sorts of sorrow, anguish, and pain; and what is worse, in the fall itself a most regretful division from God began, flight from the face of God, a servile fright and shame, a thick darkness in man's reason and understanding, a turning of the will from God, a stubbornness and hardness of heart and enmity against God, so that the prophet does not unfittingly write: *Your sins separate you from God* (Is. 59:2).

This most lamentable division and separation from God might have remained for all eternity had not the Word come between and reestablished and remade the union. God called man through the Word out of his flight to himself from darkness to light, from lies to truth, from death to life, from doubt to grace. Man was ashamed and acknowledged his hateful nakedness. God pointed out that he had overstepped his law. He ordered the serpent before him and cursed it, but took man again into grace and promised an Intercessor who would avenge him, and named this [Intercessor] the seed of woman who would crush the serpent (Gen. 3:15). In this manner, God, our gracious Father, once more took up man who had broken his word, and united him with himself. Thus, from the beginning, the implantation of the sanctifying word was nothing other than a binding and union of man with God. Thus, man's soul and mind, which by sin had been separated from God, were united with him so that the All-highest again built and established his seat and dwelling place [in him]. The word of God is the wagon on which God travels (Ezek. 1:15 . . . Zech. 6:1). Out of the mouth of God, the Word proceeds united with the Holy Spirit (Is. 59:21). If it is despised and set aside, God himself bypasses man and leaves him (1 Sam. 15:23). *Because you have cast out my Word, I have cast you out*, says he who gave the Word. The Lord God binds himself to the Word when he says: *I am with you. According to the Word by which I have made a covenant with you, My Spirit will remain with you* (Hag. 2:5 –6). How could the union with God through the Word be more clearly indicated? Indeed, the memory, honor, and service of God, insofar as it is directed to him, binds God to us as Exodus 20:24 says: *In all places where the memory of my Name is established, I will come to you and bless you*. In the Word and holy sacraments the proper memory of the Name of God is established. Therefore, he will unite with us by word and sacrament. This our Savior in beautiful and loving words affirmed: *He who loves me will keep my word and my Father will love him and we will come to him and make our dwelling-place with him* (Jn. 14:23).

Therefore, it is called a Word that enlightens our eyes (Pss. 19:8, . . . 118:27) . . . a Word of salvation (Acts 13:26 . . . Ps. 27:1) . . . a life-giving Word (Jn. 10:9 . . . Jn. 14:6) . . . a permanent seed of God . . . (1 Pet. 1:23) . . . a power of God (Rom. 1:16). God, however, is the power that works in us. Truly it is fitting that God's presence, activity, and union enlighten us, give us new birth and life. Since this occurs through the Word, it is necessary that God himself be present in and with the Word.

There come in addition the gracious promises of God, which bind and unite God and man together. *Fear not, says the Lord* (Is. 41:10), *for I am with you, be not dismayed for I am your God; I will*

strengthen you, I will help you, I will uphold you. And again in chapter
43:2: *When you pass through the water and walk through the fire I will be
with you*. With these dear consoling promises, God places himself in
our hearts. In addition to this there is the oath that he swore to us,
which is a firm bond of the union of God with man. See also Isaiah
45:23–25 . . . and Isaiah 54:9, 17. . . .

Through this word and prophecy the revelation of the Word of
God came to the apostles and prophets (1 Pet. 1:10–11; Acts 2:4,
9:14). Therefore, it is called God's word and a Voice having gone
forth from God because the Spirit of God spoke it through the
mouth of the prophets, and *holy men of God spoke inspired by the Holy
Spirit* (1 Pet. 1:22). This could not have occurred without the special union of God with man. This union is clearly shown and demonstrated in that it is written that the holy prophets and apostles
were filled with the Holy Spirit to make known the Word of God
(Lk. 1:70). In addition, God's help and presence itself belongs to
true consolation by which troubled and contrite hearts are raised up
and made living. This the prophet gives witness to in Isaiah
57:15. . . . The royal Prophet David too was satisfied with no
consolation unless he had and possessed God himself (Ps. 73:25).
The souls of those who fear God are satisfied with no good except
God himself . . . (Ps. 34:8).

Chapter Four. *The incarnation of the Son of God is the chief foundation and demonstration of the union with God*

Before his incarnation, the Son of God often appeared to the
fathers in human form so that he might strengthen and confirm
their faith and hope in the coming incarnation (Gen. 18:1ff.). Is not
the union of divine and human nature a certain and unerring mark
and sign of the union of God with man? The loving and consolatory
name "Immanuel" (Is. 7:14) gives witness of this as well. It does not
only mean a "living with" (. . . Jn. 18:26 . . . Jn. 15:4–5). Christ
lives in his members (Eph. 3:17), makes them living, and creates in
them the spiritual life as the Apostle Paul said in Romans 8:10. . . .
For this reason the apostle commands us that we are to test and seek
this indwelling in us (2 Cor. 13:5 . . .). Indeed, he considers this
indwelling of Christ in us as a certain sign of the coming glory of
which he speaks of in Colossians 1:27. . . .

The holy body of our Lord is the holiest temple and dwelling

251

in which *the complete fullness of the divinity dwells bodily* (Col. 2:9).
Thus, God made the hearts of faithful men as his holy place and
dwelling place, as the apostle indicates in Ephesians 2:22 . . . and
the Son of God made this known earlier in John 14:20. . . . Oh, the
miraculous worth of the faithful, the bodily community of blessedness that is above all things.

Chapter Five. *Concerning the indwelling of the Holy Spirit*

How great a relationship, community, and union of the highest and eternal God with man is established is clearly witnessed by
three chief works of grace: first, the creation of man to God's image
. . . (Gen. 1:26), second, the incarnation of the Son of God, third,
the sending of the Holy Spirit. Through these great works, the
Lord God revealed and made clear the purpose for which man was
created, redeemed and made holy, namely, that he might enjoy
communion with God in which the highest and only blessedness of
man consists.

Therefore, *the Word became flesh and dwelt with us* (Jn. 1:14).
Therefore, the Holy Spirit was sent down from heaven so that he
might establish this communion and union of God with man.

1. We have great need of the Spirit of God so that we might be
freed and loosed from the spirit of this world. We have great need
of the spirit of wisdom (Is. 11:2) so that we might love the highest
good. The spirit of understanding is very necessary for us so that
we might be able to wisely carry out the responsibilities of our
calling. [Likewise, we need] the spirit of counsel so that we might
bear the cross in patience, the spirit of strength and of power so that
we might conquer the world and the Devil, the spirit of understanding so that we might shun vices and evils, the spirit of
childlike fear so that we might be pleasing to God, the spirit of
grace and of prayer so that we might call upon God in all our needs
and be able to praise his grace and goodness in all his works (Zech.
12:10).

2. We have been chosen as the children of God in Christ
Jesus, as the apostle makes clear in Romans 8:16 and Ephesians
2:13. Because of this God our dear Father wished to strengthen this
great grace, which is also a spirit of God the Son, so that he might
make us partakers of the divine nature as true and proper children
who are born out of God and remain in God as is written in 1 John

4:13: *By this we know that we abide in him and he in us because he has given us of his own Spirit.* A true, natural son does not only have the flesh and blood of his parents but also has their manner of life and mind. In a like manner those who are born of God must have God's Spirit and bear something godly in themselves as Galatians 4:6 says. . . .

3. Because of his only-begotten Son, God took us up as his children. He has also established us as his heirs and co-heirs of his Son, Jesus Christ. Therefore, he gave us the spirit, the seal of the coming inheritance, with whom he sealed us for the life of his glory (Eph. 1:13).

4. He also cleansed us with his spirit in witness of the received, but still hidden, royal worth and glory (Ps. 45:8). As we have been led and directed with wisdom, doctrine, and knowledge of eternal salvation, we have received the purification of the spirit (1 John 2:20).

5. We are also purified with this oil of joy against the world and the Devil's foolishness and raging. So that we might not suffer, *the heavenly Father poured into our hearts His love through the Holy Spirit* (Rom. 5:5).

6. Because we are often spotted and unclean because of the impurity of our flesh, he also gave to us the spirit of holiness so that we might continually grow up again and be cleansed, as the apostle says in 1 Corinthians 6:11 . . . and Romans 8:9. . . .

7. Finally, because we must have a life-giving spirit against death, God our Father sanctified our bodies as the temples and dwelling places of the Holy Spirit, as the apostle teaches in 1 Corinthians 6:19 . . . and Romans 8:11. . . .

Chapter Six. *The union of God with man occurs by healing repentance or conversion to God as true regret and sorrow for sins and by faith*
Return, faithless Israel, says the Lord, I will not look on you in anger, for I am merciful . . . (Jer. 3:12) . . . (Jer. 3:1). With these gracious and loving words God our heavenly Father promises and will bring it about that man will return to him again and be united with him. Adultery breaks up the marital union and splits apart the two that should be one flesh (Mt. 19:5–6). Sin and misdeeds bring about such a spiritual divorce between God and man. Healing repentance, however, brings about spiritual remarriage and union. Therefore, our merciful God and Father, who does not wish to be

eternally angry with us, speaks to us in these words: Be converted to me for I am your man; I will be faithful to you; you have gone about with many harlots but have come back again, says the Lord.

The beginning of conversion is godly sorrow, which brings about a regret that leads to salvation that no one regrets (2 Cor. 7:10). God himself is the beginner and the cause of this healing sorrow. The prophet says this in his words in Isaiah 40:7. . . . Through this sorrow, which is awakened through the Spirit of God, the beginning of healing conversion and a return to God is made, and through faith the union is perfected and brought to its end.

Let the example of the prodigal son stand before us, the son who turned again to his own father (Lk. 15:20ff.). Beloved, what do the heart-felt embrace, kiss, and the beautiful new clothes signify, what do the ring and the new shoes signify, other than the fervent mercy, new gift-giving of lost goods and gifts, and the dear union?

Let us look at the hot tears of the poor sinner with which she washed the feet of her deserving Savior and let us look how she anointed him and how she kissed his feet (Lk. 7:38). Are not all your acts with the Lord Jesus anything other than a simple indwelling and a simple, precious bond by which they bind and tie together firmly anew the union with God?

The Lord is the only rest and enlivener of our souls. Therefore, he graciously calls to all who are invited (Mt. 11:28), not because he wishes to enliven and wash something externally with his loving joy and graciousness, but that he wishes to console them internally and pour his presence into their hearts with sweet grace and favor. Indeed, much more, he wishes to dwell in their lowly and humble hearts. He does not only truly take up the repentant, but he anoints their hearts and makes them holy so that they may be his temple and dwelling place.

Faith maintains itself firmly and strongly in such divine kindness and graciousness. It rests in these and walks before the heavenly Father with great trust and kindness in the power of the merit of Christ; it grasps him in the most loving manner; it holds to him firmly and does not let him go until he unites himself with it; it is consoled in God and is at peace. The highest characteristic of faith is that it clings firmly to God alone and does not break off from him, and sets all creatures by the side; that it enjoys God's grace alone fruitfully; that it seeks without ceasing the Lord God alone; and that God alone remains for the faithful soul a satisfaction of joy and the highest good. It is impossible to show how such things can occur without the union that has been spoken of, for faith creates out of the well of salvation, out of our Sanctifier, the only true powers of the soul, namely, salvation, righteousness, and holiness, so that the soul has for its own possession everything that is in Christ and belongs to him. In addition, faith also creates out of the well health for the body, as the evangelist in Luke 8:43 and Matthew 9:20 indicated in the story of the woman with an issue of blood who touched the hem of the garment of her great Savior. By faith in a spiritual manner she received power that went out from the holy temple of his body, was taken to her long illness, and made her healthy and new again.

From this it is clearly to be understood that the power of faith is stronger than a magnet, as our Savior said: *My daughter be consoled, your faith has saved you; go in peace.* A lovely, sweet-smelling flower gives off its odor in an unseen way. A person who is drawn by the odor to the flower will not be drawn away or taken away from the flower even if some thousand men also smell the same odor. It is the same with our flower of Paradise, the Lord Christ. He gives off an odor of his life from himself, so rich and overwhelming that by the odor of faith all faithful men are drawn to him, yet he loses nothing from it no matter how much goes out from him. A single light is able to ignite a thousand others and still remain the light. Likewise the light of faith ignited and enlightened from one light, the Lord Christ, remains always the eternal light complete and undiminished.

Chapter Seven. *The union of Christ with the believing soul occurs through the spiritual wedding and marriage*

If the bridegroom comes, the holy soul rejoices and looks closely and eagerly toward his presence. By his joyous, enlivening, and holy arrival he drives out darkness and night and the heart has sweet joy, the waters of meditation flow in upon it, the soul melts for love, the spirit rejoices, the affections and the desires become fervid, love is ignited, the mind rejoices, the mouth gives praise and honor, man takes vows, and all the powers of the soul rejoice in and because of the bridegroom. It rejoices, I say, because it has found what it loves and because he whom it loves has taken it up to himself as his bride. Oh what a love! Oh what a fiery desire! Oh what a loving conversation! Oh how chaste a kiss! If the Holy Spirit comes, if the Consoler overshadows [the soul], if the Highest enlightens [it], if the Word of the Father is there, wisdom speaks and loves and receives it in joy.

At the same time, the soul is made into a temple of God, into a seat of wisdom, into a dwelling place of chastity, into a receiver of the covenant, into a tabernacle of holiness, into a chamber of the bridegroom, into a spiritual heaven, into a blessed land, into a house of mysteries, into a dear bride, into a dear garden, into a room and chamber of the marriage, and into a Paradise garden sweet-smelling and strewn with many beautiful flowers of virtue to which the Lord of all angels and the King of honor goes, so that he might marry the deeply beloved bride who is sick with love, adorn her with the flower of holy desire, bedeck her with the apples of virtue, and wait upon his dearly beloved when he comes in his adornment. Since she shines with the crown of a pure conscience, with the snow-white cloak of chastity that she has put on, and with the precious, noble pearl of good works that adorns her, she is no way afraid before him as before the sight of a harsh judge, but her only and deepest desire is that she might see and contemplate the presence of the Lord Bridegroom for which she has carried her desire (which also the blessed hosts and the heavenly spirits of joy, the angels in heaven consider as the highest glory).

After the soul enjoys his chaste association, no creature can know how great a joy it has from this and how it feels in its heart, how fervent it is internally, how it rejoices and shouts for joy because of love, how lovely and heartfelt words and conversations come to it. No one, I say, can know this except the person who has experienced it. To feel and to experience this is possible for a man but to express it is impossible, for it is a spiritual mystery and divine matter concerning which man dare not speak so that he carry no fault against the Bridegroom who loves to dwell in the mystery and in the stillness of the heart.

Above all things and in particular, this Bridegroom has his greatest pleasure to dwell in the lowly and humble heart whose honor is a treasure of many and great graces, a daily growth and development of gifts, the peace of the conscience, the light of understanding, a spiritual exultation, a pure prayer, a justified heart and mind, a continuing faith, the power of compassion, a firm hope, a burning love, a taste of divine sweetness, a desire to learn, a thirst for virtue. This is the greatest treasure of the humble one, which no thief can take away or steal. It is his precious, noble stone, his unceasing wealth, his highest honor, his chief glory, his secret pleasure, the Bridegroom's gift, the highest adornment and the spiritual wine cellar of the bride into which the proud cannot enter, nor are the lazy and impure allowed in. Indeed, through this as through the spiritual gates the Bridegroom comes to the bride, teaches and instructs it and shares his presence with it, not through the bodily form but through the light of faith, through the beam of understanding, through the taste of meditation, through the joyous cry of exultation, through the gracious leaping of love, through the kiss of peace, through the embrace of faithfulness. At the same time the opponent does not come near to it because of the presence of the Bridegroom, and no stranger dare enter in for the soul is ringed round with many thousand holy angels that keep watch over it.

Then the humble soul is a temple of God, a seat of wisdom, a throne of the word, a house of the consoler, a room of the Bridegroom, the receiver of the covenant, a golden throne of grace, a tabernacle of holiness, a place of holy peace, a paradise of pleasure, a closed garden, a sealed fountain, an earthly paradise, a heavenly dwelling place. The heavenly spirits themselves marvel at this great worth that is given to man by God and they marvel over the love of the Bridegroom who sets aside the light of his divinity as consolation for the bride and, how shall I say, gives up eternal honor, lowers himself, and is willing to dwell in a breakable vessel not as a mighty king, nor as a lord over everything, nor as a judge over the living and the dead, but as a weak man among weak people, as a lowly man among lowly people, as a humble man enduring all insult and as a needy man with a poor bride. Behold, the holy angels say to one another: How great a difference is there between God and man, between the Creator and the creation, between the Lord and the servant, between day and night, between wisdom and ignorance, between the Word and the soul? This spiritual marriage is far beyond all human understanding, all self-will, all marital life, for it is a heavenly gift, a work of grace of the Redeemer, a lowly will of the Bridegroom, a foretaste of love, a special privilege of special love that is truly given to all those who are humble of heart, who truly know themselves, who hold themselves for nothing, and who consider themselves as unfruitful trees, as paltry and poor servants, as useless vessels, and as stinking carrion. This soul to which our Lord came so joyously, so humbly, so helpfully, if it were not adorned with the virtue of humility, and clothed with the light of purity, and ignited with the flame of heavenly desire, and enlightened with continual prayer, and continually endeavoring after all these so that it might protect its pure heart, would not have been worthy of this spiritual and mysterious wedding and marriage with the Son of God.

The soul, however, is betrothed to the Bridegroom; it hears what he says to it internally: *Arise my love, my fair one and come away* . . . (Song 2:10). The bride who is sick because of this heart-breaking, lovely conversation speaks from love: *My soul melts with love . . . my beloved is to me a bag of myrrh that lies between my breasts* . . . (Song 1:13–14). The Bridegroom once again notes the praise of the bride so that he ignited her further in love and says, *Your lips distill nectar, my bride . . .* (Song 4:11–13), but the bride answers full of sweet love: *My beloved is all radiant and ruddy distinguished among ten thousand, I will cling to him and not let him go* (Song 5:10). In this most holy of embraces many holy kisses of love are given, the joyous conversation is held that no human ear can hear, no haughty eye can see, and that comes to no human heart that thinks on carnal things. There are only those pleasures that belong to the humble. It is a hidden manna, it is a honey in honeycomb and a wine mixed in milk. If this is tasted, the heart is joyous and refreshened to such a degree that the weariness and labor of its life in this world is made easier. It would be easily offended and insulted on the way if it would not be at the same time enlivened by spiritual food, fed with milk, strengthened with visitation, directed with conversation, and bound with the physical bonds of love and love returned, for thereby it comes to understanding and tastes how many and manifold are the sweetnesses of the Lord that are hidden in the elect and promised to the humble and to those who love God with a pure heart.

This is a foretaste of eternal life, which is the highest good, the eternal joy and unspeakable pleasure, a perfect satisfaction and undisturbed peace, a true freedom, a certain enjoyment, and unceasing refreshment, an active joy and unending praise that no misfortune can disturb, no enemy take away, no time change or take away, for it is certain, continual, and eternal. The man who is made a partaker of the Lord's loveliness has nothing over which to fear that he will suffer pain, or in which he may doubt, or on which he must further hope. At all times he enjoys the presence of him whom he loves, to whom he gives homage, whom he honors, and whom he knows. His knowledge is eternal life, his kiss is the highest holiness, his love is the highest glory, his praise is unspeakable joy, and his presence is a firm possession of all goods. He who comes to this goes upon a green meadow that does not fade away. He comes to a loving pleasure that will never cease, to treasures of wisdom that will not be corrupted, to the light of truth that will not be darkened by anything, to the land of the living who praise God unceasingly, to the city of Jerusalem, which shines bright with the beam of the eternal Son, and to the holy mountain of Zion, which is adorned with the thousands of thousands of holy angels and is beautified with the choir of the saints. All these at the same time with one clear voice, with the same song, with the same thoughts, insofar as they are capable, speak to and offer praise with fervent desires to God: *Salvation and praise, honor and power, be to God our Lord from eternity to eternity, Amen* (Rev. 19:1).

Each one lays his crown before the majesterial throne (Rev. 4:10). The honor, homage, and offerings they bring to their Creator are full of perfect love grounded in humility, mixed with wonder, and fiery and fervent with the desiring enjoyment of the highest good. They drink indeed, and they still thirst; they are satisfied and they are yet hungry; they have fullness of everything and they desire to be filled; for they are made drunken by the superabundance of eternal pleasure in which they live wisely and temperately according to their pleasure from the well of life, the drink of divine sweetness, and from the light of sanctifying contemplation, the unspeakable light, as the prophet indicated in . . . Psalm 36:9–10. O holy drunkenness, which is not full of nothingness, which after its superfluity and taste lifts one to God the moment it is tasted and unites him with God so that the two become one! O well of life, which is with God and from which all those who are elected to the heavenly region and life may freely drink without any ceasing of the fountain to holy, perfect satisfaction.

259

King David had a fervent and searching desire for this spring, as he said in Psalm 42:2, *My soul thirsts for God, for the living God. When shall I come and behold the face of God?* This face is to be praised, loved, and desired above all others. There is the breadth of goodness that has no end and encompasses everything. There is the wisdom that sees into all things. There is the highness over all error. He who knows this well has unspeakable joy.

Chapter Eight. *The union of God with man is made through love given and returned*

God is love and he who dwells in love dwells in God and God in him (1 John 4:16). For love itself he became man that it might be the bond of our eternal union with God. O holy union, O holy communion, which shares the taste of love and the sweetness of pleasure with pious hearts! O sweet Lord Jesus, penetrate our hearts with the fiery arrows of your love. Break through into the closed and inner chamber of the soul and heart and enlighten it graciously with your light so that we might have in you our dwelling place, our peace, our joy, our all, our hope, our love, our exultation, our life, our refreshment, our light, our rest, our trust, and all our goods.

What is sweeter than your love? What is more healing than your goodness? What is more loving than your memory? O eternal love, without you nothing better may be sought, nothing more costly may be found, nothing more firm may be bound together, nothing more fervid may be grasped, nothing more lovely may be possessed. This, those who love you know. Your love is a source of immortality, a fountain of wisdom, a stream of pleasure, a life of faith, a depth of goodness, a paradise of joy, a consolation of those who wander in this pilgrim world, a payment of the holy, a food of love, a root of virtue, a scale of works, a strength for those who strive, a bond of union, and a continual foundation and fundament of our whole holiness. *Let him who thirsts come to you and he will receive the water of life* (Jn. 7:37, 4:14). Let him who is weary come to you and he will be revived with your love. Let him who suffers trials come to you and he will conquer by your love and will have the victory. From your fullness, O Lord, we have all received (Jn. 1:16).

Chapter Nine. *The Christian Church and its head Christ Jesus are united because of the spiritual body and his gifts*

For just as the body is one and has many members and all the members of the body, though many, are one body, so it is with Christ. For by one spirit we are all baptized into one body (1 Cor. 12:12). Our highest and only head adorns the members of his spiritual body with many gifts of grace and the spirit. He teaches them with many gifts that the spirit alone works in them. The Lord Christ lives and works in all the members of his body so that each one might receive of his fullness (Jn. 1:16), for he as the head has all the fullness of all and each gift.

Therefore, he wishes to clothe himself and transform himself in each person so that through the bond of love each person might be reformed and renewed in him and confirmed and made similar to him. Just as the pain of the head is ascribed to the members, so also is the virtue of the members ascribed to the head, so that he who honors virtue honors the head and he who suffers among the members is consoled by the head. In the insult of each individual one may consider the insult of the head and the pain will then be lessened and the bitterness made sweet if it is compared to the suffering of the head. The whole body of your innocent head suffered the cross and full tribulation for all other mortal men. If you then suffer innocently, you demonstrate that you are a member of Christ. He made himself like you so that you might make yourself like him.

You are a member of his body; he is the life of the body. Without you the body is healthy and vital and remains; without the head, however, the body can in no way live, for it lives by the spirit of the head, and has its life through the Word. The head makes the whole body alive; it makes all the members alive. Members are lifted up in the body, but the body is honored in the head and shares with the members life, spirit, and the gift of grace so that the body might enjoy the complete fullness of the head. Thus, our head gathers all the members of his Christian Church in that he shares with them the power of the spirit. By the sermons of the human voice, he wishes to gather together a church and by them he wishes also that each man might hear the Lord Christ speak in him, as the apostle pointed out in 2 Corinthians 13:3 . . . and Romans 15:18. The Lord Christ speaks internally, the instructor teaches the heart so that the sermon might be powerful. The Lord Christ speaks internally to the heart of the hearer so that the sermon of the teacher might be understood. He opens the hearts of the hearers and makes the speech powerful in the mouth of the teacher. *"Open your mouth,"* says God through the prophet, *"and let me fill it"* (Ps. 81:10).

Who wishes to believe that he could teach and preach usefully without the direction and guidance of the spirit of wisdom? The spirit of wisdom, which lives in man, speaks the mysteries through man. Therefore I do not listen to Paul for the sake of Paul; I do not believe in Paul because he is Paul. I do not listen to any man for the sake of man but I listen to man for the sake of the Lord Christ and I hear the Lord Christ speak through Paul. Therefore, our Savior says: *He who hears you hears me and he who despises you despises me* (Lk. 10:16 . . .).

The body was not only united with the head so that the body might be made rich from the treasures of the head, but this also occurred so that pain might be shared and made common between them. The true characteristic of union is that if the head is honored so are the other members and that the head suffers what the body suffers. The head said this itself: *I was hungry and I was thirsty, I was a stranger, I was naked and what you did for one of the least of these my brethren, you did for me* (Mt. 25:35). Oh immeasurable goodness! Oh unbreakable union of love! The Creator of heaven, the King of angels, the Lord of the archangels, the Praise of the saints, the Creator of all things, and the Joy of the blessed will be satisfied as a hungry man, given drink as a thirsty man, taken in as a stranger, clothed as a naked man, visited as a sick man, consoled as a prisoner, and buried as a dead man. These are above all the godly testimonies of union, goodness, and graciousness of the faithful members with the head of Christ.

Chapter Ten. *The union of God with man occurs through the desire of the highest good and through the eager longing for a heavenly life on earth*

The light of the sun is greater than all the lights of the other heavenly bodies and in a similar way the taste of divine sweetness is greater than all loveliness that arises out of creatures. No matter how beautiful, adorned, and lovely a creature is that brings joy to the heart of man, it does not satisfy it. The world with its manifold goods is indeed loved by the heart, but the heart does not set its satisfaction in these. The more a man who is inclined toward earthly things sees before himself, the more he desires to see. All those things that are not God cannot give enough for the man who loves them and cannot bring perfect rest. Man's affections and desires at all times strive in a natural way to those things that are higher until they reach that which is the best and the highest good. Many of you seek wealth, honor, pleasure, and art with great labor and endeavor but none of you who seek it grasps so much of it that through it you are satisfied to consider that you have enough. If a person gained the knowledge of all things in this world, and all the pleasures of this life came to him, he would still discover that his mind was unsatisfied and needed something, or he would still be lacking the only and highest good in which the loveliness of all pleasures and the fullness of all arts and knowledge are overflowing. Creatures can give to those who love them a temporal and momentary pleasure but they cannot satify the desires with nothing. A vessel cannot pour out any other liquid than that which was poured into it and creatures that have great need can only give to their lovers such a liquid by which they will not be satisfied nor find filling. The eye is not satisfied by seeing nor is the ear by hearing nor is the heart of man satisfied through the affections and the desires of the knowledge of desire. It seeks with anxiety that it might find something in which it can joyously rest. If the heart of man finds God, the spirit rejoices, for it is now satisfied in God . . . (Ps. 73:25) . . . (Jn. 17:3). In this knowledge consists and finally exists the true rest of the soul, the satisfaction of the heart and the eternal life.

There is a beautiful passage touching upon this: *With thee is the fountain of life; in thy light do we see light* (Ps. 36:9). *I shall behold thy faith in righteousness, when I awake I shall be satisfied with beholding thy form* (Ps. 17:15). Therefore, I hope only upon you, you who are the end of all my wishes and desires. You are my satisfaction, my inheritance, my joy, my payment, my light, my peace. You are the unceasing light, you are the eternal word, the wisdom of the Father, the adornment of angels, the bright mirror, the unspeakable light, the bridegroom of the soul, the fountain of eternal life from whose superfluity we will all be satisfied here and in heaven. We will be satisfied in heaven because we will receive the true fullness of life, satisfaction of light, unity, rest, peace, immortality, praise, and the eternal crown. You will also receive it here in that you lend and give strength to Christian warriors, help to those burdened, ease to those troubled, hope to those who are estranged, counsel to those fallen, consolation to the wretched, grace to the humble, faith to those in doubt, the word to the preacher, strength to the warriors, joy to the faithful who live together in unity, wisdom to the teachers, the water of life to the thirsty, and the taste of eternal sweetness to the hungry.

Thus, in a certain way you will enter into the hearts of the faithful and reveal yourself with the loveliness of your grace. If you do not share yourself with men and man has no unity with your presence, none of this will occur. Through your joyous presence you cast out darkness, drive away night and evil spirits into the air. The heart is then thoroughly sweetened, the mind melts with love, the tears flow forth because of joy, the spirit rejoices, the desires burn, the soul leaps, and all the powers rejoice in you. Then God will quicken you with sweetness, fill you with wisdom, enlighten you with light, ignite you in love, feed you with meditation, bring you joy in hope, strengthen you in faith, fit you with virtues, lift you up in humility. You will feel and discover that he goes with you, stands by you, speaks with you, protects you, teaches you, loves you, and embraces you with chaste love. You will experience that his words *My pleasure is with the children of men* (Prov. 8:31) are true.

Chapter Eleven. *Holy baptism is a glorious affirmation of the union with God*

1. Spiritual promise and vow occur in holy baptism. In it, Christ and the Church become one as the two become one flesh in marriage. This is a great mystery says Paul in Ephesians 5:32. . . .

2. By holy baptism we are implanted and engrafted into Christ as a branch into a tree. The branch is of one being with the tree, is united with it and grows with it, for the tree makes it living and gives nourishment to the engrafted branch so that it grows, blossoms, and brings forth fruit. In a like manner the Lord Christ preserves his members with his life-giving spirit, makes them living, and strengthens them so that they blossom and bear fruit (Jn. 15:4).

The Apostle Paul in 1 Corinthians 12:13 testifies that the Christian Church or community is a body brought into being by holy baptism . . . (1 Cor. 12:27). Because of this, Christ commanded that all should be baptized who wished to be one body with the Christian community (Mt. 3:13).

He who wishes to be a member of Christ must become one through the new birth.

3. Therefore, baptism is a bath of the new birth (Tit. 3:5) in which the members of the Church are purified through water in the Word in which all spots and blemishes are rooted out so that he might present them as one congregation holy and uncorruptible (Eph. 4:25ff.). This is the true new birth and the new creature that appears before God's face, pure and holy, cleaned and purified through the blood of Christ and the Holy Spirit without any blemish. So perfect is this washing in the blood of Christ that the Bridegroom says: *You are most beautiful my friend* (Song 1:15). Therefore, the Bridegroom takes the soul and marries himself to the soul with an eternal binding and attaches himself with as many firm bonds as a husband can attach himself to his wife with. This promise in the betrothal by which the Bridegroom betroths himself to his bride is stronger than any promise. He has so loved that he has given himself up for the soul in death. Therefore, this betrothal, promise, and binding occur in the name of the Father, in faith in the Son of God, and in the power and truth of the Holy Spirit (1 Pet. 3:21; Hos. 2:19).

4. Baptism means to put on Christ (Gal. 3:27), to be adorned and beautified with the Lord Christ's own righteousness, with his obedience and holiness. Concerning this there is much to read in Ezekiel 16:10; Psalm 45:14; Isaiah 61:10, and throughout the Song of Songs.

Just as a husband attaches himself to his wife, so the Lord Christ attaches himself firmly and strongly to his congregation and never leaves it, but he loves it deeply and he holds it in his lap so that it eats his morsel and drinks of his cup . . . (2 Sam. 13:3). O unspeakable fruit of baptism! O unspeakable, noble, and glorious marriage!

5. What is baptism other than to be baptized in the Name of God the Father, Son, and Holy Spirit, to be taken up as children and heirs of God and to receive this position, to be adorned and beautified, to be made holy and to be prepared as a dwelling place of the highly praised Trinity? This is the supremacy, acclaim, worth, praise, and honor of our holy baptism.

Chapter Twelve. *The spiritual, sacramental eating in the Lord's Supper strengthens the union of the Lord Christ with the faithful*

So that the Lord Christ, our great Savior and Sanctifier, might strengthen this marvelous union with his faithful, he established the Last Supper so that it might be a sacrament or witness of his union with the faithful. Just before he established it, he prayed for this union with fervent prayer before his heavenly Father and expressed his final wish for this in John 17:22 and explained this in the beautiful passage in John 6:56: *He who eats my flesh and drinks my blood will remain in me and I in him.* Finally, when he died he wished to confirm and establish this without doubt with his own and true body and blood (Mt. 26:25). What is the giving of his own body that he gave for us in death and of his own blood that he poured out for us other than that we might be unified with Christ in one body? We are indeed through faith and the spirit with the Lord Christ a spiritual body. It pleased our Savior in grace to also give to us a bond of this union by his final will, namely his body and blood, the ransom and payment of our redemption, which unites and binds us together by a power of faith and the spirit with the Lord Christ out of the true inner affection of love. Indeed, the spirit of the Lord Christ, God's Son, binds and unites us with our head, and with all his spiritual members with and through this spiritual bond. The body of the Lord Christ, which was offered on the altar of the cross for us, and his own blood, which was poured out for the forgiveness of our sins and is directed truly and essentially to us in the Lord's Supper, is a glorious and powerful witness of the true union with Christ and a certain confirmation and strengthening of this. Therefore, the Lord Christ in this way established an order according to his power that we eat and drink his body and blood above all ways so that all the members of his body and blood might be participants in the act and so that those who are bound to him through his spirit might also be united with him through the use and enjoyment of his essential body and blood.

What is the fellowship of the body and blood of Christ of which Saint Paul speaks in 1 Corinthians 10:16 other than a union with the head Christ? In this there is not established a community of mere bread and mere wine but a community of the body and blood of Christ through bread and wine as through the means by which essential and active offering of the body and blood, the active, true, and mysterious union, is brought out and perfected. A single offering for sins on the wood of the cross was perfected through the body and blood of Christ. By it we are purified from sin and justified before God. Our High Priest, through bread and wine, consecrates and makes this holy for spiritual food and drink so that most things that he offered up to the heavenly Father for the redemption might be applied for our renewal and fellowship with him so that his flesh and blood might be for us a true food and drink by which we were to be truly redeemed.

Satan as the enemy of the human race, as the ape of God, established and set up horrid offerings among the pagans that the people were to eat of the offering that was offered to the Devil and by this enter into the fellowship of the Devil and be one body with the Devil if they ate of this offering, as the Apostle Paul pointed out in 1 Corinthians 10:20. Since this is an abominable and horrid work, it frightened off all those who are members of the Lord Christ from the practice of the devilish offering and demonstrated against it that we with the Lord Christ are one body. According to his institution by means of bread and wine we eat his true body that he gave for us, and drink his blood that he poured out for us. We cannot at the same time be participants at the Lord's table and at the Devil's table.

In the establishment of the Last Supper, the Lord Christ truly looked to this union and its strengthening. Why other did he state and declare in John 6:56 that the faithful who are to remain in him and he in the faithful are to eat his flesh and to drink his blood, since the union in Christ occurs through faith? The foundation of wisdom and truth is made the clearest in the passage: *He who eats my flesh and drinks my blood remains in me and I in him.* Why did he not say: *He who believes on me remains in me?* He did not [state this] so that we might look at the matter more earnestly and value the greatness of the matter and the weight of the words. He wishes to unite himself with us through the eating of his life-giving flesh. If this union is truly to occur in a spiritual manner through faith, he testifies clearly that he, our Savior and Sanctifier, indicated with his finger the sacramental eating, which he instituted later in the Last Supper. He not only called himself the living bread (Jn. 6:35, 51) that those who come to him will not hunger and those who believe on him will not thirst, but he also expressly said that the

267

bread that he gives is his flesh, which was given for the life of the world, and that such flesh is the true food and that his blood is the true drink that he said and promised he would give. It seems that our Savior and Sanctifier was looking toward the Last Supper, which was soon thereafter to be instituted. Therefore, he spoke well concerning the spiritual, with the exception of the Last Supper, the sacramental eating, indeed, the life-giving use and eating of his body and blood in the Last Supper, which was to be yet established at the same time. With this shaping of words I in no way reject the meaning of our teachers concerning spiritual eating that is described in John 6, but I value it and hold that the importance of the words of our Savior indicate that he was looking toward the Last Supper. Behold, that which is given for the light of the world touches the whole man. Who is then to say that the body of the faithful are not to come into the fellowship of the body and blood of Christ? The Apostle Paul says in Ephesians 5:30, *We are members of his body from his flesh and his bones*, and he writes in 1 Corinthians 6:19 that the bodies of the faithful are temples of the Holy Spirit, which dwells in them, and that they are not spotted but are consecrated and are made holy and remain to the Lord.

Those who hereafter are united with the Lord Christ their head rejoice and come with deep affection and movement of heart to the table of the Lord, continue this union with heartfelt joy, strengthen and acknowledge it publicly. Those who are strangers of Christ and members of the devil curse and speak insults against the Lord Christ out of hate. They are guilty of his body and precious blood, which he poured out, and they must fittingly wait his proper punishment and vengeance.

Chapter Thirteen. *Man is bound with God and filled with the Holy Spirit by calling upon God, praying, and praising God*

A meditative man who prays eagerly looks to and calls upon the divine majesty. Through meditation he loves it and through the power of love he is bound and united to it. With this strong love he is led out of himself to that which he loves so that he lives far more out of himself than in himself. At the same time he is also filled with such spiritual pleasure and adornment that his soul wishes to go away from himself and to enter into the living God. A meditative man is God's friend in that he continually comes before his presence and goes into his holiness without hindrance and goes about joyously with God. I must hear our Savior's consoling statement in John 10:9: *I am the door; if any one enters by me, he will be saved, and will go in and out and find pasture.* What does the going in and going out signify other than a special and great friendship? *Behold, I stand at the door and knock; if any one hears my voice and opens the door, I will come in to him and will have my supper with him and he with me* (Rev. 3:20). Since man thus stands in friendship with God, he endeavors to give himself to our God oftentimes as his friend. O you loving goodness and friendship of God!

In 1 Samuel 3:10 it says that the Lord God called Samuel by his name three times during the night and that he answered: *Speak, Lord, for thy servant heareth.* Therefore, the Lord God also speaks in Hosea 2:14: *Behold I will allure her and bring her into the wilderness and speak tenderly to her.* Augustine says and writes: "To call upon God is as much as to call God into one's heart" (*Confes.* I,1,i). The Lord came to Abraham. He said: *Behold, I have taken upon myself to speak to the Lord, I who am but dust and ashes* (Gen. 18:27). However, when the Lord saw how Abraham humbled himself and lowered himself in prayer, he came to him yet more and spoke and conversed with him in yet a friendlier way. He said in Isaiah 66:5, *I look upon the wretched, the broken of heart and he who fears my Word.*

By such a statement of the ever-present God, the Christians who fear God, who have turned no more attention and energy to anything other than to have friendship and fellowship through prayer with God, are immediately given joy. Prayer truly binds one with God, brings joy and peace in the heart, and leads one into the choir of holy angels. All human speeches, conversations, and friendship are to be counted as nothing if they are not like this conversation with God. In how lovely and friendly a manner did God the Father go about with the prophets and apostles and speak through their mouths. How great a worth did that person have who said *the spirit of the Lord has spoken through me and his voice has gone out through my mouth* (2 Sam. 23:2). What a glory did that man have concerning whom the Lord said: *I speak with him and he sees the Lord in his form, not through dark words or likenesses* (Num. 12:8). *It is a precious thing to thank the Lord and to sing praises to your name, you highest of all*, says David (Ps. 92:1). A meditative soul senses and notes that it is a precious thing but it cannot be described with words. Prayer is precious before God's presence, for the heavenly Father brings and gives beautiful gifts that are nobler and more costly than pearls and gold. He gives an angelic life, he pours into the heart the taste of eternal holiness, and he directs man to preparation for the fellowship of eternal life.

Chapter Fourteen. *The highest blessedness or end of man is to be united with God*

The souls of those who fear God cannot be satisfied unless they have God himself, as David testified . . . (Pss. 17:15, . . . 73:25). If we are to experience only a small beginning of this blessedness in this life, our union with the highest Good is a good indication of it. Spiritual joy and the taste of divine sweetness are witnesses to it and is discussed throughout the Psalms and the prophets.

Truly, meditative hearts that have given themselves to God taste nothing except God. Everything except God is to them tasteless, bitter, and dead. Therefore, holy souls have a desire for the living fountain that flows forth into eternal life to green meadows that can be found in no place outside of Christ. This is an image, indeed, a beginning of eternal life, in which God will be All in all (1 Cor. 15:28), he will be our dwelling place, our food, our satisfaction, our clothing, our love, our delight, our loveliness, our rest, our wisdom, our praise, our life. Then the glory of the children of God, which is yet hidden, will be revealed. We will see the Lord as he is, says the apostle in I John 3:2. Who will tell of God's being or the essential goodness of God, which is the total and infinite goodness? To see God is to enjoy God; to see God as he is means to participate in the complete fullness, and to be filled with the immeasurable and unending goodness of God. This fullness we know and embrace and taste in the Lord Christ. We will praise it with all the saints and holy angels, filled with the glory of Christ and with the joy of the Holy Spirit in all eternity. Of this we have said enough above in chapter 7.

Therefore, dear soul, prepare yourself, that your heart may be God's dwelling place. Unite yourself with God in this life . . . (Ps. 132:4–5). He who is united with God through true conversion in this mortal life before the soul leaves [the body] will remain united with God in the immortal life in all eternity, for God chooses to dwell in the elect and the saints and to fill them with eternal blessedness and indivisible light and glory. In a word, the soul that breaks off from the body, if it is united with God, will remain united with God in all eternity.

Chapter Fifteen. *The greatest and highest misery of man is to be eternally cut off from God*

Those men who give themselves up to the pride, covetousness, and pleasure of this world and are completely drunken in the vices of this world are not converted. They not only walk and turn themselves away from God and close off any entry to the Holy Spirit, but they are also united with the Devil. Those who cling to the Devil are not only refugees of the Devil but are also united with him eternally, for their soul is turned away from God, from the true light, rest, and joy.

The damned soul will wish for the light, but outside of God there is no light. [For them] there is and will remain an abominable and eternal darkness. They will indeed wish for rest but outside of God there is no rest for the soul, but only fright and terror. They will wish for joy but outside of God there is eternal sorrow. They will wish for refreshment but outside of God there is no refreshment, but dread and sorrow. They will seek consolation but outside of God there is no consolation, but continual martyrdom and pain and the unceasing gnashing of hell. The Devil will live in the godless, fill them with devilish fullness, with suffering, vices, stupidity, fear, horror, evil spirits, serpents' fangs, dread, pain, darkness, shame, and eternal doubt. Therefore, when the man's soul that is made impure with the Devil leaves the body, it will remain united with him in all eternity. The Devil will live in all the damned.

The soul must be redeemed from the Devil through repentance and conversion in this life, for after death there is no redemption and separation from the Devil. In a word, the soul that departs from the body that is united with the Devil will remain with the Devil in all eternity. However, if it is not blinded by the Devil and the world, if its will is not twisted, if its memory is not spotted, the Lord God will prepare a worthy dwelling place for it.

JOHANN ARNDT

Part Three

[Three chapters containing statements of faith concerning the Holy Trinity, the incarnation of the Son of God, Jesus Christ, and the Holy Spirit and his gifts.]

Book Six

[Dedicated to the mayor and council of the city of Danzig on June 10, 1620.]

Foreword to the Christian Reader

[In the first four books of true Christianity I have described the Christian life and have indicated how this is to grow from the inside and to flow out of the heart. Some people have misunderstood it, have suggested that I teach that justification is based upon works. This is not in any sense true. Because of this I wrote the Fifth Book, a book of doctrine and of consolation. I have written as well this Sixth Book to clarify my position.]

Part One

[Short defenses of each of the chapters of the first three books of *True Christianity*.]

Part Two

[Nine open letters by Johann Arndt discussing the Christian life.]

Part Three

[Two Essays on the *Theologia deutsch*.]

First Essay

[There is a need to practice the doctrines of the Christian faith and not simply discuss them. Far too many of those who call themselves Christians write books and discuss the merits of books and ideas out of pride or the search for position. The *Theologia deutsch* is not such a book however. The short discussion of the *Theologia deutsch* is contained in expanded form in the Second Essay.]

JOHANN ARNDT

Second Essay to All Lovers of True Godliness

In the publication of this and other of my books, dear Christian and good-hearted reader, it is not my intention to desire to seek my own gain or honor by them and much less to wish to help to fulfill the present need of the world with unnecessary books. [It is my intention], however, to lead men firmly to the one Book of Life, our Lord Jesus Christ, and to teach the true, proper Christian life and godliness from him as he commanded us in Matthew 11:29, *Learn from me*, and Matthew 16:24, *If anyone will follow me, let him deny himself and take up his cross and follow me*.

Without this following and denial of oneself, no one can be Christ's disciple or lover or be a true Christian. [What a true Christian is and how true Christianity must come about], these chapters teach in a completely spiritual and clear way. If you do not allow yourself to misinterpret this freely or reject my advice, you will be a lover of Christ and of true godliness.

In this book, you will not find much polemic, useless shouting, artless affectation, or harsh words, but pure, clean love, desire for the highest, eternal good, denial and rejection of the world, offering of your own will, mortification and crucifixion of your flesh, conformity with Christ in patience, meekness, humility, suffering, sorrow, and persecution. In a word, as you die to yourself and the world, Christ will live in you.

Much has been written, disputed, and argued concerning Christian doctrine but little concerning Christian life. In regard to disputation, I leave what is valuable and I do not attack it other than in its misuse. Other places I have written against polemical, antagonistic, theological argument over words, which is of no use, and against the many useless and unnecessary books and disputations by which true Christianity has not been served. The holy prophets and apostles at all times placed doctrine and life together and they zealously upheld both together. What are doctrine and life? A tree without fruit, a spring without water, clouds without rain? What is true repentance other than a change of the Adamic life and conversion from the world to God? What is true repentance and faith other than that one die to the world and live in Christ?

It is because of the great patience and long suffering of God that in so many places he allowed his Word to stand where yet great unrepentance and self-certainty existed and had fully taken the upper hand. However, if we are not righteously repentant, God will take away his Word and pure doctrine from us even if we compose enough polemical books and disputations to cover our ears. Many a man thinks he truly knows Christ if he can dispute much about the person of Christ. Yet if he does not live in Christ, he deceives himself. The person who does not have Christ's humility, patience, and meekness in his heart, and does not experience it, does not know Christ nor does he have him in a proper fashion nor does he taste him properly, and he who preaches the doctrine of Christ and does not follow his noble life preaches but only half of Christ.

Therefore, the holy Apostle Paul gathers together Christ's teaching and life in 2 Timothy 1:13: *Follow the pattern of the sound words which you have heard from me in the faith and love which are in Christ Jesus*, and the holy Apostle Peter testifies to the same thing in 2 Peter 1:5–6: *We are to walk in faith, in patience, in godliness, and love so that we might not be unfruitful in the knowledge of Jesus Christ*. Here the apostle teaches us that the knowledge of Jesus Christ consists more in practice—namely, Christ lives in us and we in him—than in knowledge and theory.

In the living and working faith and in the following of the holy life of Christ, the true living knowledge of Christ consists. Christ is the eternal life of the Father, and God is love itself. How can you properly know God and Christ if you have never tasted love in your heart?

These chapters teach how you are to take the noble life of Christ and living active faith to yourself, indeed, how you are to allow Christ to live through faith in you and to do all things. If you read through these often, and practice them continually in your life, as a flower is changed into its fruits, you must confess that it is the proper, true, living Christianity and that there is no more noble, precious life than the holy life of Christ. You must also confess that a Christian must be a new creature or he does not belong to Christ, as Saint Paul says in 2 Corinthians 5:17: *If any man is in Christ he is a new creature*.

In this renewal in Christ, in this spiritual, heavenly, godly truth, everything is set. This is the end of all theology and the whole of Christianity. This is the union with God (1 Cor. 6:15), the marriage with our heavenly Bridegroom, Jesus Christ (Hos. 2:19), the living faith, the new birth, Christ's dwelling in us, Christ's noble life in us, the Holy Spirit's fruit in us, the enlightenment and healing of the kingdom of God in us. This is all one thing, for where true faith is, there is Christ with all his righteousness, holiness, merit, grace, forgiveness of sins, adoption of God, inheritance of eternal life, that is, the new birth that comes out of faith in Christ.

Christ and faith are so united with one another that everything that is Christ is ours through faith. Where Christ lives through faith, there he brings about a holy life and that is the noble life of Christ in us. Where Christ's life is, there is pure love; and where love is, there is the Holy Spirit; and where the Holy Spirit is, there is the whole kingdom of God. If a man has one thing he has everything, but if he does not have one thing he has nothing. If he does not have from Christ a holy, noble, and new life, he has nothing from Christ, from faith, or from the new birth. *But if Christ lives in you and works and dwells in you, all the good which you do is not yours but that of the indwelling king in you* (Eph. 3:17). God's power works this in you. Therefore, you cannot ascribe it to yourself. The end and goal of the author of this *Theologia deutsch* is that a man ascribe everything that is good not to himself but to God. Much less do you earn anything with your good works, because they are not yours but God's, from whom everything that is good comes, namely, from God into us and not from us into God in such a way that he would be our debtor.

First, it is to be seen in this book that the true enlightenment and living knowledge of Christ is not to be achieved without true repentance and conversion to God, without following after the holy life of Christ, without true godliness and without a rejection of this world, for:

1. What has light to do with darkness (2 Cor. 6:14)? Unrepentance is darkness and, therefore, the light of the true knowledge of Christ has no fellowship with this. It is impossible that those people might be enlightened with the spirit and light of eternal truth who live in the darkness of unrepentance.

2. The Lord says in John 12:35: *Walk in the light while you have it so that the darkness does not come over you*, and in John 8:12: *I am the light of the world and he who follows me walks not in darkness but has the*

light of life. The following is to be understood from the life of Christ, and the light of life that followers of Christ have is the light of the true knowledge of God. From this it is clear that those are not able to be enlightened with the spirit and the light of eternal truth who do not follow Christ in his life.

3. The wisdom of God speaks in Wisdom 7:27: The Holy Spirit flees the dissolute; *he gives himself fully to holy souls and makes them prophets and friends of God*. The Holy Spirit, our only and heavenly doctor who leads us into all truth, the only light who enlightens our darkness, flees the godless. How can we then be enlightened? The Lord says: The world cannot receive the Holy Ghost, that is, because of its impenitence. Therefore, God in Jeremiah 2:13 complains: *They cast out me, the living source, and dig for themselves wells which bring forth no water*.

4. Paul says in Ephesians 5:14: *Awake you who sleep and Christ will enlighten you*. Therefore, those who do not awake from the sleep of sins in this world, from the lust of the flesh, the lust of the eyes, and the pride of life cannot be enlightened by Christ.

5. Peter says in Acts 2:38: *Be penitent and you will receive the gift of the Holy Spirit*. Therefore, the Spirit of God, which enlightens the heart, cannot be received without repentance.

6. All prophets and apostles had to reject the world and deny themselves, and give up everything they had, if they wished to be enlightened and to receive the Holy Spirit from above.

7. Saint Bernard said: The streams of grace flow under you and not over you. How is the grace of light and knowledge of God to come to man who does not walk in the humble life of Christ, but in the way of Lucifer?

In a word, the union with Christ through living faith, the renewal in Christ through the mortification of the old man, is the end and goal of this book. Insofar as a man dies to himself, Christ lives in him; insofar as he gives up his evil nature, grace comes into him; insofar as he mortifies the flesh, the spirit is made living in him; insofar as the work of darkness in man is extinguished, man is enlightened; insofar as the external man is done away with and dies, the inner man is renewed; insofar as self-affections and the whole fleshly life in a man dies, such as self-love, self-honor, wrath, covetousness, and pleasure, Christ lives in him; insofar as the world leaves a man, such as the lust of the eyes, the lust of the flesh, and the pride of life, God, Christ, and the Holy Spirit enter into that man and possess him; and on the other hand the more that nature, the flesh, darkness, and the world rule in man, the less is grace, spirit, light, God, and Christ in him, thereby each man is to test himself. Therefore, one cannot be enlightened without true repentance.

Such old, short books that lead to a holy life all lie hidden in the dust as Joseph in prison. Truly, years ago there were people, more than in the present old and cold world, who hungered and thirsted for Christ, and those who practiced the noble and holy life of Christ in simplicity, purity of heart and pure love were among the most enlightened. Joseph was released from prison by a dream. So by God's gift such books were sought out, found, loved, and brought forward. As Joseph when he was released from his imprisonment still had on his old servant's cloak, so this old *Theologia deutsch* steps forward in its rude German farmer's cloak, that is, in its old, rude speech in which it still teaches very high spiritual and lovely things, namely, to take on Christ's life, to practice the teaching of Christ in life, how Christ is to live in us and Adam is to die in us. If our present, soft German ears are thus to hear it speak, they would not truly understand it and would cast out its teaching with its language. Therefore, because of the present world, which loves good-sounding and lovely words, which looks more to the adornment of speech than to the Spirit of God and a holy life, I have made its cloak a little better and made its heavy tongue a little lighter so that the spiritual understanding might shine forth a little better. As a powerful spirit was hidden under the heavy tongue of Moses, so is it also here.

This Joseph, however, does not teach you to go about with Potiphar's wife, that is with this world, but he teaches you to reject the world and to seek the highest good. In their Christianity more people seek temporal things than Christ himself, more love the lust of the flesh, the lust of the eyes, and the pride of life than the kingdom of God. They commit adultery with Potiphar's wife, who grasped Joseph by the cloak. He let the cloak go and fled from her. Thus, the present, proud, lustful, carnal world, all its class standards, wishes that the heavenly Joseph, namely, Christ himself, should commit adultery with it in a worldly manner. Each proud servant of the belly seeking after gold and the world grasps after him and wishes to hold him and says: Here is Christ; I am also a Christian. No. The heavenly Joseph let go of his cloak, that is the external letter, appearance, name, and title. He flees from them and is not grasped by them unless they are repentant in their hearts, take on the humble life of Christ and walk in it.

If the First Book [of the *Theologia deutsch*] appears to you dark and difficult to understand, the second will clarify it. You will also find good and useful discussion [of it] in my *True Christianity* and *Paradise Garden*. This is all I have to say for the present; more will follow. In the meantime, take this with love and pray to God for me.

Index to Introduction

Index to Text

Wisdom, 75; example of, 22, 40, 54, 62, 64, 65, 68, 78, 80, 92, 93, 127, 202, 205, 206, 207, 208, 217; fellowship of, 163, 266, 268; following of, 22, 24, 42, 60, 64, 66, 71, 80, 82, 85, 92, 93, 95, 133, 162, 164, 165-166, 168, 171, 174, 175, 176, 201, 202, 205, 206, 217, 227, 276, 277, 279; God in, 66, 111, 213, 247; glory of, 100, 205, 206, 210, 215, 217, 247, 253, 270; High Priest, 82, 267; humanity of, 31, 50; image of, 165, 206; image of God, 31, 76, 77, 85, 248; incarnation of, 39, 150, 209, 236, 246, 251, 252, 272; inheritance from 38, 39, 45, 47, 50, 90, 252, 253, 278; as light, 54, 64, 68, 163, 164, 165, 169, 175, 233, 263, 278, 279; man in, 21, 22, 36, 39, 43, 44, 46, 47, 50, 58, 66, 70, 76, 80, 87, 89, 93, 121, 137, 167, 168, 177, 247, 253, 267, 276, 277; mercy of, 202, 203; merits of, 42, 43, 45, 47, 53, 55, 56, 59, 80, 89, 113, 115, 130, 131, 133, 153, 167, 168, 180, 203, 205, 235, 243, 254; obedience of, 31, 39, 67, 89, 203; patience of, 22, 39, 56, 58, 62, 66, 67, 76, 84, 85, 93, 126, 139, 164, 171, 277; pays for sin, 56, 57, 59, 67, 77, 106, 114, 167, 168, 203, 266; as physician, 55, 56, 58, 139, 153, 195; power of, 101, 111, 204, 205, 217, 254; promise of, 71, 117, 153, 243, 246; Redeemer, 139, 146, 148, 231, 257; redemption through, 33, 77, 131, 194, 216; as remedy, 201, 202; renews man, 36, 37, 39, 40, 47, 58; resurrection of, 40, 43, 51, 58, 209, 233; reveals God, 31; righteousness of, 118,

235, 278; sacrifice of, 203; and salvation, 25; Sanctifier, 48, 68, 126, 139, 247, 266, 267, 268; as Savior, 65, 68, 111, 126, 254, 255, 262, 266, 267, 268, 269; second coming of, 214; sorrow of, 206, 207; suffering of, 22, 40, 56, 57, 67, 80, 145, 148, 181, 202, 206, 207, 209, 214, 215, 216, 217, 227, 236, 261; turn to, 23; union with, 46, 51; in us, 21, 22, 25, 39, 41, 43, 47, 50, 51, 66, 67, 70, 71, 76, 83, 117, 118, 165, 177, 196, 204, 206, 216, 217, 247, 251, 253, 261, 277, 278, 279, 280; will of, 31; yoke of, 42, 43, 64, 67, 74, 75, 128, 156.

Christianity, and disputations, 174; and faith, 21, 104, 145; false, 62; growth in, 118; and image of God, 184; and love, 145; true, 68, 104, 176, 184, 195, 196, 203, 231, 276, 277.

Church, 260-262.

Cicero, 165.

Colossians, 1:16, 231; 1:17, 231, 233; 1:27, 251; 2:9, 252; 2:13, 188; 3:3, 24, 71; 3:5, 41; 3:10, 39; 3:14, 134; 3:17, 96.

Conscience, and Christian, 53, 54, 81, 105, 111, 123; evil, 121, 122, 123; and existence of God, 52, 53, 190; and final judgment, 52; good, 122, 123, 126, 175; joy of, 122; and love, 123, 126, 129, 240; and natural law, 52, 53, 54, 189, 190; and natural righteousness, 52; and pagans, 53, 54, 190; and peace, 121, 122, 131, 168.

Contrition, 24, 55, 56, 58, 99, 103, 106, 247.

Conversion, through Christ, 25, 116, 121, 166, 184, 204; from Devil, 271; to God, 209, 253,

286

254, 270, 276; and Holy Spirit, 41; lack of, 53, 122; and parables, 204; and repentence, 115, 121; from sin, 55, 114, 163; true, 42, 168.

1 **Corinthians,** 1:19, 172; 1:30, 40, 104, 111, 118, 153; 2:2, 120; 2:14, 193; 2:16, 62, 66; 3:9, 142; 4:7, 195; 4:10, 142, 4:20, 151; 6:11, 253; 6:12, 104; 6:15, 277; 6:17, 156, 177, 247; 6:19, 222, 253, 268; 6:19-20, 83; 9:7, 141; 9:9, 135; 9:22, 148; 10:12, 183; 10:16, 266; 10:20, 267; 10:23, 104; 12:12, 261; 12:13, 264; 12:27, 264; 13:1, 150; 13:1ff, 124; 13:2, 134; 13:3, 137; 13:4, 185; 13:4ff, 145; 13:4-7, 145; 13:8, 124; 15:1ff, 173; 15:22, 39; 15:42-52, 231; 16:4, 125.

2 **Corinthians,** 3:16, 163, 172; 3:17, 39, 129; 3:18, 165, 184, 185; 4:4, 172; 4:13, 87; 4:16, 41, 66, 87, 104; 4:18, 93, 5:15, 70; 5:17, 177, 277; 5:21, 46; 6:9-10, 106; 6:14, 163, 278; 6:15, 171; 6:16, 247; 7:10, 56, 104, 107, 109, 179, 254; 8:9, 74; 9:8ff, 173; 12:9, 101, 102, 183; 13:3, 261; 13:5, 247, 251.

Covenant, ark of, 50; blood of, 56-57; of grace, 203; new, 54; received, 256, 257; renewed, 246; and Word, 250.

Creation, cf. Man; 236, 245, 246; six days of, 232, 233-235.

Creatures, 143, 262, 263; new, 21, 37, 39, 43, 44, 50, 51, 58, 66, 80, 106, 151, 194, 204, 205, 243, 244, 265, 277; old, 76; serve man, 236, 237, 238; signs of God, 97, 213, 231, 232; use of, 232.

Cyprian, 223.

Damnation, 44, 53, 87, 101, 105, 130, 131, 167, 168, 183, 188.

Daniel, 60, 74, 178.

Daniel, 1:8, 74; 4:33, 98; 9:7, 113; 9:26, 60.

David, 33, 84, 93, 99, 100, 114, 132, 138, 147, 160, 181, 203, 212, 224, 231, 251, 260, 270.

Death, cf. Christ, Sin, World; 253; Christian, 119; eternal, 70, 72, 105, 137, 188; natural, 70, 76, 85, 91, 92, 107, 108; redemption of, 112; of self, 70, 74-76, 78, 81, 83, 84, 85, 87; spiritual, 70, 104, 107, 188, 205; temporal, 204, 217.

Delilah, 76.

Deuteronomy, 4:41-43, 114; 6:5, 185, 186; 6:15, 110; 28, 170; 30:19, 90; 32:4, 185; 32:21, 170; 32:32-33, 46;

Devil, 65, 142, 186, 222; children of, 34, 65, 88, 126, 204, 245; conquering of, 155, 172, 182, 194, 216, 217, 227, 252, 253; as enemy, 133, 189, 191; fellowship of, 267, 268, 271; and idolatry, 208; live in, 68, 70, 76, 87, 166, 171, 211, 271; power of, 249; redemption from, 112, 162, 165; seed of, 196; and self-love, 150; treachery of, 47, 187; turn from, 47, 211; works of, 65; yoke of, 67, 108, 188, 190, 191.

Diogenes, 121.

Ebion, 173.

Ecclesiastes, 7:4, 179; 9:4, 107; 10:15, 108; 12:12-13, 176; 24:29, 157.

Ecclesiasticus, 24:27-28, 160; 39:21, 179.

Egypt, 23, 74, 95, 108, 183.

Egyptians, 23.

Election, 170, 216.

Enlightenment, in Christ, 163, 164, 165, 166, 171, 175, 176, 194, 210, 255, 260, 278, 279;

mercy of, 30, 31, 47, 56, 59, 99, 101, 102, 111, 112, 115, 116, 126, 139, 148, 162, 170, 180, 181, 183, 203, 204, 205, 213, 214, 215, 216, 234, 246, 253; as Mother, 214; name of, 96, 190, 197, 244, 246, 250, 265; nature of, 75, 252; and new birth, 37, 43, 45, 47; pleasing of, 29, 39, 59, 100, 101, 120, 124, 125, 128, 150, 151, 152, 178, 179, 180, 182, 186, 207, 208, 223, 224, 227, 236, 247, 252, 264; power of, 46, 101, 102, 111, 112, 162, 170, 175, 202, 210, 215, 233, 234, 235, 243, 278; presence of, 72, 159, 193, 212, 222, 223, 250, 251, 269, 270; punishment of, 22, 52, 96, 110, 180, 205, 208, 215, 237; rejection of, 170; as rewarding, 52; righteousness of, 46, 52, 53, 56, 111, 112, 113, 126, 186, 188, 189, 202, 207, 210, 217; and scriptures, 49, 50; seed of, 47, 49, 121; seeking of, 96, 223, 224, 225, 227, 252, 255, 260; service of, 110, 111, 116, 125, 132-133, 147, 157, 236, 238, 243, 250; Son of, 56, 57, 60, 64, 65, 139, 165, 173, 206, 216, 232, 235, 246, 248, 251, 252, 253, 258, 265, 266, 272; as source, 101, 221, 223, 236, 248; Spirit of, 66, 83, 117, 155, 156, 157, 165, 193, 251, 253, 254, 279, 280; thanks to, 96, 115, 116, 182, 190, 206, 236, 244; trust in, 45, 83, 111, 189, 190, 192, 212, 215; turn from, 32, 33, 35, 38-41, 43, 53, 65, 85, 90, 96, 123, 143, 160, 162, 178, 188, 208, 249, 271; turn to, 43, 45, 46, 90, 121, 158, 192, 193, 204, 209, 210, 221, 222, 223, 236, 254, 270;

visible, 31; will of, 23, 30, 31, 42, 49, 62, 66, 111, 128, 161, 179, 185, 189, 197, 207, 214, 216, 224; Word of, 21, 37, 45, 47, 49, 51, 53, 54, 57, 58, 72, 76, 99, 112, 121, 129, 132, 146, 154, 155, 156, 157, 159, 160, 164, 171, 173, 178, 188, 203, 206, 211, 212, 213, 214, 215, 216, 233, 243, 249, 250, 251, 276, 277; wrath of, 22, 41, 53, 55, 56, 57, 96, 110, 113, 114, 215, 235.

Golan, 114, 115.

Gomorrah, 50, 97.

Gospel, 95, 156, 167; abuse of, 21; conformity to, 21, 174; consolation of, 24, 196; and God's grace, 41, 170; light of, 172.

Grace, and Christ, 37, 56, 59, 74, 89, 163, 168, 204, 212, 227, 234, 257, 264; consoles, 43, 101, 102, 163; and faith, 23, 38, 45, 102, 115, 171, 254; and forgiveness, 130, 167; gift of, 57; from God, 47, 75, 83, 89, 100, 101, 102, 103, 106, 111, 115, 116, 119, 156, 166, 167, 168, 180, 183, 196, 213, 215, 216, 227, 231, 235, 249, 250; and holiness, 23, 29, 153; ignored, 54, 57; and knowledge, 69, 103, 111, 165, 196; light of, 215, 225, 279; prevenient, 118; promised, 47, 48; rejected, 169; removed, 170; and righteousness, 46; and Scripture, 41, 213; seat of, 50, 99, 111, 245, 257; seeking of, 58, 99, 102, 116, 243; and sin, 45; works of, 252.

Haggai, 2:5-6, 250.

Heaven, bread of, 155, 156, 160; and Christ, 80; consolation of, 214; desire for, 262; gifts of,

members, 87; of mind, 87; of
Moses, 82; and sorrow for sin,
56; of spirit of life, 88; and
worship, 110.

Leah, 72, 73.

Leviticus, 10:1-2, 110; 10:9, 113;
21:14, 82; 25:23, 92.

Life, bread of, 157, 159, 267, 268;
carnal, 67, 68, 189, 201; Christ in
us, 21, 22, 25, 39, 41, 43, 47, 51,
67, 70, 71, 76, 83, 117, 118, 165,
177, 196, 204, 251, 253, 261,
277, 278, 279; in Christ, 21, 22,
36, 39, 43, 44, 46, 47, 50, 58, 66,
70, 76, 80, 87, 89, 93, 121, 137,
154, 167, 168, 171, 177, 247,
253, 276, 277; of Christ, 22, 62,
64, 65, 66, 67, 68, 80, 83, 84, 92,
93, 156, 164, 165, 166, 174, 175,
202, 205, 207, 209, 217, 245,
255, 277, 278, 279, 280;
Christian, 24, 58, 60, 61, 64, 70,
72, 80, 83, 84, 85, 91, 92, 106,
112, 113, 117, 118, 119, 137,
142, 154, 159, 164, 168, 174,
175, 178, 184, 195, 201, 202,
221, 224, 245, 276;
contemplative, 202; crown of, 88;
eternal, 30, 39, 45, 68, 70, 71,
76, 77, 79, 80, 81, 87, 92, 94, 95,
96, 97, 104, 105, 108, 113, 126,
133, 134, 135, 136, 151, 157,
159, 166, 168, 170, 178, 179,
184, 188, 194, 204, 217, 225,
236, 258, 259, 270, 271, 277; 278;
false, 68; fountain of, 263; fruits
of, 176; in God, 66, 69, 90, 96,
101; improvement of, 44, 104,
105, 106, 107, 113, 114, 116,
117, 166; light of, 64, 164, 168,
171, 279; new, 44, 45, 64, 66, 68,
115, 124, 151, 161, 177, 244,
250; perfect, 78, 224; righteous,
55, 159; rule of, 22, 39, 70, 95,
117, 178, 193, 214; spirit of, 88;
tree of, 145, 157, 163; of

ungodly, 21, 22, 50, 53, 57, 60,
61, 62, 169, 174, 175, 176, 177,
271; water of, 260, 264; well of,
259; Word of, 165; of world, 62,
92.

Lot, 50, 113, 142; wife of, 50.

Love, cf. Holy Spirit; of
Bridegroom, 255-258, 265;
Christ is, 111, 164, 165, 278; for
Christ, 22, 67, 73, 74, 81, 82, 85,
126, 159, 165, 207, 222, 240;
256, 259, 260, 264, 270; of
Christ, 58, 68, 81, 93, 112, 125,
127, 129, 134, 135, 139, 142; of
Christians, 25, 117, 124,
125-144, 149, 154, 164, 171, 173,
174, 175, 197, 205; and
commandments, 123, 124, 125,
126, 130, 133, 134, 137, 148; for
enemies, 42, 50, 135, 137-140,
148; and faith, 23, 25, 79, 95,
123, 124, 125, 127, 128, 145,
151, 152, 153, 175, 177, 240; and
freedom, 129; fruits of, 145-149;
God is, 68, 69, 116, 124, 133,
150, 163-164, 177, 185, 208-209,
248, 260; for God, 62, 72, 78, 79,
83, 97, 98, 112, 116, 123, 124,
125, 126, 127, 128, 134, 141,
143, 144, 154, 157, 181, 185,
186, 189, 192, 208, 212, 221,
224, 225, 226, 235, 237, 238,
239, 240, 248, 258, 259, 264,
268; in God, 185; of God, 30, 31,
41, 56, 71, 75, 79, 97, 99, 101,
111, 122, 125, 126, 128, 129,
130, 133, 135, 141, 142, 156,
158, 160, 182, 186, 208, 209,
210, 211, 214, 216, 234, 236,
237, 248, 253; and holiness, 148;
Holy Spirit is, 111; marks of,
209, 214; of neighbor, 97, 112,
123, 125-136, 141, 143, 144, 145,
147, 148, 154, 182, 186, 208,
224, 226, 238; and prayer, 125,
136; proper, 239; and Satan,

293

128; seeking for, 96; for self, 31, 32, 34, 41, 42, 78, 79, 81, 82, 84, 85, 150, 204, 224, 239, 240; and wisdom, 75, 222; of world, 76, 79, 81, 83, 92, 93, 97, 98, 113, 123, 125, 141, 142, 143, 157, 159, 176, 206, 209, 225, 226.

Lucifer, 150, 165, 279.

Luke, 66

Luke, 1:48, 100; 1:50, 48; 1:53, 156; 1:79, 92; 4:22, 146; 6:38, 130; 7:22, 24; 7:37, 102; 7:38, 254; 8:7, 58; 8:43, 255; 9:23, 24, 42, 83, 84; 9:55, 38; 9:56, 182; 9:58, 84; 10:3, 147; 10:16, 262; 10:20, 183; 10:21, 148; 11:13, 117; 11:27-28, 146; 11:42, 147; 12, 63; 12:9, 60; 12:20-21, 92; 12:34, 97; 12:37, 119; 12:44, 119; 12:50, 128; 13:32, 36; 14:26, 42, 49, 78, 82; 15:7, 59; 15:10, 148; 15:18, 58; 15:20ff, 254; 17:21, 49, 221; 17:32, 50; 18:1, 245; 18:8, 60, 159; 18:13, 58; 18:23, 166; 19:41, 147; 19:42, 106; 22:27, 84; 22:61, 147; 23:31, 101; 23:34, 125, 139, 148, 182; 23:40-42, 114; 24:47, 40.

Luther, Martin, 173.

Majorists, 25.

Mammon, 157.

Man, cf. Life, World; Adamic, 34-35, 37, 38, 39, 58, 65, 67, 68, 71, 84, 85, 276; battle in, 87, 88, 189; bodily, 29, 30, 87, 102, 107, 186, 201; corruption of, 65, 66, 67, 139, 147, 192, 193, 194, 204; creation of, 30, 52, 76, 77, 94, 97, 130, 141, 187, 191, 193, 235, 236, 238, 240, 246, 248, 252; die to self, 70, 74, 75, 76, 78, 81, 83, 84, 85, 87, 172, 175, 195, 227, 276, 279; as earthly, 34, 35, 196, 223; fall of, 33, 35, 39, 52, 65, 89,

187, 209, 210, 211, 237, 246, 249; God in, 66, 67, 69, 102, 116, 127, 209, 222, 223, 225, 246, 247, 248, 250, 252, 254, 257, 260, 271, 280; in God, 79, 87, 111, 127, 246, 247, 260; of God, 96; godliness of, 178; growth of, 117-122, 167; happiness of, 32, 45, 79, 91, 106, 121, 125, 135, 157, 159, 161, 191, 240, 249, 263, 269; heirs of God, 47, 253, 265; image of God, 29, 30, 31, 32, 33, 34, 35, 36, 39, 47, 50, 51, 52, 65, 76, 77, 85, 97, 98, 116, 117, 121, 184, 186, 187, 188, 189, 191, 194, 197, 211, 231, 236, 238, 243, 247, 248, 249, 252; image of Satan, 34, 35, 36, 37, 187, 188, 189, 191, 192, 194; immortality of, 30, 237; inner, 87, 92, 117, 118, 122, 157, 158, 180, 254, 261, 279; merits of, 45, 46, 85, 102, 168, 226; mind of, 29, 33, 37, 117, 185, 189; nature of, 65, 66, 67, 101, 195, 204, 227, 279; new, 37, 41, 49, 50, 65, 66, 67, 76, 83, 89, 106, 201, 202; new birth, 21, 37, 38, 39, 40, 43, 45, 46, 49, 50, 51, 58, 64, 68, 76, 77, 83, 87, 88, 96, 105, 117, 150, 169, 184, 189, 190, 192, 194, 196, 243, 246, 250, 253, 265, 278; as nothing, 99, 100, 101, 102, 180, 190, 208, 224, 227, 247; old, 37, 41, 49, 66, 68, 76, 82, 83, 84, 106, 184, 201, 202; perfection of, 180, 184, 204, 221, 243, 249; physical birth of, 33; powers of, 237, 238; puts on Christ, 50-51; renewal of, 36, 37, 39, 40, 47, 49, 58, 65, 76, 77, 83, 89, 116, 117, 118, 184, 186, 189, 194, 195, 211, 225, 243, 261, 277, 279; and self-hatred, 78-79, 82, 85, 205, 240; sins of, 40, 41, 46, 47, 54, 56, 57, 58, 65, 74, 79,

82, 88, 102, 106, 107, 114, 183, 189, 192; Son of, 182; spiritual, 29, 30, 67, 87, 107, 129, 169, 192, 201; and temporal goods, 90, 91, 92, 94, 95, 96, 97, 104, 105, 107, 108, 109, 143, 157, 158, 176, 178, 179, 280; testing of, 90, 91, 95, 118, 129, 130, 144, 181, 206, 215, 216; turned from God, 32, 33, 35, 38, 39, 41, 43, 53, 65, 85, 90, 96, 123, 143, 160, 162, 178, 188, 208, 249, 271; unhappiness of, 32, 78, 101, 102, 156, 223, 240, 241, 271; united with Christ, 145, 146, 177, 225, 245, 254, 255, 258, 264, 266, 267, 268, 278, 279; united with God, 32, 45, 47, 65, 66, 127, 179, 204, 225, 226, 239, 243, 245, 246, 247, 249, 250, 251, 252, 253, 254, 259, 260, 261, 264, 270, 271, 277; will of, 29, 30, 31, 33, 34, 37, 42, 65, 66, 79, 81, 88, 153, 175, 179, 180, 185, 188, 190, 197, 204, 209, 211, 213, 221, 224, 248, 249.

Manna, 155, 158, 159, 160, 161.
Marcedonius, 234.
Mark, 8:38, 22, 76; 14:38, 88.
Mary, 50, 100.
Mary Magdalen, 102, 167.
Matthew, 2:19-20, 71; 3:7, 34; 3:13, 265; 3:16, 137; 3:17, 31; 5:16, 164; 5:44, 135; 5:44-45, 137; 6:21, 97; 7:6, 36, 77; 7:7, 245; 7:12, 134; 7:14, 109, 176; 7:19, 177; 7:20, 176; 7:21, 44, 154, 222; 7:23, 22, 61, 75; 8:2-3, 180; 8:20, 84, 93; 9:2, 181; 9:12, 55, 195; 9:12-13, 55; 9:20, 255; 11:5, 167; 11:24, 53; 11:28, 254; 11:29, 39, 42, 67, 128, 159, 276; 11:30, 74, 156, 12:30, 62; 12:42, 53; 13:25, 176; 13:45-46, 81; 16:24, 24, 276;

16:26, 77; 18:19, 136; 18:35, 130, 131; 19:5-6, 253; 19:17, 30, 143; 19:20, 105; 20:28, 67, 73, 147; 21, 61; 22:37, 186; 25:12, 75; 25:34ff, 183; 25:35, 134, 262, 26:25, 266; 26:41, 88.

Mephibosheth, 205.
Messiah, and Old Testament, 110; and prophets, 172.
Micah, 172.
Micah, 6:8, 115, 132; 7:1, 63.
Michal, 99.
Miracles, 51, 134, 145.
Mortification, and faith, 58; of flesh, 24, 41, 42, 43, 58, 71, 72, 95, 104, 107, 116, 151, 155, 171, 178, 179, 195, 201, 224, 276, 279; of old man, 184, 202, 279; of pride, 41; of self-love, 41; of sin, 58, 189, 226; and sorrow, 24.
Moses, 74, 82, 90, 95, 114, 115, 135, 137, 170, 183, 212, 231, 280.
Nebuchadnezzar, 98.
Nestorius, 173.
New Testament, 50, 110, 214, 231.
Nicolites, 234.
Noah, 49, 113, 121.
Numbers, 5:6, 144; 11:1, 95; 11:1ff, 96; 12:3, 138; 12:8, 269; 21:8, 58.
Old Testament, 110, 124, 173, 205, 214, 231.
Papists, 25, 154, 173, 176.
Paradise, 114, 145, 155, 187, 249, 255, 256.
Paradise Garden, 197, 281.
Patience, of Christian, 23, 42, 84, 85, 112, 127, 158, 163, 176, 179, 183, 202, 206, 214, 215, 216, 217, 224, 225, 226, 252, 276, 277; and God, 47, 137, 197, 205, 215; helps to, 215; and love, 133; of martyrs, 128; and mercy, 112; of Moses, 137; and neighbor,

112, 148; of new man, 66; original, 185; and trials, 216.

Paul, 24, 39, 46, 52, 53, 54, 55, 60, 61, 62, 64, 66, 70, 71, 75, 80, 83, 87, 88, 93, 96, 99, 101, 102, 104, 106, 107, 109, 112, 117, 120, 123, 132, 133, 134, 135, 137, 141, 145, 149, 163, 164, 165, 168, 170, 171, 172, 173, 174, 175, 176, 182, 183, 186, 193, 215, 221, 251, 262, 264, 266, 267, 268, 277, 279.

Peniel, 72.

Pericles, 138.

Peter, 40, 93, 147, 165, 166, 167, 177, 181, 277, 279.

1 Peter, 1:3, 40; 1:5, 175; 1:10-11, 251; 1:18-19, 40; 1:22, 251; 1:23, 37, 250; 2:21, 64; 2:22, 93; 2:24, 24; 2:25, 40; 3:21, 4:14, 181; 5:5, 156, 163, 165.

2 Peter, 1:4, 75; 1:5ff, 177; 1:5-6, 277; 1:5-8, 166; 1:8, 133, 165; 1:9, 167; 2:19, 129; 3:5, 234.

Pharisees, 65, 173.

Pharoah, 74, 108, 169, 170.

Philipians, 1:11, 133; 1:20, 45; 1:21, 70; 1:29, 74; 2:5, 62; 2:10, 115; 2:12, 23; 4:4, 186.

Phocion, 138.

Piety, through Christ, 47, 243; command of, 147; and God, 47, 215; lack of, 21; and love, 148; of man, 175, 211.

Plato, 52, 95, 165.

Potiphar, wife of, 142, 280.

Praise, of creature, 30; of God, 30, 32, 121, 147, 214, 215, 224, 232, 233, 244, 252, 259, 260, 270; of man, 224; of self, 146, 239; of virtue, 183.

Prayer, 184; basis of, 212; to Christ, 180; and Christian, 75, 176, 202, 212, 221, 244; and consolation, 212, 213, 244; and contemplation, 202, 208; continual, 211, 212, 245, 258; for enemy, 84, 93, 123; and faith, 23, 50, 136; failure in, 211, 212; to Father, 180, 197, 226, 266; and forgiveness, 243; fruits of, 213; and gift, 195, 197; to God, 180, 212, 213, 215, 244, 269, 270, 281; guide to, 211-212; heard, 213, 215; as help, 217, 245, 252; helps to, 213, 244; and Holy Spirit, 226, 244; and humility, 208; and knowledge, 207, 211, 244; lost, 137; and love, 125, 136, 209; as request, 136, 226, 244, 252; steps of, 207; true, 211; unfitting, 152; weakness of, 194, 213.

Pride, 43, 56, 57, 58, 62, 66, 70, 76, 84, 87, 93, 139, 155, 163, 176, 181, 190, 194, 195, 196, 197, 201, 204, 208, 216, 222, 239, 271, 279, 280.

Prophets, 24, 43, 57, 58, 84, 99, 114, 132, 146, 156, 160, 172, 173, 174, 232, 235, 249, 251, 254, 259, 262, 269, 276, 279; false, 154, 172, 173, 174.

Proverbs, 1:29, 118; 8:31, 29, 246, 264; 16:32, 87, 140; 18:10, 115; 18:21, 106; 21:2, 152; 30:7-8, 75.

Providence, 190, 235.

Psalms, 203, 214, 270; 1:4, 109; 5:4, 122; 5:10, 91; 6:24, 188; 7:10, 118; 14:1, 189; 16:5, 125; 16:11, 160; 17:4, 125; 17:14, 96; 17:15, 263, 270; 17:18, 125; 18:2-3, 123; 18:26-27, 129; 19, 231; 19:8, 250; 22:7, 84; 23:5, 159, 160; 27:1, 101, 250; 32, 24; 32:2, 45; 32:2-5, 48; 34:5-7, 122; 34:8, 251; 34:9, 112, 160; 34:18, 245; 36:8ff, 160; 36:9, 263; 36:9-10, 259; 38:24, 188; 39:12, 92; 42:2, 260; 42:4, 107; 45:2, 146; 45:8, 253; 45:14, 265; 48:10, 96; 49:18, 107; 49:20, 92; 50:15,

190; 51, 24; 51:2, 180; 51:7, 114; 51:17, 132; 51:19, 103; 63:3, 69; 63:4, 160; 63:11, 186; 66:20, 245; 70:4-5, 160; 73:25, 251, 263; 73:25-26, 123, 270; 74:19, 63; 77:8-11, 48; 80:2, 247; 80:6, 107; 81:10, 262; 84:1, 160; 84:1-2, 120; 84:2, 69, 93; 84:2-3, 186; 84:3, 120; 85:9, 122; 85:11, 168; 85:11-12, 102; 91:1, 23; 92:1, 269; 92:12, 120; 92:12-15, 117; 92:13, 147; 94:9, 113; 102:18-20, 245; 102, 24; 102:5, 107; 102:7, 63; 103:1, 181; 103:7, 115, 148; 103:8, 137, 185; 103:9-10, 146; 103:17, 104, 231; 109:22, 206; 111:10, 174; 112:6, 183; 112:7, 23;118:27, 250; 130, 24; 130:3, 113; 130:7, 180; 132:4-5, 270; 133:3, 136; 139, 231; 143, 24; 143:2, 113; 145:17, 179; 145:18, 245; 146:8, 147; 147:3, 58.

Publius, 138.

Punishment, cf. God; deserved, 215; eternal, 206; fear of, 44; and love, 237; and pride, 208; of self, 127; for sin, 102, 169, 180, 226, 244; and wrath of God, 96.

Purification, 44; and baptism, 265; through Christ, 265; and faith, 225; and Holy Spirit, 177; of human nature, 192; of man, 65, 118, 159; from sin, 57, 167, 180, 181, 267; and sorrow, 118, 122; of spirit, 253.

Rachel, 72, 73.

Ramoth, 114, 115.

Rebecca, 81.

Reconciliation, 144.

Redemption, through Christ, 59, 77, 131, 153, 182, 266, 267; and faith, 45; final, 23; fruits of, 207; and glory, 74; and God, 97, 214, 217, 246, 252, and law, 111; loss of, 131; from misery, 182; and repentence, 162, 168, 271; self-,

153; from sin, 112; and wisdom, 211.

Renewal, cf. Man; 184; in Christ, 36, 37, 66, 76, 77, 89, 186, 192, 195, 261, 277; daily, 83, 117, 118, 184; and faith, 40, 58, 184; and God, 65, 211; and Holy Spirit, 77, 189; and image of God, 36, 116, 117, 184, 185, 189, 194, 211, 248; of inner man, 279; of life, 114, 117, 118, 243; of man's nature, 39; and mortification, 41, 66, 104, 279; and redemption, 267; and repentence, 40, 112, 113; and word of God, 21.

Repentence, cf. Righteousness, Sin, Sorrow; 184, 190, 240, call to, 53; and Christ, 40, 43, 59, 89, 113, 145, 153, 175; and Christian life, 201, 221; continual, 162; and conversion, 121, 175, 253, 271; daily, 51, 168, 202, 221; doctrine of, 201; and enlightenment, 279, 280; examples of, 205; and faith, 162, 195, 253; and forgiveness, 57, 58, 111, 113, 114, 115, 116, 127, 168, 243; fruits of, 24, 67, 195; and grace, 153; healing, 253; and holiness, 104; and Holy Spirit, 41, 165; inner, 42, 43, 44; joy in, 148; and knowledge, 113, 115, 116; lack of, 24, 53, 58, 65, 68, 81, 89, 93, 163, 174, 176, 187, 277, 278; and mortification, 41, 42; moved to, 204, 205; preaching of, 57; sermon of, 147; and Son of God, 39; and Spirit of God, 279; true, 21, 25, 41, 43, 44, 47, 55, 57, 64, 66, 68, 89, 104, 107, 112, 115, 116, 166, 168, 173, 174, 175, 189, 196, 201, 203, 215, 243, 276; unfitting, 152; work of, 24.

Resurrection, of Christ, 40, 43, 209, 233; of dead, 173, 231; first,

297

51; fruit of, 43; image of, 217, 233; of man, 40, 233; use of, 58.

Revelation, 1:6, 102, 245; 2:10, 88; 2:17, 155, 156, 183; 3:12, 183; 3:20, 102, 159, 269; 4:10, 259; 7:17, 108; 14:11, 108; 14:13, 96; 18:2, 36; 19:1, 259; 21:8, 36; 22:15, 36.

Righteousness, cf. Christ, Faith, God; through Christ, 33, 38, 43, 45, 46, 47, 55, 111, 133, 159, 168, 184, 203, 265; Christian, 24, 45, 46, 118, 133, 147, 186, 196, 201, 255; divine, 29; fruits of, 21, 24, 25, 133, 201; is gift, 46; and God, 47, 111, 121; and Holy Spirit, 111, 121; of life, 55; and love, 130; of man, 115, 212, 227, 247, 248; natural, 52; original, 33, 52, 185, 186, 188, 246; and repentence, 24, 201, 277; true, 29; and works, 46, 47, 186, 227.

Romans, 1:16, 250; 1:20, 189; 1:21, 53; 1:28, 54; 1:32, 53; 2:4, 145; 2:5, 53; 2:14-15, 52; 2:15, 52; 2:15-16, 53; 3:13, 191; 3:21ff, 173; 3:23, 183; 3:25, 245; 4:1ff, 173; 5:3, 106; 5:5, 112, 124, 253; 5:10, 137; 5:19, 33; 6:1-18, 71; 6:3, 40; 6:4, 40, 184; 6:6, 24; 6:11, 41, 58; 7:18, 88; 7:23, 87, 88; 7:24, 102; 8:1, 88; 8:6, 87; 8:9, 117, 253; 8:10, 251; 8:11, 253; 8:13, 71, 157; 8:14, 117; 8:15, 111; 8:16, 156, 252; 8:22, 231; 8:26, 118, 244; 8:38, 46; 8:38ff, 142; 8:39, 148; 9:3, 135; 9:18, 170; 10:12, 115; 11:20, 196; 12, 124; 12:1, 24, 107; 12:9, 134; 12:20, 125; 12:21, 106, 135, 182; 13:8, 132; 13:8-10, 132; 13:10, 123, 148; 13:12, 64; 15:18, 261; 15:33, 136.

Sabbath, 86, 120, 166, 175, 224, 225.

Sacraments, 37, 58, 169, 204, 231, 246, 250, 266, 267, 268.

Sacrifice, of body, 24, 107; of Christ, 132, 180, 203; eating of, 115; and faith, 50; fire of, 110, 113; of Moses, 115; pleasing, 180; and sorrow, 103; unfitting, 152.

Salvation, and Christ, 25, 147, 255; knowledge of, 253; and prayer, 136; and repentence, 24, 104, 109; and sorrow, 254; and Word, 250.

Samson, 76.

Samuel, 160, 269.

1 Samuel, 3:10, 160, 269; 15:8, 71; 15:23, 250.

2 Samuel, 6:22, 99; 9, 205; 13:3, 265; 14:25, 33; 16:6, 147; 16:10, 138, 181; 16:11, 84; 16:12, 181; 18:33, 33; 23:2, 269; 23:15-17, 224.

Santification, 184; of body, 253; and Christ, 40, 55, 111, 127, 153, 250; and contemplation, 259; by faith, 42, 47, 203; and Holy Spirit, 38, 212, 253; and new birth, 37; and sorrow, 105, 179.

Sarah, 71.

Satan, cf. Man; 33, 42, 50, 54, 65, 66, 87, 88, 128, 133, 167, 171, 176, 178, 184, 187, 188, 189, 191, 192, 193, 194, 197, 216, 245, 267.

Saul, 71.

Scriptures, 24, 34, 35, 49, 50, 51, 71, 87, 144, 152, 154, 157, 176, 184, 186, 190, 195, 204, 213, 215, 221, 231, 240.

Seneca, 138, 165.

Severus, 134.

Shimei, 84, 138, 147, 181.

Sidon, 157.

Sin, cf. Adam, Forgiveness, Knowledge, Man; absolved, 114; battles with, 88, 211; and Christ, 142, 148, 192, 243; of Christians, 54, 56; covered over, 45, 89; dead in, 46, 51, 93; as desire to be God, 31, 33, 34, 41, 208; die to,

Theologia deutsch, 275, 278, 280, 281.

Theology, 21, 171, 221, 276, 277.

Theophilus, 64.

1 Thessalonians, 1:5, 46; 2:2, 45; 4:1, 112; 5:5-8, 164; 5:23, 186.

2 Thessalonians, 2:9, 171; 2:10-12, 170; 2:11-12, 54.

1 Timothy, 1:5, 123, 175; 2:3, 182; 4:7-8, 178; 6:7-8, 90; 6:11, 96; 6:19, 183.

2 Timothy, 1:12, 46; 1:13, 175, 277; 1:13-14, 173; 1:15-16, 183; 2:19, 63; 3:5, 60, 61, 174.

Titus, 138.

Titus, 1:9, 173; 1:16, 174; 3:5, 37, 39, 117, 265.

Tractat de antique Philosophia, 159.

Trinity, blessings of, 210; and faith, 272; image of, 29, 139, 246, 248; in man, 247, 265; and soul, 222, 224.

True Christianity, 281.

Truth, and act, 68, 74; belief in, 54; and Christ, 80, 81, 111, 175, 267; and Christian, 66, 68, 173; and doctrine, 175, 176; eternal, 68, 111, 113, 163, 214, 278, 279; and faith, 173; God is, 111, 113, 217; and God, 112, 113, 126, 189, 203, 209, 212, 213, 214, 233, 235; and Holy Spirit, 111, 173, 265, 279; and life, 162; light of, 259, 278, 279; and love, 148; path to, 176; spirit of, 278, 279; and Word, 243.

Turks, 54, 171.

Tyre, 157.

Virtue, and Christ, 165, 166, 205, 208, 261; Christian, 23, 118, 119, 133, 135, 164, 165, 167, 178, 182, 196, 224, 226, 264; divine, 52; and faith, 23, 145, 164, 167, 205, 224; and God, 126, 140, 183, 187; and grace, 166; highest, 140, 150, 208; and justification, 24; light of, 193; of love, 123, 133, 140, 145, 148, 150, 205, 208; and pagans, 165, 193; practise of, 119, 133, 134, 135, 145, 164, 167, 183; and righteousness, 133; soiled, 135; source of, 124; value of, 52, 133.

Wisdom, 1:5, 165; 7:27, 165, 174, 279; 11:21, 185; 12:19, 59.

Wisdom, and Christ, 22, 75, 111, 153, 203, 267; divine, 30, 179, 185, 206, 248; eternal, 75, 113, 119, 159, 185, 233, 246; of Father, 263; God is, 111, 202, 211; of God, 112, 113, 119, 185, 210, 211, 233, 234, 235, 236, 243, 246, 247, 279; heavenly, 79; and Holy Spirit, 111, 175; and love, 75, 222, 260; of man, 42, 79, 124, 154, 190, 222, 246, 247, 264; and prayer, 222; and repentence, 203; righteous, 159; and soul, 75, 185, 256, 257; spirit of, 252, 253, 262; and Word, 256; and world, 21-22, 68, 79, 171.

Works, of Christ, 25, 47, 257, 278; Christian, 106, 178, 180; of darkness, 54, 62, 166, 279; dead, 39, 46, 47, 55, 124; external, 193; and faith, 51, 95, 124, 208; false, 75; of God, 41, 46, 51, 52, 100, 203, 216, 225, 245, 246, 252, 278; God in man, 30, 31, 32, 180, 196, 250; good, 137, 173, 256; and Holy Spirit, 213; and humility, 227; and justification, 24, 192, 275; of light, 39; lost, 137; and love, 124, 125, 154; of man, 24, 158, 186, 203, 227, 236; pleasing, 46, 208; and rebirth, 39; and righteousness, 46, 47, 186, 227; of soul, 186; of truth, 164.

World, cf. Love; carnal, 280; children of, 62, 76, 93, 108, 183;

and Christ, 22, 80, 145, 171; and
Christian, 75, 93, 98, 119, 122,
142, 206; clinging to, 155, 160;
coming, 112; conquering of, 46,
47, 88, 135, 155, 158, 247;
darkness of, 166; desires of, 71;
die to, 24, 42, 43, 58, 70, 71, 74,
75, 76, 85, 155, 223, 224, 276;
evil of, 145; foolish of, 94, 142;
friendship of, 75, 76; God of,
208; and God, 231, 236, 237;
guest in, 86, 90, 91, 92, 93; and
Holy Spirit, 165, 279; honors of,
85, 93, 95, 142, 157, 183, 232;
invisible, 92; life of, 268; light of,
164, 165, 171, 278; nothingness
of, 82, 141; opposed to Christ,
62; pleasing of, 81; pleasures of,
55, 67, 75, 76, 77, 85, 90, 91, 92,
95, 97, 104, 106, 107, 113, 122,
157, 158, 160, 209, 226, 263;
rules in man, 67, 90, 98, 119,
166, 280; sins of, 57, 130, 132,
164, 279; sorrow of, 106, 107,
108, 109, 157, 179; as test, 90;
turn from, 42, 43, 55, 62, 73, 75,
77, 78, 108, 120, 165, 195, 209,
223, 226, 252, 276, 278, 279.
Worship, destroyed, 174; false,
110; and forgiveness, 115;
greatest, 237; lost, 137; of Old
Testament, 124;
pleasing, 180; true, 110-116, 132,
245.
Zacchaeus, 153, 167.
Zechariah, 6:1, 250; 12:10, 244,
252.
Zion, 259.
Zodiac, 235.

DATE DUE

30 505 JOSTEN'S